301.08
P25

77367

DATE DUE			
Mar 21'80			

The Participant Observer

THE
PARTICIPANT
OBSERVER

EDITED BY

GLENN JACOBS

George Braziller

NEW YORK

ACKNOWLEDGMENTS

The editor and publisher wish to thank the following for permission to publish certain essays in this volume:

Aldine Publishing Company for "The Home Territory Bar," from *Liquor License*, by Sherri Cavan.

Social Casework for "The Reification of the Notion of Subculture in Public Welfare," by Glenn Jacobs.

Social Problems for "The Poolroom Hustler," by Ned Polsky.

Trans-action for "Time and Cool People," by John Horton.

Little, Brown and Company for "A Field Experience in Retrospect" from *Tally's Corner*, by Eliot Liebow.

"The surest way to know men is to have simple
and necessary relations with them."
                              —CHARLES HORTON COOLEY

We see it with our eyes, and smell it with our
noses,
                                        the world
but just exactly what it is we never know.
Creatures of passion
our wishes color our judgments
in anything that matters.

Shall we go some special place and
fix everything so
we can see what goes on;
like the cat under the street light
where it's plain to see.
                              —ED GAUTHIER

Preface

"There is a game of puzzles," he resumed, "which is played upon a map.
One party playing requires another
to find a given word—the name of a
town, river, state, or empire—any
word, in short, upon the motley and
perplexed surface of the chart. A
novice in the game generally seeks
to embarrass his opponents by giving
them the most minutely lettered
names; but the adept selects such
words as stretch, in large characters,
from one end of the chart to the
other. These, like the over-largely
lettered signs and placards of the
street, escape observation by dint of
being excessively obvious; and here
the physical oversight is precisely
analogous with the moral inappre-
hension by which the intellect suffers
to pass unnoticed those considerations
which are too obtrusively and too
palpably self-evident."

—EDGAR ALLAN POE

As social scientists become more conscious of themselves, they
become more aware of their subject matter. Often, however, like
the novice in Poe's puzzle game in "The Purloined Letter," they
have a penchant for the specialized and the obscure, and are thus
prevented from reaching beyond their flatland toward more
promising horizons.

To stretch the analogy further, the cartography of the research environment itself becomes more detailed once the researcher surrenders himself to the subject of his study. But it
is questionable if the scientist can any longer afford the luxury
of a mystique separating the knower from the known. The atti-

tude of mind which is intended to facilitate his mastery of the
data reflects the very same mystery-mastery dualism operating in
the pretheoretical world of everyday life, the world in which he
seeks an understanding hidden from its participants by their
own games of mystery and mastery.[1] The methodology of the
social sciences rests upon an assumption of prediction and
control. This, in turn, assumes that, as in everyday life, knowledge is power; a transposition of the "one-upmanship" theme.
The social scientist strives to understand people, but the pre-
sumption of social distance between the researcher and his
subjects vitiates that which he seeks to understand.

Content in the belief that the average man takes the world
for granted, he proceeds to fragment it without seeming to
realize he has merely ripped data out of context. His approach
to social reality might be likened to a man (the sociologist)
pacing alongside a bus and shouting for information from his
friend (society) in the bus that progressively outdistances him.
As Erik Erikson and many other social scientists have asserted,
society will not hold still long enough for us to get a solid grip on
it. How often we sacrifice the richness of context for the
security of precision.

In this regard everyman and the sociologist resemble each
other. The former accepts the social world as given and is secure
in its apparent factuality. The latter is dimly aware of its elusive-
ness and precariousness but satisfies himself with the knowledge
that he has nailed some of it down. One takes comfort from the
"is-ness" of social reality, the other from the apparent manage-
ability of data. In either case the result is the same; neither has
scratched the surface of the ordinary, one with his wholesale
subscription to its premises, the other with his reconstruction of
a new puzzle from the ruins of those premises. Indeed, some
foreign sociologists have characterized their American cousins
as having reified themselves into a corner.[2]

How do we find our way out of this predicament? The answer
seems apparent, even too simple: by not interposing anything
between ourselves and the objects of our inquiry. We interpret
the hallmark of science, empiricism, literally; that is, we take
it to mean what some writers call surrender of the self to the
phenomenal world so that our experience of it is circumscribed

as little as possible.[3] I am not suggesting that we cast out the standard scientific criteria of relevance, internal consistency, replicability, objectivity, and so on. I mean simply that these should not be idolatrized, for they are merely tools ancillary to ourselves as research instruments. To the extent that we cannot escape participating in the experience of those we observe,[4] we must always more or less be participant observers.

To be a participant observer does not preclude the use of elaborate methodological techniques. Rather, it posits a criterion of ontological fitness similar to that advocated by William James when he outlined his pragmatic philosophy; namely, we allow phenomena to be our masters and to determine our means of assessing them. As regards the social world, we observe it first by the most direct means possible—ourselves—and then parsimoniously develop extensions (methods) to the degree that our existential involvement needs supplementing. Such a view presumes a radical empiricism in place of scientism, a disciplined skepticism about any substitute for man as his own measure. It refers to the "human coefficient" the sociologist Florian Znaniecki spoke of in distinguishing the cultural from the natural sciences: once the sociologist abstracts himself out of the phenomena he studies he is left only with deracinated data.[5]

Moreover, such a view does not merely carry the stipulation that the sociologist be wary of himself as a contaminant of what he studies; it means that he is necessarily an interacting part of a total field of experience. In surrendering ourselves to social phenomena we have made a choice which simultaneously commits us to suspend belief in, and expand our awareness of, the social world.[6] We are thus permitted to observe and participate in the development of experience. The real skill of the sociologist lies in his perfection of that which is essentially social in his ability to "take the role of the other." This was G. H. Mead's expression signifying the process by which we develop selves, in effect become human, through empathizing with other selves.[7]

The research experience can now be interpreted as a widening of one's breadth of perspective, and the professional socialization of the sociologist can hopefully be viewed as a "meta-socialization," transcending the internalization of a guild's norms. What is advocated here is a kind of transcendence; the sociologist; he must be more than a professional. A humanistic sociology can resonate on many levels of meaning.

The contents of this book offer a diversified sample of the world of the ordinary. They are studies in social contexts written by people who to a considerable degree were denizens of the environments they wrote about.

There are many to whom I am indebted for having opened my eyes to the ordinary. They have all been my teachers, directly or indirectly. Teacherhood, like parenthood, is an arduous task, for it involves luring the novitiate into a progressive disenchantment with the satisfactions derived from a given level of understanding so that he may rise to another level despite its indefiniteness and ambiguous rewards.

I would like to thank first the man who defined sociology as real for me—Alfred McClung Lee, my intellectual gadfly and teacher and friend as well, although he has never let friendship get in the way of criticism. Professor Lee taught me the virtues of intellectual forthrightness and the dangers of intellectual narcissism.

Other explorers of the ordinary from whose voyages I have benefited are: Edouard Gauthier, philosopher of "what's going on," who lives where he thinks; Celia Young, poet, who understands that social reality is an artifice; James Lorence, historian, who wants to keep everything honest, equable as he is; John W. Ford, anthropologist, sometime misanthrope *because* he is an optimist who sees things as they are; my sister Sherry, full of guts and sensitivity; my father and mother, who are on my side; Leo P. Chall, editor of *Sociological Abstracts*, at the heart of the sociology of knowledge; Gail Finsterbusch, sociologist and joyful agnostic; Andy Olson, student who sees and is radiant; and Edwin Seaver, editor-in-chief, George Braziller, Inc., for his encouragement and help.

Finally, I wish to thank my wife, Ada, who was a source of constant support in the preparation of this work. And to my little son Brian Lee, who always makes me smile, I want to express my gratitude for showing me my feelings.

G.J.

Contents

Preface   vii

On Context and Relevance   3
    Alfred McClung Lee

i

SOCIAL PROBLEMS INSIDE OUT

1. How Black Enterprisers Do Their Thing: An
    Odyssey Through Ghetto Capitalism   19
    Desmond Cartey

2. The Needle Scene   48
    Harold Tardola

3. Birth of a Mini-Movement: A Tenants' Grievance
    Committee   64
    John W. Ford

4. The Gilded Asylum   92
    Corrine Huesler

ii

THE PURSUIT OF LEISURE

5. Time and Cool People   125
    John Horton

6.   Urban Samurai: The *"Karate Dojo"*   140
     Glenn Jacobs

7.   Poker and Pop: Collegiate Gambling Groups   161
     David McKenzie

8.   The Home Territory Bar   179
     Sherri Cavan

iii

CAREERS STRAIGHT AND OTHERWISE

9.   Summertime Servants: The *Shlockhaus* Waiter   203
     Mark Hutter

10. The Hustler   226
     Ned Polsky

11. Life in the Colonies: Welfare Workers and
     Clients   246
     Glenn Jacobs

12. A Field Experience in Retrospect   260
     Elliot Liebow

Index   293

The Participant Observer

On Context and Relevance

Alfred McClung Lee

The current youth rebellion dramatizes a basic conflict we have
never resolved or dissipated. It has dogged those involved in intellectual pursuits throughout human history. Now, under spectacular conditions of affluence, of inequalities of opportunity,
of wasted resources, of environmental pollution, and of irresponsible warfare, vast numbers of youth are temporarily caught
up in this conflict in the course of their intellectual and emotional explorations. They see vividly and painfully—for the time
being—contrasts between the promises or ideals of human society
and the practical procedures customary among those who exercise social controls. They also perceive that many of their elders
ignore or rationalize those contrasts. They discover that many of
their elders do not object to the unchecked continuance of in-
equality, waste, pollution, and warfare. They even learn—often
not from their formal instructors—that many of their elders
benefit from waste and destruction. What had been the concern
only of a few sensitive poets, artists, and scientists has now become that of far greater numbers.

Each intellectual tradition has embedded within it, as its most
vaunted justification, ideals of service to the field or to humanity

or to both, of respect for accomplishment and creativity, and of individual autonomy and integrity. When followed, such ideals are said to take one on a high road, to make possible an admirable life here or hereafter. In the study of society, this means dedication to an ideal of perceiving human affairs more accurately, fully, precisely, and verifiably and thus differently from the way they had previously been seen. It means setting oneself to modify myths by which people live. It means placing oneself at odds with those who call for a critical reexamination and revision of knowledge about society in the interests of special purposes. It means attempting to reexamine, revise, and broaden our knowledge of society in terms of a humanistic discipline serving popular needs.

On the other hand, in the worlds of the politician, the general, the business tycoon, the church leader, and the educational administrator, such ideals of novelty or modification in ideas often fall into quite different perspectives. "Practical" men like novel ideas which will be sure to serve their enterprises. They also have their ideals that dedicate them to social leadership, to the construction of organizations and of other social controls, and to the maintenance of a growing, stable society. They thus may regard more "objectively"—perhaps chiefly as ploys—the ideals of intellectuals not directly involved in entrepreneurism or administration. They may find such ideals useful as part of a protective image for their enterprise and for the inexpensive motivation of valuable but quixotic types of employees. The ideals of entrepreneurs do not preoccupy them directly with the modification of our cultural heritage. They largely accept our culture as basic to their social environment and trust that it will continue to serve to make that environment reasonably stable. Their ideals justify procedures they use in making their politico-economic affairs go forward efficiently, profitably, in an orderly manner, and with social tolerance or even recognition.

Wielders of controls over social power need not worry about why others do not share their ideals or look upon them personally as cynics or hypocrites. They can reward rationalizers who justify their course of action. They feel quite free to offer enticements, when expedient, to those who accept a plausible compromise of a creative intellectual's idealism with the idealism or practicality of the entrepreneur. The acceptance of the enticement may change the character of an intellectual's work. It may even destroy its creative character. But whatever an intellectual may have to offer to society can scarcely be as important in an entrepreneur's view as the pressing problems with which he is trying to cope. Thus, when necessary, entrepreneurs may even reward —occasionally with overnight fame or fortune—those who will serve as their instruments, those who will work to help them maintain some aspect of their social controls or expand those controls through manipulating ideas, things, and other people.

This is not at all to say that "practical" men are scheming cynics. A few fancy that they are, but cynicism is not a common pattern in any group. There are many sets of ideals in human society, and society's processes gain vitality by people trying to mount different types of status ladders through being dedicated to different sets of ideals.[1] The conflict we are talking about in this paper is thus, like so many human conflicts, one due to a lack of tolerance and understanding, a refusal to accept the multivalent character of human society. Ideological syntheses that appeared to resolve such multivalence at certain historical periods—whether those of Thomism, Calvinism, or Soviet Communism—were at best façades, constantly in need of patching and even governmental and military enforcement.

In a less disturbed period than the present, intellectuals were typically nurtured within an environment in which awkward implications of traditional ideals were not laid bare. When vocational training is not questioned by its recipients as it is now, its rationale has as a most significant consequence the repressing or blunting of idealistic mandates. Each vocational cult has such verbal magic, plausible especially to those who have developed a vested interest in the cult's job-giving potentialities. Thus the basic conflict we are discussing underlies contrasts between the teachings of scientific ideals and of engineering "realities," between an artist's aspirations and those of a commercial "artist," between a philosophical or sociological or literary pursuit of wisdom for its own sake and the training protocols for clergymen, journalists, lawyers, physicians, schoolteachers, social workers, and social research technicians. Investigators report that, in any of these vocations, novices in each succeeding year of training typically show a lessening concern with problems of idealistic commitment and greater "maturity" in their acceptance of durable "professional" attitudes—of "more mature" ideals.

How does this most profound, timeless, and timely problem relate to my present concern here with context and relevance? The connection I see is that—especially in the study of social affairs—context and relevance both are all too often casualties in the intellectual's struggle to work out a practical *modus vivendi* within his chosen field. Before exploring some of the ramifications of this problem further, let me first state what I mean by context and relevance.

Somehow the records of the social scientist's perceptions must carry with them as full a sense of their contexts or settings as possible. Selections of what to consider and to record must be made. What is to be reported? The social scientist willy-nilly approaches all social situations with preconceptions as to what they are. How is he to move beyond those preconceptions to more accurate understandings? What questions should he have in mind? How should he confront those with whom he is to interact as he participantly observes their behavior? How does each person involved interact in a given social situation? Of what significance are physical and social environment, other circumstances, tradition and custom? As much as possible of all the observer does not record in a final report or even in his field notes must still somehow enter his consciousness and influence his evaluations of data and his conclusions.

Social science is a struggle to see ever more clearly and to report ever more accurately what we think we have seen and to relate it to whatever other contexts we can—to make it as relevant as possible to human understandings and concerns. It is the best way we have discovered yet to check, revise, and even reorganize traditional social ideas we learn from childhood in any social status group. It is our only adequate basis for criticizing constructively as well as destructively the kind of more or less enlightened social theories by which people live and by which the world's affairs are guided. The data of social science are endlessly and intimately complicated and intertwined. They defy measurement or even precise determination. But they are what we have to work with to try to cope with human problems.

As Francis Bacon[2] noted in 1620, we should not reject "difficult things from impatience of research, sober things because they narrow hope, the deeper things of nature from superstition, the light of experience from arrogance and pride, lest [one's] . . . mind should seem to be occupied with things mean and transitory, things not commonly believed, out of deference to the opinion of the vulgar." In short, one should be aware that "human understanding is no dry light, but receives an infusion from the will and affections."

How can we best perceive social behavior in context? How can we best substitute more precise social knowledge for traditional folk wisdom? As Herbert Blumer[3] forthrightly puts it, we "must go to a direct examination of actual human group life." He contends that the "task of scientific study is to lift the veils that cover the area of group life that one proposes to study." For this, there is no substitute for participant observation: "No theorizing, however ingenious, and no observance of scientific protocol, however meticulous, are substitutes for developing a familiarity with what is actually going on in the sphere of life under study."

Participant observation is only a gate to the intricacies of more adequate social knowledge. What happens when one enters that gate depends upon his abilities and interrelationships as an observer. He must be able to see, to listen, and to feel sensitively the social interactions of which he becomes a part. He must be able to grow with his experiences. He must question time and again whether he has perceived enough and whether his understandings are as accurate as he can make them. He must be able to understand his own impact upon the social situation he studies and what influences other participants and the situation have upon him. He must learn to expect a personal sense of culture shock,[4] a confusing and possibly a painful experience, as a symptom that he is bringing new perceptions of situations into focus and that he is becoming able to assimilate those perceptions into his modifying understandings.

As William Foote Whyte said of his own remarkable study, *Street Corner Society*,[5] "It would have been impossible to map out at the beginning the sort of study I eventually found myself doing." His work "depended upon an intimate familiarity with people and situations," and he was able to learn "to understand a group only through observing how it changed *through time.*" He had to explore his way along, to inspect carefully each situation in which he found himself, to record unobtrusively what he found, to make and revise many times his research objectives as well as his plans of work, and constantly to think and rethink the implications of what he was learning. He used whatever methods of observation, listening, interviewing, participation in discussions and activities, collection of life-histories, manuscript materials and other records and documents, and data processing appeared useful for the expansion and verification of his knowledge of street corner life and its contexts. In other words, Whyte fulfills, in my estimation, what Blumer[6] prescribes as the characteristics of a scientist studying human relations: "a high order of careful and honest probing, creative yet disciplined imagination, resourcefulness and flexibility in study, pondering over what one is finding, and a constant readiness to test and recast one's views and images of the area."

The observer can best strengthen his competence as a social scientist by seeing human behavior in a variety of contexts— in different age groups, among deviants (whether criminal, neurotic, psychotic, or just strange), in a foreign culture, and in crisis situations. Particularly instructive to the observer are the contrasts between various types of verbalization in human interaction and spontaneous responses to crisis situations or to manipulative efforts. I have called this type of observation the clinical study of social interaction.[7]

The clinical study of human relations is the crucial aspect of participant observation. The first patterns of interaction the observer usually perceives in a social situation are the cultural modalities common to the society—the conventions and morals —that the persons involved typically exhibit to an outsider. People behave before new associates much as they think societal mandates prescribe for them to behave. As the observer becomes more intimately participant, more identified with a group, he becomes initiated into the group's operating folkways and mores. These patterns and more individual practices and habits gain dimension for him through time by his comparison of verbal and other reactions to ranges of stimuli and especially of spontaneous reactions to unexpected problems. The clinical study of groups thus helps to provide the leverage of comparison through which the observer can strip away many a veil obscuring other participants' potentialities for action and thus their thoughts and emotions.

To learn how to do clinical study in human relations requires at least as much training and experience as does its individual parallel, psychoanalytical interviewing. Our best clinical students have been largely self-trained, but fortunately there is a growing awareness among sociologists of ways in which formal training can aid to stimulate the development of such basic contributors to social science.

Experience in firsthand observation in a variety of contexts equips the social scientist to understand and to use more fruitfully as well as more accurately the reports of other observers. For example, when I turned in the early 1930's from the firsthand clinical study of the daily newspaper as a social instrument in order to read available social scientific reports on that subject, I was shocked by the superficiality and inaccuracy of many of them. The writings on the press of Robert E. Park[8] stood out for the intimacy with which he had observed processes of newsgathering, editing, and newspaper manufacture, merchandising, distribution, and reading in their human and mechanical ramifications. Like Park's, my work on the press reached many conclusions at odds with or beyond both those in other previous social scientific reports and those of the professional apologists for commercial interests.[9]

If an investigator were able to achieve an adequate grasp of his data in context only through firsthand observation of a continuing and intimate sort, comparative and historical approaches to social and sociological problems would be sharply limited. As I have suggested in the case of the press, participant observation in general as background and in the particular area under study helps to make other types of data more meaningful. This is a point that cultural anthropologists, with their strong emphasis in professional training upon field experience, have many times demonstrated.[10] It was the basis on which the very strong University of Chicago sociology department of the 1920's and 1930's was built.[11] On the other hand, while the Human

Relations Area Files contain items from more than 240 cultures, organized in terms of a basic set of categories, they have often been criticized for lack of context. The neatly filed items "are wrenched out of context by coders unknown to the reader or to the original ethnographer. Items which should be treated separately are lumped together and those which should be lumped together are counted as examples of different traits."[12] In other words, for documents to be useful to the social scientist, as Florian Znaniecki[13] put it, they "are always 'somebody's' never 'nobody's' data." They all contain a "humanistic coefficient" which needs to be known as a qualification of the nature of the material.

Granted a broad basis for comprehension of comparative data in participant observation, cross-cultural and cross-temporal comparisons are most useful in the study of sociological problems. How can one understand fully the nature of the human family in any society except by seeing families in the contexts of many different types of society? Violence, war, and political and economic organization all take on new significance in the light of comparative data replete with their contextual concomitants. For example, how can one understand white "Anglo-Saxon Protestant" racism without gaining a social-historical grasp of its roots, persistences, and modifications? How does it relate to myths of class, religion, and "race" during some one thousand years of Anglo-Saxon, Anglo-Norman, and English conquests and exploitations? How similar the treatments were of the Cockney worker, the Irish peasant, the Indian, and the American Negro? Like participant observation in a variety of groups, the use of cross-cultural and cross-temporal comparisons yields significant data on social flexibility and adaptability and on the pervasive influence of context, both in time and in current environment.

From my discussion of context in sociological research and thought, it is apparent that I regard it as being closely related to the currently magical word, relevance. As used in debates about the black and the student rebellions, relevance is taken to stress the sense of being germane to important human concerns, concerns with what lies behind veils obscuring the behavior of problematic groups. Those who demand greater relevance in education, politics, business, religion, and civic affairs ask social scientists to develop social theory as a guide for their own action to change those fields. Fortunately, social scientists as such concern themselves with the development of data and theory that are above all as accurate and as verifiable as they can make them. Accurate descriptions, conclusions, and generalizations may run counter to the prejudices and special interests of many who call loudly for relevance, but those are a scientist's best products.

Social scientific investigations are relevant to pressing social problems through taking the form of sociologically defined problems underlying important social issues.[14] As such, they are always relevant to the criticism and modification of extant social conceptions—both popular and "scientific." Criteria of relevance for the social scientist rule out abstract methodological exercises. They set aside speculative "model building" that has little reference to social possibilities or verification. They relegate to others, if others should wish to engage in them, flights of statistical fantasy. They put in a category of academic futility such trivia as needless replications of inconsequential studies, elegant schemes for the construction of concepts, and transpositions into the social realm of terminologies and concepts from other disciplines (systems analysis, theory of games, physics principles).[15]

This is all easy enough to say. Many of the extant social conceptions in need of revision are not mere academic properties to be dug into casually or irreverently. They are deeply held social prejudices in which powerful interests have entrenched their controls. Others are so intimately a part of an American social scientist's personality, of the myths with which he lives, that change would have fundamental personal as well as social consequences. Thus, to be relevant today in a significant way in social science requires not only real courage and dedication, or even foolhardiness, but also freedom from enchantment with myths of the "social system"[16] and of the scientist's own self.

Until students revolted in the mid-1960's, how many social scientists explored actively the irrelevancies of much university educational method, content, and certification? When the Blacks rebelled in the 1960's and shook the universities, how many social scientists were not taken unawares? In the face of crude and brutal politico-economic manipulations in this country as

well as abroad, how many social scientists have probed the nature of American social control structures and procedures relevant to such machinations? It is easy to dream up and even
sketchily to document an American "establishment" which "decides" major policies, but it is much more significant to discover
how irresponsibly and even irrationally by happenstance many
major decisions are made and by whom. Finally, with military
interventions taking the lives of thousands of American men and
women and of hundreds of thousands of others, and exacerbat-
ing by neglect our domestic social problems, how many social
scientists are researching realistically—for people and not for
manipulators—these questions: Why are we fighting at all?
What interests benefit from such adventures? How effective are
conscientious objectors and war resisters in stirring up American
antipathy to our country's militarization? What practical devices
might we now develop and use to divert our politico-economic
entrepreneurs from military recourses or projects that lead to
military interventions?

To make an impact on current social understanding, the
participant observer need not go so far afield as some of my
questions appear to suggest. Fully seen, the study of any group
can yield disturbingly useful data on such problems as these:
How do its members respond to failures of organized education?
How have they contributed to the rankling black-white contro-
versy? What aspects of their personalities, their thoughts, emotions, and actions, help our society's manipulators to continue
to get away with outworn crudities? How do they react to the
draft and, for that matter, to participation in war through the
payment of taxes, through certain types of investment, and
through war-related civilian employment? So long as one is
studying an apparently important aspect of human behavior in
its contexts, relevant to a pressing human issue of our time, one
can fruitfully study it in terms of any appropriate group of
people.

As I have emphasized, the study of human behavior in context and in terms relevant to important social issues requires a
degree of idealistic dedication that raises practical problems of
self-maintenance and of social influence. To some few, endowed
with funds from sources involving no special obligations (if such

sources actually do exist) and also endowed with adequate motivation, there is no conflict between commitment and *modus vivendi*. At times and depending upon specialty, intellectuals employed as university professors continue to interpret their financing as implying no breach of their idealism, as involving no obligations other than those to student and to human welfare —until one of their products (usually a statement or a student) falls afoul of a person with power.

This matter involves a great many subtleties. To illustrate, it is simple enough to permit one's work to fall more and more into noncontroversial areas. In such areas, one can deal with abstractions that have contexts fully known only to a few *cognoscenti* (if any) and that have allegedly profound but actually obscure relevance to pressing human problems.

A great many social scientists also enter into what they perceive to be clever and somewhat surreptitious relationships with representatives of the world of the status quo in the manner of Dr. Faustus dealing with Mephistopheles. They contract (often through their university's tax-free "research foundation") with a detergent manufacturer or oil company official or advertising agent to do a social investigation ("sociological research") on terms that will permit or encourage the investigator to write up the resulting report in two ways. One version is to satisfy the immediate needs of the paymaster, and the other, often rendered anonymous as to paymaster and his interests, is given an academic character and comes to repose in the pages of a "learned journal" or of a "research monograph." More prestigiously, the contract would be with a foundation which is also quite likely the creature of more general but quite real vested interests. Increasingly honorific, too, are investigations ("sociological research") made under contract for governmental commissions and nonprofit voluntary associations, regardless of how special and even questionable socially the actual interests forwarded by such investigations might be—so long as they favor the powerful.[17]

That a Dr. Faustus is not really subservient to such a contract is both his conviction and his contention. That his products are useful to a manipulator of society serving a specific interest justifies his paymaster's confidence and subsidy. Whether stipends provided in such contracts for graduate students are useful educational opportunities or perversions of educational processes is a controversial issue too often foreclosed in discussions by practical considerations. What the social consequences of such probably biased efforts might be is a more complicated problem. At any rate, such efforts have contributed little or nothing to scientific sociology as a subject despite the extent to which they have in recent years preoccupied sociologists as members of the professional cult. They have given vast numbers of sociology graduate students the impression that their discipline requires them to become well-drilled technicians available as instruments of the powerful rather than autonomous explorers, inspectors, and critical ponderers.

Such self-conscious ways of keeping a foot in each of two worlds are only necessary for those desirous of Faustian rewards. For less ambitious but equally cautious sociologists, protective colorations are built into their cult's moral image in society as well as into its operating mores and thus into their own sentiments. Like other sophisticated intellectual cults, the sociological profession provides an array of ways in which to hang one's clothes on a hickory limb and thus appear to be a swimmer in sociological waters—without wetting one's feet and ignoring "parental" warnings against treacherous societal currents, rocks, and sinkholes. Thus, social scientists fall into ways of avoiding contextual specifics and of giving pretentious substitutes for social relevance.

Let us look at a very few examples:

Studies of prostitutes rarely involve their services to "legitimate" business on an expense-account basis. Journalists have occasionally pointed to the utility of prostitutes as sales bait for giant as well as small business enterprisers, but social scientists have not explored further the ramifications this suggests.

Just how illegal gambling is made possible through the knowing cooperation of legitimate banks and communications agencies does not figure in the textbooks.

During Prohibition, huge legitimate manufacturers made tremendous profits on synthetic alcohol wholesaled to bootleggers. Would not that have helped to explain and characterize the nature and growth of gangsterism during the 1920's and early 1930's in this country?

Occasional incidents of police brutality do not succeed in damaging popularly the policeman's "image" in this country. Just what do the police do with the largely unchecked grant of armed force we entrust to them—presumably in return for "protection"? Only in rare instances, such as police brutalities to reporters, cameramen, and rioting white students during the 1968 Democratic National Convention,[18] do mass communicators become temporarily rebellious about the character of our police. Innumerable examples of abuse to Blacks and Puerto Ricans,[19] to alcoholics,[20] and to "criminals"[21] are all too easily justified or brushed aside.

Studies of crime usually give criminals the appearance of being outcasts in an underworld quite separate from "decent" society. How different crime would appear were it to fit facts available to participant observers! It would then be seen as a worrisome ingredient of practically all facets of social life.

Am I taking the position that what really important scientific sociological work is done is accidental, accomplished by the ruggedly independent, or stimulated by fortunate windfalls of funds? That is about the situation, as I see it. The life and work of such a great American sociologist as William Graham Sumner[22] illustrate all three of these points. His protective coloration as a member of Yale's powerful Skull and Bones society and as an Episcopalian clergyman kept the Yale administrators from suspecting that they were accidentally employing an austerely honest student of society. He had several windfalls of funds. One, given to him by a wealthy undergraduate classmate, permitted him to study in Switzerland, Germany, and England. The act of the Yale Corporation that gave him continuing tenure on the faculty was the other. Later, during bitter controversies over the text use of Herbert Spencer's *The Study of Sociology*[23] and over his anti-imperialistic position on the Spanish-American War, his status as a tenure professor protected his freedom to continue to investigate, to teach, and to write. There have been many others who had Sumner's advantages, but only a few, such as Robert S. Lynd and C. Wright Mills in sociology have used them in as courageous a manner. Such others as Thorstein Veblen and W. I. Thomas had to follow less secure life courses, dogged by objections to their fundamental contributions.

This is neither a counsel of absolute perfection nor one of despair. It is an assertion that the student of society has to face the problems of context and relevance fully, honestly, and openly. It is a contention that the student of society has no choice but to follow the necessarily idealistic mandates of social science as knowingly and as well as he can or not to contribute significantly to his field.

i

SOCIAL PROBLEMS
INSIDE OUT

1

How Black Enterprisers Do Their Thing:
An Odyssey Through Ghetto Capitalism

Desmond Cartey

The sociologist Alfred Weber said that in order to understand capitalism one had to assume that exploitation was intrinsic to it and could not be naïvely separated from laissez faire; he said this clinically, not polemically. Desmond Cartey gives us a picture of some forms of enterprise indigenous to the ghetto. In demonstrating the impossibility of distinguishing legal from illegal behavior and legitimate from illegitimate enterprise, he fleshes out Weber's dictum —and the implications it presents for the formation of public policy regarding the welfare of the ghetto population.
Mr. *Cartey is Coordinator of the Brooklyn College Work-Study Program and was formerly Assistant Director of the Office of Technical Assistance, Human Resources Administration, City of New York.*

During the 1968 presidential election campaign, Richard M. Nixon presented "black capitalism" as the sum and substance of his domestic policy for the cities. In a speech on April 25 he explained: "By providing technical assistance and loan guarantees, by opening new capital sources, we can help Negroes to start new businesses in the ghetto and to expand existing ones." He added that this sort of program would involve little government money and produce as a dividend "a firm structure of Negro economic opportunity." The irony of these statements can be appreciated only by an understanding of the history and character of ethnic succession in the United States.

Scholars of American society, especially those concentrating on ethnic minorities, have long been aware that depressed groups have to find their economic opportunities where they can. As successive waves of immigrants landed on our shores, they found life in the new environment tantamount to a fight for survival. To accommodate themselves to these circumstances they often engaged in quasi-legitimate and illegitimate enterprises, which were adaptive in that they provided a foothold for the assimilation of future generations into the larger society. The Irish, Italians, and Jews, for example, made defensive alliances with local politicians and received patronage and personal assistance in return for votes and funds, some of which derived from "criminal" activities.[1] In many cases, the ward-heeling politician, like his old-country feudal counterpart, the patron or squire, was a familiar face at important family and community functions. He was a fixer or mediator between the immigrant community and a strange, threatening outside world. Also, the avenues opened up to these groups by stable, organized crime enhanced their chances for mobility out of the ghetto. Eventually, with the rise of minority groups came a concomitant withering away of certain political machines (boss systems) and ethnic criminal hegemonies—or at least, the absorption of some forms of illicit activity into the economic structure.[2]

In the case of the American black, this pattern is checkered, both in terms of the now familiar background of discrimination and exploitation and, more specifically, in terms of the history of Negro city politics. Northern Negro political affairs have been characterized by conflicts of interest between the individualistic black politician and the civil rights-minded Negro organizations. In the 1920's, both political and civic leaders tried to break into established white organizations. However, beginning in the 1930's, the goals and interests of these two black groups diverged. The former focused on maintenance of the white-dominated political machine (which included the black politician), while the latter was preoccupied with the attainment of racial goals. This pattern was typical in New York and Chicago, for example.[3] Though criminal activity flourished in the black ghetto, blacks usually occupied the lowest rungs on the ladders of organized crime. Those black enterprisers who did exist could not accumulate the capital necessary for legitimate enterprise. Furthermore, with the repeal of Prohibition, in cities such as Chicago, the profits of organized crime began to dwindle

and led to a period of forced mergers in which Italian gangs began to exert monopoly control over what had been a rather competitive set of Negro gambling enterprises. Most of the important Negro gamblers were killed or driven out of town or into retirement. The result was the closing off of an important source of Negro capital formation, which, during the 20's, had worked to the advantage of Negro voluntary associations (including the NAACP and the churches, which received large contributions from the gamblers), as well as to the advantage of the politicians.[4]

Thus, one of the most important opportunities traditionally open to ethnic groups was wrested from the hands of the black man. The notion of "black capitalism" from this perspective, then, ignores some basic historical facts about American society as well as the particular problems that an ethnic community faces.

Within the black ghetto today, furthermore, there are important patterns of association that defy classification: they are neither purely "legitimate" nor totally "criminal." In this connection, the language of morals and conventions naïvely distinguishes between "good guys" and "bad guys," but bears little relation to the facts of life in the urban milieu. Rather, the two merge to form a network within which individuals and groups compete and cooperate to perform functions of mutual benefit of which they may not even be conscious. It was this realization that became a working hypothesis for Robert E. Park and his colleagues of the famous "Chicago School" of sociology in the 1920's and 1930's. For them, the city was a social laboratory consisting of "natural areas," analogous to the animal communities studied by ecologists. They differed from animal communities insofar as human communication enables purposeful, collective action.[5]

Viewed in this light, the common conception of the ghetto as an area of "social disorganization" belies the complexity of the community network. It is true that the ghetto lacks overall organization, but it is no more unorganized than other communities in our society. It is merely organized differently. It may be useful to visualize the ghetto as an area of intersecting careers, games, and pastimes. Individuals and interest groups, as players, influence one another reciprocally and gain from each other's activities without the direction of any single authority.[6] Specifically, this implies that so-called criminals do not simply remain in a "subculture," but travel in many circles, associating with those whom we would ordinarily type as "law-abiding" and typical Americans.

As we shall see, two prominent underworld types in the ghetto, the professional thief and the numbers man, frequent establishments we would consider "legitimate"—beauty shops, shoeshine parlors, bars, poolrooms, and pawnshops. These businesses function as staging areas, markets, depots, and meeting places indispensable to their activities. Furthermore, the police and law enforcement apparatus also cooperate routinely with the racketeers. They are thus part of the criminal enterprise. In addition, it is possible even to trace indirect relationships between numbers racketeering and the religious institutions of the ghetto. Then, too, when we consider that white-dominated enterprises, both legitimate and illicit, working with the rackets and the law enforcement agencies, combine to result in a flow of capital out of the ghetto, the themes of racial discrimination and black power take on new meanings. The fact that whites profit from the status quo contradicts the very operational assumptions behind "black capitalism."

Our odyssey through the ghetto begins with a beauty parlor, and moves into a world of class rivalry, a world of number-runners, thieves, pimps, prostitutes, fortune-tellers and ministers, and a world of dilapidated shoeshine parlors, pawnshops, poolrooms, bars, speakeasies, religious stores, and storefront churches —a checkerboard world over which the pieces as players move in deceptively crazed patterns.[7]

Black Beauty Parlor

The beauty parlor specializes in a new craze among Blacks called the "Weev," an abreviation for "Hair-Weev," which refers to a process of weaving commercial human hair onto one's natural hair to impart to it fullness and length or to disguise bald spots. The process permits unlimited hair-dressing possibilities and enables one to keep up with the latest hair styles. The Weev was invented in 1949 by Clara Gray, who claimed that the innovation was a God-sent revelation; soon it became a craze.[8]

The cost of the Hair-Weev varies according to the amount, grade, and blend of hair needed. Usually the price ranges from seventy-five to three-hundred dollars. The hair costs the beauty parlor owners between thirty-two and fifty dollars a pound, and the entire process takes about four hours to complete. About a half pound of hair is usually sufficient to complete an entire Weev of average length. When complete it resembles a wig, but it is fixed to the scalp.

One particular beauty parlor is owned and operated by a young couple: Charlie, the husband, born in the West Indies, came to the United States about three years ago; his wife, Jane, is American. Charlie came from a lower-middle-class family and was one of thirteen children. He completed high school, and he characterizes himself as ambitious, always seeking to better himself socially and financially. Charlie does not consider himself a success, however, and blames his father for his misfortune. His explanation is that his father sired too many children, thus shackling his mother to the home and Charlie to the family's finances.

Jane is a tense, ambitious, and arrogant woman, competent at managing her business and preoccupied with making money. She, too, came from a large family and was forced to assist her divorced mother in caring for the four other children. Although she did not complete high school, she exhibits shrewd business acumen, sometimes visible in a selective selfishness toward her family and a calculated liberality toward strangers.

At the time of this study, they had been married a year; before that they had lived together. Their ideas, attitudes, and values were so far apart that many conflicts resulted. Charlie admits that he married Jane only because the immigration authorities were on his back. Jane, on the other hand, felt she was getting old, and since most of her friends were already married, it appeared to be a good idea. Many of the habitués of the beauty parlor see the roots of their conflict as sexual; others contend it is economic or cultural. Charlie explains his involvement with Jane:

I came to the United States in September of 1962 on a vacation. From the information I received about the United States while in my native country and on my arrival here, I decided that I would remain in the U.S. at all costs. There were two possibilities: either I enroll in an accredited school, or get married. Both possibilities caused me serious problems because both required money which I did not have. I finally decided to enroll in the La Belle's Beauty School. In this way, it was possible for me to attend school and at the same time shop around for a suitable companion. I was not interested in falling in love with anyone. Jane was a student at this beauty school and by becoming friendly and later marrying her, I was able to solve the problem.

Such situations are typical, especially among students. The immigration law stipulates that a student cannot work without first obtaining permission from the immigration office, but he is not eligible to apply until he has established residence for six months. Since he has to subsist he is forced to break the rule, and since many of the better jobs require citizenship, he is relegated to menial work in hospitals and factories. A frequent way out of this bind, therefore, is the route that Charlie took.

Lower-class American and West Indian blacks find it very difficult to secure employment. They are marginal workers— uprooted. Their income is low and uncertain. A large proportion of them are on public assistance. Those who work engage in unskilled or semiskilled occupations as domestics, waitresses, cooks, and factory workers. The West Indian and the American blacks, however, exhibit strong cultural differences. West Indians come from a different cultural background and therefore cannot fully understand the Afro-American. The slave trade was abolished in the West Indies in 1807, but emancipation did not occur until 1834. From 1834 onward, the average West Indian was poor, but he was never confined to any particular area; he was free to choose any form of religion that he desired, and he has not suffered from the extreme discrimination that the American black has. The West Indians became assimilated into the white man's culture, which made a great deal of difference in their attitudes and values. These factors contribute to the differences between American and West Indian blacks.

Class Versus Class

The beauty parlor customers can be classed in two status groups, the professional and the nonprofessional. They also differ ethnically—American, West Indian, and African. The professionals consist mainly of nurses, teachers, secretaries, and housewives whose husbands' occupations fit into this category. The nonprofessionals consist mainly of welfare recipients, waitresses, and factory workers.[9] All live in Brooklyn, Queens, Manhattan, and the Bronx, and were informed about the beauty parlor through advertisements in the *Amsterdam News*.

Many of the nonprofessionals are divorcees or live in "common law." Their group cultural values are at strong variance with the professionals', especially with regard to their mores of sex and of status-seeking. Most of them came to the beauty parlor for the Weev, which with its cost and maintenance can be a financial burden for them; every appointment after the initial one costs twenty dollars. Most are willing to pay the price since it gives them the opportunity to "make style on their friends." Paradoxically, the nonprofessionals' competitiveness is not oriented toward social mobility but toward the gaining of status and recognition within the group to which they already belong.

This they accomplish through the acquisition and display of material goods such as jewelry, furs, and other means of adornment.[10]

The nonprofessionals are the most active patrons of the numbers game and the most avid customers of the professional thieves who also frequent the beauty parlor. They spend freely out of limited resources and thus diminish their chances for interclass mobility. William Foote Whyte, in his classic study of an Italian slum, describes an analogous situation in which the "corner boys" nurture and maintain indigenous ethnic values in order to enhance their status within the community, simultaneously preventing themselves from moving between social strata. On the other hand, the "college boys" in the same study set their sights on managerial or professional positions outside of Cornerville.[11] This state of affairs has been called the "ethnic mobility trap"[12]; that is to say, the nonprofessionals, in upholding their own group mores, automatically and unwittingly prevent themselves from climbing the social ladder.

The nonprofessionals do not conform, moreover, to middle-class sexual norms. They are not ashamed to discuss their sexual experiences in front of the group, and, from their conversations, it is obvious that they do not restrict their sexual relationships to one race. In fact, they seem to prefer people of different racial origin because of the money and luxuries they can get from them. Many unabashedly admit that they have sex relations with their employers. It is difficult to distinguish between the married and single women, for all speak about their "lovers." Yet they try often to justify their sexual escapades as if they do indeed worry about their promiscuity. Such philandering entails also the risk of violent reprisals from a jealous husband. In this connection, the owner of the beauty parlor is a willing accomplice, acting as confidant and intermediary for her patrons. When a husband calls to find out what time his wife left the beauty parlor, she knows what to say because she already has specific instructions and information regarding the wife's destination, the phone number to call in case of emergency, and the time she is expected to return home.

For the most part, the nonprofessionals dislike the professionals. They are tolerant toward the American middle-class blacks but dislike the West Indians and Africans. The West Indians are referred to as "monkey chasers" and "black Jews," the latter invective denoting their ambitiousness. The Africans, because of their strange dress, their aloofness, and better treatment in society, are equally resented. When these are present at the beauty parlor, tension pervades the atmosphere. Often, the nonprofessional's derogatory remarks center around the difference in life styles and spending habits, as for example when Jane inveighed against one customer: "You see the gal who just left here? She is so damn cheap, and she is making so much money. She and her ol' man are teachers but they do not spend a bad penny. She leaves a seventy-five cent tip on a ten dollar job. I'd rather she keep it!" Another customer then chimed in: "You could see that she is cheap. Did you see the dress and shoes she was wearing? I'm sure she got them at Gimbel's basement."

The middle-class professionals are more conservative spenders, conscious of their status, and concerned about an appearance of stability. Their main objective is upward mobility, although among the professional women there is a great deal of frustration about finding a mate, since professional men are scarce and they look askance at sexual involvements with men of lower status. The married professional women are also concerned about their husbands' philandering. Here the situation is reversed, or apparently so, for the husbands generally carry on affairs with divorcees and people of other racial backgrounds.

Particularly interesting is the reason why the middle-class women come for the Weev. Most explain that this is owing to the nature of their jobs; they often come into contact with the public and want to look attractive. Unlike the nonprofessional, they are not appear interested in competing among themselves. They are not as extravagant as the nonprofessionals, although their salaries average at least fifty dollars a week more.

The majority of the African women are not employed and derive their status from their husbands, many of whom are diplomats. They display an attitude of aloof superiority and seldom communicate in English. They make it a point not to socialize with Americans or West Indians, especially those from the lower class. The Africans tend to associate with their own people or with those of similar interests, regardless of race, color, or ethnic attachment. As foreigners more respected than the American black, they are not forced to live in the ghetto and can afford to pay higher rents. Thus, even though the Africans are nonwhite, their social background, economic resources, and national pride and identity lead them to segregate themselves from the general American black population.

More Than a Beauty Parlor

The men who frequent the beauty parlor include the owner and very few customers; most are either purveyors of stolen goods or numbers collectors. Although some of the men are of different racial origin, they all appear to be familiar with one another and interact freely.

Many of the male habitués of the beauty parlor frequent the establishment to buy or "fence" stolen goods. The professional thief is a familiar visitor. Like other professionals, his status is relative to that of his cohorts, based upon technical proficiency, financial standing, personal influence, and comprehensive knowledge of the community. These are reflected in his dealings with other criminals, the police, and businessmen.

The peddling of stolen goods in the Bedford-Stuyvesant section is highly organized. Consequently, the skills of the thief are more important in two areas: the planning and execution of crimes and the disposal of stolen goods. In the beauty parlor, stolen goods are trafficked by black and white men and black women: the goods are stolen only if there is an order and a market. During the week, the items sold in the beauty parlor comprise primarily foodstuffs, stockings, cigarettes, and other sundries. On weekends, however, "big" items pour in in large quantities: television sets, cameras, watches, appliances, and furs. The retail prices of the items are generally slashed by 50 percent, but if the thief is in dire need of money (usually because of debts to loan sharks or of having to leave town to avoid the police), he may consent to cut the price to one third. The following table provides some typical examples of the "discounts" available to customers of the beauty parlor:

Item	Retail Price	Selling Price
Television	$210.00	$75.00
Camera	100.00	45.00
Wristwatch	75.00	30.00
Iron	8.00	4.00
Portable hi-fi	75.00	40.00
Typewriter	120.00	45.00
Mink coat	800.00	250.00
Mink stole	200.00	100.00
Suit	85.00	40.00
Raincoat	40.00	15.00
Shoes	20.00	8.00
Dress	15.00	6.00
Perfume	5.00	2.00
Lipstick	1.00	.75
Toaster	10.00	6.00
Liquor	7.00	2.00

A typical transaction may go as follows: "Hi Jane, I have a watch to sell for fifty dollars. You want it?" "What kind?" "A Bulova." "You want too much money for it." "Well, how much will you give me?" "Fifteen dollars." "Twenty. I need money. I'm leaving town for a few days." "Fifteen." "Okay. Give me the fifteen."

Money is available as easily as stolen goods, but the interest rates are exorbitant; the loan sharks charge 30 percent on the dollar. Generally, the loans are short term, and the payment must be prompt or else the debtor leaves himself open to brutal reprisals. Charles, a professional thief, related these experiences with loan sharks:

Last week, I borrowed $350 from them people. I lost it all in a poker game. I went back to them and borrowed another hundred. They told me don't go to heavy if I know that I cannot meet the payments. I felt that I had a chance to win back some money. I win back about $200 but I was still out about $250. [He had been gambling for three nights consecutively.] I promised them I would pay them back in a week. When the time came I did not have the money to pay. They came looking for me. I hid from them for a few days but I was losing out in my business. One day I took a chance and went out. Somebody tip them off. They came for me. I did not have much money on me. I knew what I was in for. There were three of them. One say "get him." They beat, kick me up. One took out a gun and tell me, "get that money to me in three days or things going to get worse." Man, I had that money for them not in three days but in three hours.

Charles obtained the money to repay the loan sharks by bringing stolen items to the beauty parlor.

The owner of a beauty parlor or a shoeshine shop acts as a liaison between the professional thief and the customer. The beauty parlor owner recommends her clients to the thief. Although the price is presumably fixed, she may be in a position to have it reduced; she can also purchase the best items at a lower cost for herself. This particular one had furnished her apartment, as well as acquiring personal goods for her family, in this manner.

While the professional thief participates in a group culture, crime in this milieu is not organized in the melodramatic sense of the "Syndicate," "Mr. Big," or "Cosa Nostra." Its organization emerges out of the network of informal relationships crisscrossing the community. These include "fixes" with the police and ties with "legitimate" operations. The professional thieves have established procedures for dealing with the law enforcement agencies; police pressure is considered part of the routine course of business. Through these agencies, for example, thieves with the right connections can have their cases brought before judges who are known to be lenient. The thief, often realizing the symbolic value of arrests, will try to be cooperative when dealing with police officers. Those thieves who operate alone and do not have the advantage of the right connections engage in petty theft of used items and so are more prone to land in jail and suffer harsher penalties. A professional thief gave the following account of his dealings with the police:

I know the policeman on the beat. He knows the stores that we are going to rob. He usually tells us if there is a new cop on the beat. If a new cop is on the beat, he would bring him around and introduce us. If the cop is straight he informs us when he has his night off. When we are about to enter the store the cops move away from the area. When we get the goods from the store, the cops take what they want. Then on top of that, we have to turn around and pay them off. Some cops make at least $170 a week. They usually share this money with the cops who drive the patrol cars. The sergeant makes about $100 [per week]. We also have to pay off the cops in the area where we sell the goods, but not so much.

Good "Fences" Make Good Neighbors: Other Depots

The beauty parlor is an apparent nucleus and point of intersection of daily routines. Other nuclei can be discerned, however, and offer interesting variations within the neighborhood. As one would expect, these turn out to be shoeshine parlors, pawnshops, poolhalls, bars, and after-hours joints (speakeasies). Many of the personnel already familiar to us at the beauty parlor also turn up at these haunts.

Shoeshine Parlors

There are four shoeshine parlors in the neighborhood. The interiors are dilapidated and small; the decor consists typically of pictures of nude women and baseball and football stars and newspaper clippings dealing with civil rights issues. Among the loiterers, conversations usually center around gambling, numbers, drinking, and partying. Many of the faces are familiar as patrons of the beauty parlor, especially the numbers-runner.

On Saturday, there are twice as many clients as midweek; for example, on one occasion only thirty-three people could be seen entering for actual service. Figuring from this, the four parlors could collectively make only fifty dollars on busy days, yet the owners dress well and drive expensive cars. The clientele, then, falls into two categories: those who come ostensibly for some service and remain no longer than fifteen minutes, and those who use the shoeshine parlors as hangouts to carry on other business, of which there are several varieties of illegal activity, including the sale of stolen goods and numbers-writing. Suspicious types move in and out and surreptitiously deposit parcels, probably stolen goods.

Pawnshops

Pawnshops, though owned exclusively by whites, are patronized solely by blacks. They also mesh in with the network of the criminal culture. For example, the beauty parlor proprietor owns a lot of expensive jewelry and household items bought from the professional thief. Her husband, who is usually in debt, steals the jewelry from his wife and pawns it; the pawnbrokers accept these goods without question. More significant, however, is the direct relationship between the thieves and the pawnbroker. Many of the people who traffic in stolen goods in the beauty parlor or in the shoeshine parlors also deal with the pawnbroker. Sometimes, when a beauty parlor client reneges on an order, the thief will dispose of the item at the pawnshop. The pawnbroker will generally ask for proof of ownership, but once one has established initial contact by pawning one item, he is no longer asked to supply this information. Every time an item is pawned it is checked on the patron's card.

Pawn tickets are sold freely in the neighborhood, although buying one can sometimes be a risky proposition. For example, an individual may pawn an item for five dollars and then forge a "2" in front of the "5." The original value of the item may have been twenty dollars at the time of the theft. The "Smart Man" may then approach someone and convince him that he has something worth seventy dollars. He will, however, accept thirty dollars for the pawn ticket. When the new owner then goes to the pawnshop to claim the item he becomes aware of the con. One would ordinarily surmise that these shops are patronized mostly by the poor; it is clear that this is not the case. The chief patrons are the thieves and the "suckers" just mentioned.

The Poolroom

As in the cases of the other establishments, the poolroom is usually crowded and is a focal point of several activities. The men who frequent the poolroom are all blacks ranging in age from twenty to thirty-five years. There are also a few adolescent boys utilized as messengers or decoys. In general, the poolroom functions as a hideout and gathering place for criminals, numbers men, and dope peddlers. As a rule, women do not frequent the poolroom, and the few who do come in are often looking for their "sweethearts," who they may not have seen for several days, even though they probably share the same room.

Joe is known as a pimp and con artist; he is a prominent poolroom personality. He dresses well, although he often appears worn out due to the fact that he has a "Jones"—that is, he is a narcotics addict. In order to satisfy the demands of his habit he engages in varied illegal activities, including the sale of stolen goods. He also controls between five and seven young teen-age prostitutes who surrender half of their daily take to him: he rationalizes the exploitation by claiming that he gives them "protection." He has a friend who maintains a large seven-room apartment, and the prostitutes pay three to five dollars a visit to use it. If they stay longer than the allotted time, the fee is increased. The economics of these transactions usually proceed as follows: if a girl earns thirty dollars, she hands Joe fifteen, gives the owner of the apartment between five and seven, and keeps the remainder for herself.

Characters such as Joe abound in these places, but they rarely stay around long. They generally wind up in the hospital because of taking drugs, in jail for pushing drugs, or in another community to establish a similar operation.

Bars and Speakeasies

Within the nine-block area five bars can be counted, all owned by whites but operated and patronized by blacks. Rather than serving as mere places of relaxation and conversation, they function as centers for illegal activities where one can meet "contact men" such as racketeers and thieves. The women present are largely barmaids and prostitutes. Many men use a bar as a staging area for illegal operations. The barmaid, who plays a significant role in these operations, is familiar with the communication codes used. As in the case of the beauty parlor, the women exhibit their expensive furs and jewelry and gossip about other women.

The bars open at 9 A.M. and close at 3 A.M. the following morning. In the morning and early afternoon business is slow. The people who enter in the morning are usually on specific missions; they confer with the bartender or barmaid and exit quickly, or drop off a parcel containing clothing, jewelry, or drugs. Around 2 P.M., business picks up and the drinkers and "after work" crowd make their entrance, the latter being mainly numbers men and thieves. At six o'clock the group's composition changes, the patrons crowd in, and the prostitutes take up their regular positions around the room. The prostitutes do not remain in one bar the entire evening, but usually frequent several bars in the same vicinity.

Occasionally, unescorted women who are not prostitutes will enter the bar; they appear lonely and are often looking for a boyfriend. They will accept a drink but are not available for money. For them, the bar is a place to socialize and find a new mate. The prostitutes who come to the bar, unlike those in the poolroom, do not "slave" for a pimp. They are older, have their own apartments, and are more able to fend for themselves.

The speakeasy joint functions as a storehouse for stolen goods, a depot for the collection of numbers, a haven for the alcoholic, a hotel for male and female transients, and a rendezvous for professional thieves. Most of its business is done after the liquor stores close or on Sundays and holidays. A profit of seventy-five cents to a dollar above the retail price is made on each flask of liquor; the added profit on a case of beer is about two dollars. The liquor is generally procured at cost price from a liquor store, or it is stolen. A liquor store owner will often recommend the speakeasy to his customers for after-hours drinking.

One speakeasy, located in a large apartment building, is owned and operated by a West Indian woman, who, like the beauty parlor owner, is well informed about the community and able to acquire stolen goods at the lowest cost. She exercises a great deal of influence among the male patrons, lends money, and runs other businesses. Money naturally flows into her hands since she sells food, receives a cut on every poker game played in her house, and is given large tips by her clientele. She also helps consume the liquor she sells to her men customers. In addition, she is an expert on abortion and knows other people in the field. Finally, she maintains a cooperative relationship with the police, who know that her joint exists.

The Numbers Racket

The relationship between the aforementioned establishments and personnel might be better understood if the role of the numbers man and the part played by the numbers racket in the ghetto were examined; for they evince clearly the networks of human association in the ghetto, as well as its relationship to the outside world.

The role of the numbers man or "runner" is a prominent one, for aside from his major function he is also a repository of valuable information, such as where to locate vacant apartments, where to find the speakeasies, where and for how much stolen merchandise can be purchased, where to find a pawnshop to "dump" stolen goods, and where the doctors and nurses in the area who perform abortions can be contacted.

Like the thief, the numbers man is one of the more affluent figures in the vicinity. He sports expensive clothing and jewelry and drives a fashionable late model car. His weekly income from the numbers alone varies between two hundred and fifty and three hundred dollars; "moonlighting" can yield him an extra eighty to one hundred dollars. These other sources generally come under the headings of the various "hustles" described.

For the numbers, each runner has his own circumscribed area or route, which involves servicing at least two hundred and fifty people a day. Since it is impossible to see these people individually, he utilizes various depots, such as the beauty parlor, the shoeshine parlor, the poolroom, etc. Virtually all of these establishments are related to the numbers racket in some way. The player leaves his money with a trusted person who holds it for the runner. The numbers are collected in the morning and taken to the "bank" headquarters; the staff consists of a bank lieutenant, bank supervisor, and the number-runners. The role of the lieutenant is to bail out the runner if he is caught and to pay off lucky winners.

The game is a well-organized business and operates smoothly. On most winning numbers the bank pays six hundred to one. The runner receives a twenty-five cent commission on each number bet, and he also receives tips from the winners. The lucky number is taken from mutual reports and comprises the last three digits of the day's total mutual handle, published in the city's daily newspapers. Thus, on a given day, if the total handle at Aqueduct is $3,587,153, the number is 153. A bet on a three-digit number is called a "straight play"; a "combination" is a wager on all six numbers of three chosen digits. A player who makes a combination wager of a dollar and a half on 153, for example, has twenty-five cents "riding" on numbers 153, 531, 351, 513, 135, and 315. If any of these win, he will collect approximately $125.

Some players resist the big payoff for the prospect of more frequent hits at lesser odds. In a single action the player takes only one digit, that is, bets on the first, second, or third digit of the day's number, allowing himself one chance in ten of winning. The payoff is then six or seven to one above his original investment: he is thus returned seven or eight dollars for each dollar bet. A player may also bet on the first or last two digits of the day's number; this is known as a "boledo" or "bolito" and has one chance in a hundred of winning. The payoff odds are between 50 and 64 to one depending on the bank.

The numbers man often makes contacts in local bars, many of which have ingenious devices for this purpose. For example, several bars have toilets whose doors can be opened from the outside only when the bartender presses a button activating an electric switch. When a player wants to make a wager, the button is pressed, requiring any suspicious policeman to break down the door in order to ensnare the parties making the transaction. Concealment of the collector's slips is crucial. Most of them write the numbers on thin metal foil, contending that it is easy to swallow and regain. In the event of an arrest, special lawyers are available to handle the case and bondsmen are specified by the bankers for bail for offenders. Any banker who shirks the responsibility of providing legal protection for his employees is boycotted by the collectors of his own "precinct" and of the adjoining areas.

The police, one runner claims, are aware of the racket and are paid off each week, in amounts commensurate with rank: a patrolman nets about ninety dollars, a sergeant one hundred and fifty dollars, and the lieutenants and the captain over two hundred dollars. The upper echelon officers' payments are handled by the "office," although they receive their share indirectly from a trusted patrolman or sergeant. Should a collector be arrested, no money is paid to a winner on his route, since the collector has been marked. One numbers man explained his relationship with the police this way:

> The local police don't molest me, but every now and then a tactical force from downtown makes a raid. The local police can't prevent the raids but they often learn of them early enough to give a warning to us. If a raid on a section is under way, the radio car in the neighborhood tells us which section they will raid next. One of the signals that a section has been raided was to see a police car in the neighborhood with its hood up and the patrolman inspecting the car, thus warning us to stay off the block.

Ex-Police Commissioner Michael J. Murphy pointed out, in an interview on June 26, 1964, that effective police work could reduce the activity of numbers racketeers to a great extent, but never by itself dry up the flow of money from numbers players to crime organizations. He urged public vigilance as the necessary factor in the elimination of the racket and attempted to validate this point by asserting that the quarter and half-dollar bets were also helping to support other nefarious operations, such as the narcotics trade and prostitution. The public at large probably would agree with this. However, given the above information, any major crusade to solve the so-called problem—as in the case of our periodic "crime waves"—would be abortive because gambling in the form of the numbers racket is a victimless crime. The laws prohibiting victimless crimes such as gambling, homosexuality, narcotics possession and use, abortion, and prostitution have proven to be virtually unenforceable since these practices often prevail in social contexts which support them. In addition, repressive laws and their enforcement often exacerbate the conditions they were designed to eliminate since they either directly or indirectly aid in the growth and operation of the prohibited practices: in the case of narcotics addiction, for example, the prohibition against possession of opiates and their dispensation by physicians to addicts results in the growth of an illicit trade in narcotics, and secondary crime on the part of addicts in order to enable them to purchase the drugs they require at the black-market price; in the case of the numbers racket the compliance of the police plus the tremendous community support of the racket render the prospect of enforcement an absurdity.

The numbers racket is interconnected with other activities besides law enforcement. Noteworthy among these are the religious practices, beliefs, and establishments in the ghetto. Many people will bet on a number as a consequence of a dream or a consultation with a reader. Dream books containing interpretations and lucky numbers are compiled and published under such colorful pseudonyms as "Madam Fu Fattam," "Professor Knoje," "Red Witch," and "Moses Magical." Within the community the relationship between the numbers game and quasi-religious practices is clearly a symbiotic one. Each profits from the other, although the participants in each are not necessarily aware of the cooperation. As George J. McCall has noted, the numbers racket "has become a 'multi-situated game,' requiring a vast proliferation of goals, roles, and strategies beyond those of the 'gaming encounter' itself. Many of these extrinsic game-elements are oriented toward the ecological struggle with other games of the community—the law enforcement game, the ecclesiastical game, the hoodoo game, etc."[13]

The Religious Game

Apart from the preceding, religion plays an important role in the lives of both middle-class and lower-class people in the ghetto. Among the beauty parlor patrons, for example, the middle-class (i.e., the professionals) are mainly Baptists and do not attend the storefront churches; instead, the majority are active in their own church organizations. The roles they play in church enhance their status among their friends and other members of the congregation. Their attendance is high and they donate money freely. After Sunday morning services, most of the gossip, in fact, involves invidious comparisons between donations made by parishioners. The institution supports this in its emphasis on money during the service, since the collection plate is passed around at least three times and lists indicating the amounts donated by members are circulated. The Baptist churches are usually larger, newer, and better furnished than the storefronts frequented by the lower classes.

The church is an outstanding social institution in the black community; it is the only large organization, aside from the black press, over which the black exercises much control. It functions as more than a religious organization as well, insofar as middle-class blacks use it as a base for self-expression, recognition, and leadership. The church offers opportunities to gain prestige, develop abilities, and preserve self-respect.

The middle- and lower-class West Indians are mostly Protestants, but their ties to church are of a different character and not as strong as those of the American Blacks. Many are skeptical about the emphasis placed on money in the American churches. As one West Indian puts it: "In the West Indies I went to any Anglican church. I did not have to give money to the building fund, organ fund, pastor's vacation fund. All of the people who give money are real hypocrites. They give money so that the pastor can read their names every Sunday."

The Storefront Church

The small storefront churches that dot the area mean a great deal to the people who participate in them; they serve as a place where people seek identification and the opportunity for self-expression. One preacher asserts that the church is a relief to the troubled soul, a concept revealed in the testimony of one woman:

I was very, very sick, and I was sure that I was going to die. I
began to pray to God; I never prayed hard before. Later that day a
friend of mine came to see me. She told me that somebody did "put a
hurting on me." She left and went for Pastor James. When Pastor
James came, he told me the same thing. So he pray, and pray and
then he give me some medicine. In a few days I was better. I will
never leave the Church. Pastor James is a miracle worker. He saved
my life.

At the end of the testament the congregation clapped and
shouted "Amen" and "Yea, Lord."

The sociologist Franklin Frazier believed that the storefront
churches flourished in the North because:

In the large churches, the Negro from the South, being lost in the
mass of members, has no status and longs for the . . . sympathetic
relationship which is provided in the face to face association in the
small church. Some ministers are, of course, charlatans, who take
advantage of the ignorance and simple faith of their followers. Then
there are the so-called "jack-leg" preachers, untrained and seeking
an escape from manual labor, who find in the "storefront" church a
chance for employment or a chance to supplement their regular
income.[14]

In a four-block span of the area there are fourteen such
churches. They are close to each other (sometimes so close that
one can attend one and follow the service in another) and in
some cases adjoin a bar, restaurant, garage, or factory. The
buildings that house them are dilapidated, and the pictures
representing Christ and the disciples are crudely executed.
Their notices and advertisements concerning the church's activities are often chalk-written on small blackboards and frequently contain misspellings.

Nine of the churches accommodate no more than thirty
people, and five hold between sixty and one hundred. The fur-
nishings consist mainly of stools, folding chairs, and benches.
Some have a very small table draped in white satin with vases,
bells, Bibles, and water tumblers resting on them. In all but three
the clergymen are male—all are called "Reverend." The complement of musical instruments accompanying a service depends
upon the church's prosperity; some have organs, others have
pianos, and as one goes down the line, trumpets, drums, and
tambourines. Handclapping is used throughout a service to

demonstrate approval of the hymns and of words expounded by the Reverend. The members all refer to each other as "brother" or "sister," possibly as a demonstration of the solidarity of the congregation. The majority of these congregations are women.

All the churches in the area except one hold services on Sundays. On hot days services are conducted with the doors open. The services seem disorderly when compared to those of the major denominations. The women dress in white with white head ties, and the men wear ordinary suits. The ministry in these churches appears to be largely self-ordained and without much formal education. The typical sermon appears extemporaneous; many of the themes center around the childhood experiences and hardships of the minister. From the standpoint of rational exposition, the sermons are often confusing and the biblical quotations and interpretations oft awry. Words are mispronounced, sentences omitted, and the whole body of the sermon is difficult to follow. It is obvious that the flock's enthusiasm is generated by something other than the techniques of conventional elocution.

The key element at the base of the emotional fervor of these services is the emphasis on spontaneous expression and the strong interaction between the congregation and the pastor; the excitement is heightened by the accompaniment of musical instruments. The fervor mounts to what seems almost an orgasmic pitch when finally the "spirit" manifests itself in the members, who sway rhythmically in all directions. Soon their bodies begin to vibrate with arms rigid at the sides or stretched out before them until the movements become so intense that they resemble epileptic convulsions. The frenzy lasts for approximately fifteen minutes, when the climax finally subsides and the more "sober" people assist in the revival of their brethren by fanning them or giving them water. During the seizure state they may have screamed or called on God to help them, or on deceased relatives. However, at the termination of the trance they seem to suffer amnesia about the whole experience, which makes the whole thing all the more convincing for the group as an audience and collectively validates the experience. The Reverend is gratified by this, since their performance, in turn, affirms his role, like that of a conductor whose musicians have superbly executed a symphony.[15] It is this kind of heightened group consciousness and expression which the sociologist Durkheim characterized as the quintessence of religious feeling, and it is ironic that such "avant-garde" phenomena as "underground churches," psychedelic cults, and emerging quasi-religious encounter groups are struggling to recapture the elements epitomized by "primitive" religious forms such as the storefront church.

Since the congregations of these churches are small, the pastors must have other jobs to subsist; many, in fact, work in factories and hospitals. The more skillful among them send representatives, usually women, into the community to beg for money. They are usually dressed in uniforms similar to those worn by Roman Catholic nuns, although they are more disheveled. Occasionally a child or a crippled man will be sent into a busy area. The women will often beg in bars and in front of barbershops, liquor stores, and subway stations; it is a thriving business, with funds often collected on the pretense that they will be utilized for renovating or building a church. Occasionally the pastor and his disciples may be seen driving a large, expensive limousine with a sign on the sun visor marked "clergy." The sign protects the pastor from being ticketed for illegal parking. Some of the pastors carry on sexual relationships with the women in their "flock." One minister was accused, but not convicted, of cohabiting with the entire group of women in his congregation. In some sense, one might comfortably say that the mildly exploitative practices of the clergy in areas such as this are merely caricatures of the baleful practices of the larger, established denominations throughout history. Ironically, as in the cases of the numerous unorganized and, hence, unprotected mixed bag of small-time criminals in these areas, their visibility and unsophisticated petty transgressions make them easy game for small-time critics and social reformers who take them to be the quintessence of the immorality lying at the roots of the ghetto's problems. At least three churches, in this respect, retain a vitality that the large denominations have lost in favor of bureaucratic respectability, a respectability which only more skillfully conceals their "white collar" style of economic predatoriness.

In sum, Negro churches are of many varieties and serve many interests, reflecting the diverse forces affecting them. The church is the predominant social institution in the community, the only one that can provide effective organization. Ghetto dwellers, like other lower-class urban groups, rarely join voluntary associations which would offer opportunities for the promulgation of common interests. The church, then, must be construed as an organization which fulfills needs otherwise unmet by private or public agencies.

Religious Stores, Readers and Advisers

In addition to the storefront churches there are religious stores which do not represent any particular denomination. Their windows are filled with exotic items such as: "Seven Seas Water," "Luck Hand Incense," "Dragon's Blood Incense," "Attraction Incense," "Success Oil," "Indian Horoscope Bath," "Three Wise Men Lucky Charm Bath," "Lover's Bath," "Cleopatra Powder," "Aunt Sally Lucky Dream," "Double Luck Incense," and "Des PoJo Oil-Protection Oil." Often hortatory statements, such as "God is Love, Let us trust in the Lord," are written after the product names. These stores thrive since they emphasize self-prescription for personal problems: pastors, readers, and advisers are consulted for the solution of more pressing and complex problems.

Black and "Indian" readers and advisers also do a lucrative business in the neighborhood. They prescribe herbs and medicines often bought in the religious stores. The cooperative relationships between these institutions reflect the conventional relationship between physician and pharmacist. The readers and advisers try to drum up business by distributing handbills like this one:

> Come to the House of Prayer
> MADAM STELLA [sic.]
> Reader and Helper
> Gives Lucky Days to Lucky Numbers

See this remarkable healer. You'll bless the day you did. If suffering, sick, in need of help, don't fail to consult her. She heals the sick, removes all pain. She is an ordained mistress and with God's help, she helps all who come to her. She is a faith healer. Her prayers remove all pain. She will reunite the separated. She asks you for one visit to prove to you she is the Divine Healer for whom you have been looking.

Hours 9 A.M. to 9 P.M. for appointment call ST 3-0000 HALF PRICE with this ad.

All of the advisers are women: on their signs the "Indian" advisers identify themselves with designations such as "Indian Woman" or "Hindu Woman."

The Indian readers are more transient: they stay in the area for a few months at most. As soon as one moves out, the place may be occupied by another Indian reader. Many have children who roam the streets and look filthy: these urchins are not accepted by the black children and consequently travel the neighborhood alone. The black children regard them as inferiors; members of one oppressed group thus oppress the members of another. Their transience obviously contributes to their lack of acceptance on the part of the community. On holidays such as Christmas, Easter, and Thanksgiving, the Indian families usually beg or sell artificial flowers, and on spring and summer evenings the elder family members sit in front of the store to attract clients. The door is usually left ajar, allowing passersby a glimpse of the "mysterious" interior, which is usually dirty and sparsely furnished.

Like her children, the Indian reader gets harsh treatment from her peers. In order to attract a potential customer's attention she may ask for a cigarette. A person familiar with this tactic may still respond if she is young and attractive, or dismiss her with a profanity. Responses of this sort are fairly typical and probably anticipated. Middle-aged people form a large part of the Indian reader's clientele, and thus she is often able to avoid surly young male clients. If she is engaged for a reading, she immediately gazes at her customer's palm, asks a series of questions, and then launches into various interpretations. Some herbs and potions may be prescribed, some advice given, and the client requested to return on a specified date.

The black reader's mode of operation offers a strong contrast to that of the Indian reader. For one thing, she seldom solicits business on her doorstep. Her place is cleaner, and the children are kept indoors. Unlike the Indian reader's children, the children of the black reader have strong ties with the neighborhood children; in fact, they gain high status because of their parent's occupation. One ten-year-old boy who proudly apprised me of his mother's role in the community explained that she was respected as a counselor for the troubled, similar to the pastors of the storefront churches.

It can easily be demonstrated, then, that astrologers, advisers, fortune-tellers, and others of that ilk actually do succeed in providing services of a genuine psychotherapeutic nature.[16] In the ghetto, where despair runs high, this kind of quick and inexpensive therapy works well within the cultural context of the community, and may offer comfort to the bruised spirit.

Thus we complete our tour through the ghetto. Admittedly, no attempt has been made to establish any statistical representativeness—that was not our aim. Our aim was to bring into relief some of the context from which the plethora of bloodless statistics is captured, and to illustrate by example and by contrast the nakedness of a notion promulgated as a panacea for a complicated social problem. We have seen the interconnectedness of ordinary business establishments, albeit many of them marginal, with such operations as professional thievery and the numbers game; we have witnessed the cooperation between those operations and the police; and we have noticed how these operations drain large amounts of money out of the ghetto. We have also noted the way in which these practices dovetail with the values and religious practices of the ghetto population. The examples, then, typify what might be called the character of ghetto enterprise.

Anthropologists have long noted that customs and technologies foreign to a given society will only be incorporated into the society if they can fit, often with major modifications, into the indigenous cultural configurations. The fate of such contrivances as "black capitalism," therefore, will be influenced and shaped by the extant networks of the ghetto; that is to say, quite apart from the intentions of policymakers, the implementation of such a program can only result in its incorporation into, or rejection by, the dominant patterns of ghetto entrepreneurship.

The overlapping of quasi-legitimate and illegitimate enterprise with conventional "games" makes it impossible, therefore, to apply the usual simplistic criteria of growth and economic development to the ghetto. The ghetto, like its neo-colonialist counterparts in the Third World, continues to be economically depressed partially as a result of the lack of legitimate entrepreneurship. But even more important is the factor of economic exploitation and the lack of opportunity for training its population for gainful employment and participation in the economy. Black capitalism, as it is normally defined, cannot be *the* solution. Only a small proportion of the total population at large is self-employed, and the disparity increases drastically with respect to the black American. The problem, therefore, is one of providing jobs, not businesses. Moreover, black capitalism, a concept which, incidentally, even conservatives embrace, is predicated upon the theory that a major source of the American black's problems is the disproportionately small black middle class. This is superficially true, but what must also be considered is the tremendous hostility between classes in the ghetto and the consequent lack of credibility of black middle-class spokesmen: accordingly, the slight increase in affluence of a slightly expanded black middle class is likely to exacerbate tensions rather than quell them.

In addition, it is not likely that such a program could succeed, even in a limited way, for the mortality rate of small business is high, and the attrition would probably be even greater in the ghetto. Furthermore, supposing the black middle class does arrive at a parity with the rest of American society, the black market (no pun intended) will become increasingly attractive to large corporations who can easily outcompete indigenous business. In a sense, black capitalism, as conceived by the Nixon administration, hangs as a specter over the ghetto much in the same way that American foreign investment is an anathema to underdeveloped nations. That is to say, if we accept the notion as policy, we must also accept as an eventuality the continuation of exploitation. It is not at all difficult to visualize this kind of solution as a continuation of black economic and political powerlessness.[17]

The idea of "black capitalism," then, is a slogan which seems to be overshadowing, but which is, in fact, the operational equivalent of "urban development," of "urban renewal," of "citizen participation."[18] It is at the very least naïve, and at most akin to the folkloristic notion of pulling oneself up by one's bootstraps. Such chimeras arise from success myths which have ignored the cultural pluralism of our society, and which, like all myths, serve to validate prevailing ideologies and to "energize" bureaucratic operations. Clearly, any attempt to ameliorate existing ghetto conditions must go beyond the formulistic thinking which has passed for problem-solving in public life.

2

The Needle Scene

Harold Tardola

*Participant observation is useful, even to quantitatively oriented
social scientists, in bringing to the surface in-depth information about communities, groups, social situations,
and the like. The observational method can also yield a
bounty in the form of the case study, transforming drab
generalizations about social phenomena into more colorful
and perceptive analyses. Harold Tardola presents a case-
study analysis of the world of the narcotics addict followed
by additional observational and case-study material on a
therapeutic milieu in which the treatment process proceeds
through the use of group processes and active participation
of addicts and ex-addicts. It is an example of how the
compelling quality of case materials effortlessly leads to
more generalized observations and assessments of a given
phenomenon.*

*Mr. Tardola currently heads the Disadvantaged Student Program
at the Rock County Campus of the University of Wisconsin.*

The hypothesis that the drug addict is functionally related to
his community as a supplier of stolen merchandise at a reduced
cost is the basis for the following study. However, in the testing

of this hypothesis it was necessary to investigate other related areas, such as the general subculture of drug addiction and the interrelationship between the addict and his community, which involves the interaction between the addict and his relatives, friends, and peers. Also involved is the process of how the addict is exploited and utilized in certain urban areas.

The Addiction Process

There are many drugs that are habit-forming and people who use them can be addicted psychologically as well as physically. The individuals discussed below are or were psychologically and physically addicted to heroin.

The World Health Organization defines drug addiction as "a state of periodic or chronic intoxication produced by the repeated consumption of a drug (natural or synthetic). Its characteristics include: (1) an overpowering desire or need (compulsion) to continue taking the drug and to obtain it by any means; (2) the tendency to increase the dose; (3) a psychic (psychological) and generally a physical dependence on the effects of the drug; (4) an effect detrimental to the individual and to society."[1]

Tolerance and dependence are the critical factors of the addiction process. An addict must know how to use drugs, and this involves awareness of how to administer the drug and the recognition of its effects.

Beyond this, one must have some motivation for trying the drug—whether to relieve pain, to produce euphoria, to please a loved person, to achieve acceptance in a group, or to achieve some other goal. The goal need have little to do with the specific effects of the narcotic. Moreover, the motivation or goal of initial drug-use must be sharply distinguished from the motivation to maintain a drug habit. The latter is a product of learning which seems to depend on the interaction between the drug effects, especially in the first experience of withdrawal, and the self-conception of the drug user.[2]

Generally, tolerance refers to the process through which the body adapts to the effects of a drug such as heroin. In order to maintain the effectiveness of the "kick," the user must increase his dosage progressively. With each successive increase there is a proportional increase of bodily tolerance (physiological dependence) so that the user's bodily system requires the drug to function normally. When the user recognizes that the acute distress accompanying withdrawal of the drug (e.g., stomach pains, muscle spasms, nausea, and so forth) can only be alleviated by maintaining his dosage, he has effectively become an addict.

It must be emphasized that soon after the initial experiences an addict no longer experiences physical pleasure (kicks) from the use of heroin. It is the fear of withdrawal symptoms and the psychological dependence on drugs that maintain the addiction process.

Street Addicts

Gaining the trust of the addict is essential in any study of his problem. He is wary of everyone except other addicts, and sometimes he mistrusts even them. It is almost impossible to get viable information from him in the traditional institutional setting; an addict interviewed in jail will only give information which he feels will help his cause. Information for this paper was gathered from observing some addicts in their daily social environment, and interviewing others in an untraditional institutionalized setting which allows and encourages freedom of expression.

First case: Harry W., a thirty-seven-year-old Negro, living in the Bedford-Stuyvesant area of Brooklyn, New York, has been a heroin addict for twenty years. As a member of a teen-age gang, Harry was introduced to drugs and later developed burglary skills. In the initial stages he was typical of young addicts of the early 1950's. When many of these were interviewed in 1952, they were still in the early stages of their addiction.

They were "snatch and grab" junkies supporting their habits through petty thievery, breaking into cars, shoplifting, and a variety of "scheming," such as "laying a story" on a "sucker" in the hope of gaining sympathy and some cash. Some enterprising ones actually had girls out "hustling" for them through "boosting" (shoplifting) and "turning tricks" (prostitution). Despite the ragged state of their clothing and the harried nature of their existence, they regarded themselves as members of an elite, the true "down cats," on the best "kick" of them all, "horse" (heroin). Many of them were still living at home, although they had long since exhausted the last reserves of patience of their families and "fenced" much of their movable property. Few, if any, of them had finished high school, and, on the average, they had little or no employment experience. Their attitudes towards work and the daily routine that steady employment presupposed were entirely negative. Their number one hazard was the "man" (the police). Once they became "known junkies"—that is, known to the police—they were frequently picked up and sometimes sentenced—mostly for misdemeanors and, consequently, for short sentences. . . . The impression gained from interviewing them was that these addicts were petty thieves and petty operators who, status-wise, were at the bottom of the criminal population or underworld.[3]

Today Harry uses these skills to get money to support his habit. In his endeavor to keep it under control he occasionally has himself institutionalized. Sometimes he allows himself to be arrested; at other times he voluntarily enters rehabilitation programs. Harry is proud of the fact that he has never been arrested for burglary. In conversation, he will relate that he is an expert burglar and that he is capable of breaking and entering any residence. Most of his crimes take place outside of the Bedford-Stuyvesant area because he feels there is very little to steal there. However, if he is desperate, he will steal from his neighborhood. He associates mainly with heroin addicts; all others he considers "square," but he still maintains a strong relationship with his mother, who is not addicted.

Harry takes his stolen goods to either a pawnshop or a "fence" (a receiver of stolen goods), who sells these items to stores and individuals in the Bedford-Stuyvesant area at approximately one-tenth of their value. Because of his limited resources, he does not allow his habit to become more than fifteen dollars per day.

Second case: Miguel R., a Puerto Rican, born in Brooklyn, first became acquainted with heroin when he was in junior high school, and has been an addict for ten of his twenty-three years. He is tall, extremely good-looking, and most attractive to women. He supports his thirty-dollar-a-day habit by carnal pandering, and has women (six of them) ranging in age from fifteen to thirty-five working for him. They each average approximately one hundred dollars daily of which his share is half. These women are also addicts.

In addition to heroin, Miguel has other expensive habits—his fifty $200 suits and his 1970 El Dorado Cadillac. From the ages of thirteen to fifteen he resorted to theft. When he was sixteen, he became romantically involved with a twenty-five-year-old woman addict. She was supporting her habit by prostitution and readily agreed to support his as well. Through her, Miguel was able to meet other women who were also willing to prostitute themselves for him. In return, his function is to supply them with drugs and to provide satisfaction in terms of their personal sexual needs.

If it is true, as the sociologist Kingsley Davis and others suggest, that prostitution is functional within any social system, then Miguel can be said to have a functional relationship to the Bedford-Stuyvesant community.

Third case: Thomas F. is thirty-eight years old. As a member of a teen-age Negro gang in Bedford-Stuyvesant, Brooklyn, he learned how to smoke marijuana, also what the effects and expectations of heroin were.

Although the use of heroin was prevalent in his neighborhood at that time, Thomas' first experience with the drug was during the Korean War when he was on leave in Tokyo. His addiction was discovered, and he was given a dishonorable discharge. He also served time—five years—in Lexington, Kentucky, where he learned more about the use of drugs and the illegal means of obtaining them. Today, in order to support his habit, he is involved in various illegal activities. His hustling involves petty thievery, purse-snatching, pickpocketing, breaking into pay telephones, and the like.

Thomas has a twenty-five-dollar-a-day habit, which he supports mainly by pushing or selling drugs. (He hustles in order to support his daily living needs, not his drug habit.) He sells his drugs openly on one particular corner in the Bedford-Stuyvesant area, and is able to do this by sharing part of the proceeds with the police in the area.

Fourth case: Johnny B., age twenty-eight, has been an addict for the past fourteen years. His first experience with heroin was at a dance in the Palladium ballroom in Manhattan, in the men's room, he took a fix on a dare from his friends. Johnny, also Negro, works as a mechanic in a gas station in Bedford-Stuyvesant. He is married to another addict; they do not have any children. He tries to bring in the extra thirty-five dollars, his wife and he need daily to support their habit, by working overtime at his place of employment.

If he is unable to earn this amount, he occasionally steals a car and sells it in the neighborhood. These automobiles are stolen upon order of the prospective buyer. When Johnny is in need of money, he will let it be known that he will obtain any kind of car requested; he steals only new cars and only on order. Since he has access to the gas station's garage at night, he is able to repaint and change some of the features of the car he has stolen before he makes his sale. Part of the profits are shared with the owner of the garage. He usually charges one-half the list price of the stolen automobile, and the buyer must present proof of his ability to pay cash for the goods. Johnny considers himself an expert car thief; however, he limits this activity for fear that overinvolvement would lead to his arrest and conviction. His social acquaintances are other drug addicts. His wife does not have any means of supporting her habit, but on rare occasions she practices prostitution to support his and her habits of twenty dollars and fifteen dollars a day respectively.

Fifth case: Wallace L., age thirty-three, has been a user for the past seventeen years. When he was nine years old he ran away from home and began living on the streets. From that time until he was eighteen, he was in foster homes or reform schools, or on the street where he gathered the knowledge and folklore of hustling. This involved petty thievery, purse-snatching, various forms of the "con game," and other activities designed to beat the system. An adequate description of this type of activity can be found in Harold Finestone's article, "Cats, Kicks, and Color."

He achieved his goals by indirection, relying, rather, on persuasion and on a repertoire of manipulative techniques. To deal with a variety of challenging situations, as those arising out of his contacts with the police, with past and/or potential victims, he used his wits and his conversational ability. To be able to confront such contingencies with adequacy and without resort to violence was to be "cool." His idea was to get what he wanted through persuasion and ingratiation; to use the other fellow by deliberately outwitting him. . . . The image of himself as "operator" was projected onto the whole world about him and led to a complete skepticism as to other persons' motives. He could relate to people by outsmarting them, or through open-handed and often ruinous generosity, but his world seemed to preclude any relationship which was not of a "scheme" or did not lend itself to an "angle."[4]

Wallace learned to use addicts to gain his own ends; although he used heroin, he never became addicted to it. He became a "joy popper" (one who takes drugs only occasionally). Because he could control his intake, he was able to enter into the subculture of drug addiction and make the necessary connections to begin his career as a pusher.

Today he is looking forward to a point in his career where he will be able to accumulate enough money to become a "big-time operator." With $20,000 he will be able to purchase one pound of heroin, set up his own "factory" (a clandestine residence where heroin is cut), redistribute this merchandise to other junkie-pushers, and make a profit of $80,000.

The cases mentioned above are all members of the Bedford-Stuyvesant community, and belong to the special subculture of the addict.

The social world of addiction contains a loose system of organizational and cultural elements, including a special language or argot, certain artifacts, a commodity market and pricing system, a system of stratification and ethical codes. The addict's commitment to these values gives him a status and an identity. In addition to these direct links to the world of addiction, becoming an addict means that one assumes a number of secondary status characteristics in accordance with the definitions the society has of this activity. Some of these are set forth in federal and local laws and statutes, others are defined by the stereotypic thinking of members of the larger society about the causes and consequences of drug use. The addict's incarceration in correctional institutions has specific meanings which he finds reflected in the attitudes adopted toward him by members of non-addict society and by his fellow addict. Additionally, as his habit grows and the demand for drugs gets beyond any legitimate means of supply, his own activities in satisfying his increased craving give him direct experiential evidence of the criminal aspects of self. These meanings of self as a criminal become internalized as he begins to apply criminal argot to his activities and institutional experiences. Thus, shoplifting becomes "boosting," the correctional settings become "joints," and the guards in such institutions become "screws."[5]

In brief, the subculture of addiction reinforces and maintains the process. However, the addict is not an entity within an isolated system. The subculture of addiction is also related in a direct way to the community at large. This relationship involves the supply of certain goods and services which the community desires. It also involves the utilization of the addict as an exploitative instrument by certain segments of the community. To corroborate this, the writer interviewed five ex-drug addict residents of Daytop Village in Staten Island, New York, to study the addict's relationships in other communities.

Ex-addicts

Daytop Village is a private institution which was established several years ago to provide the type of therapy which would help the individual addict to return to his community as a healthy person. An attempt is made to treat the emotional problems causing the addiction. Such treatment consists of massive group therapy. When an individual wants to enter Daytop Village, he must seek his entrance through an intermediary— in most cases, the New York State Narcotic Addiction Control Commission. If he is recommended, he must be able to pass other examinations in order to be accepted. These examinations are probe sessions, in which the subject is questioned by resident ex-addicts who have had more or less the same social, criminal, and economic experiences. Thus, a subject entering with a criminal history of armed robbery is initially approached by a resident who has had the same criminal background. This probing takes place within a group context, and the function of the resident is to question the addict in such a way that he is unable to use subterfuge or self-deception. He will try to maintain his "tough-guy" image as long as possible, but confronted with someone with the same image from the group, he is forced to be truthful.

The importance of the probe session is threefold: to acclimatize the entering addict; to make him realize that he must always be truthful while at this institution and that he will be invariably confronted with whatever lies he may tell; to make him review his own life and become aware of who he is and what he is.

If the probe sessions have been successful and the addict remains at Daytop, he is then allowed to participate in the encounter sessions. These sessions allow each resident to express how he feels about himself and others in the group. The next step is the marathon sessions, which sometimes last as long as three days (normally they run fourteen hours). In the marathon sessions each member tells everything he can remember of his life, so that all can see the patterns of his experience and thus be helped to understand how and why they themselves became involved with drugs.

There is a strict regimentation of duties for each resident. When he enters the Daytop community he is given the most menial task—dishwashing—and is assigned to a more experienced resident who has the title of expediter and to whom he is held responsible. The expediter must know where the addict is and what he is doing at all times. His self-improvement and success within the group therapy sessions and on the job are used as indices of his ability for promotion to a more responsible position. The residents are never given jobs which are easy for them; they have to prove themselves under stress. Their "As If" program involves the placing of an individual into an occupational position where he has no experience or knowledge. He must act out this role under supervision "as if" he knew what he was doing, on the premise that a large part of doing a job is the will to do it.

After several weeks the Daytop Village resident has acquired some ability to relate to the realities of his life. He is able to tell others of his experiences in a sincere and truthful manner. The following were interviewed:

First case: Freddie G. is from Newark, New Jersey, of Italian descent, and is thirty-five years old. He first got in trouble with the law at the age of ten. When he was twelve, he was using "goof balls," amphetamines, and marijuana, and at the age of fifteen became a heroin addict. Freddie grew up in Newark's North Ward, a predominantly Italian neighborhood. His family consisted of his father, mother, sister, and himself. His father used to beat Freddie viciously and try to eradicate the effects of the beating by excessive expression of love. The boy's reaction was alternately to love and hate his father. His mother consistently spoiled him; when she disagreed with some directive of his father, she communicated this feeling to her son behind his father's back—for example, if Freddie wanted to stay out later than usual or go to a movie without his father's permission, his mother said yes behind his father's back and provided the necessary money. Freddie's reaction to his mother was to be excessively dependent on her. He was incapable of self-discipline because of inconsistent treatment from his parents.

Freddie went through three phases in his criminal career. The first was investigative, the second his actual career and associative values, and the third the breakdown of his criminal skills and ensuing desperation. In his teens he was involved in many types of criminal activities—petty thievery, armed robbery, car theft, burglary, carnal pandering, and general hustling. Eventually he became a specialist, and his specialty was the check game. Through association with people whom he could trust—that is, other addicts—he became part of an elaborate criminal organization. Individuals in this organization would contact and be contacted by outsiders who had stolen blank checks from factories, stores, and other businesses. Freddie would then provide expert forged identities and correct forged stamps for the checks. These checks and the forged identities were then cashed by other members of this organization and the remuneration would be shared by all.

Freddie was proud of his skills and the respect of his associates. He was finally arrested for dealing with "hot paper" (blank checks that were stolen for over a sufficiently long period to permit the original owners time to report and describe this material to the police) and served five years in prison. Once released, he lost his nerve for fear of becoming a third-time loser. He returned to drugs and began to hustle, passing a bad check now and then, petty thievery, car theft—any means of

obtaining money to support his habit. During this period he under-
went a personality disorientation which further contributed to
his desperation. Finally, when he felt he was no longer able to
continue his criminal career, he applied to and was accepted at
Daytop Village.

Second case: Charlie H. is a sixteen-year-old Negro youth who
has been at Daytop Village for two months. Charlie comes from
the Lower East Side in New York and first began using heroin
at the age of thirteen, having been introduced to the drug by his
friends while attending high school. He supported his habit by
car theft, armed robbery, purse-snatching, and general hustling;
his specialty was stealing cars on order. Charles was never
arrested for his criminal activities; he was caught giving himself
an injection of heroin in the boy's room of his high school, and
was recommended to Daytop Village by the Juvenile Court.

Third case: Gary S. is a white twenty-five-year-old male from
a middle-class area in Staten Island, New York. He has a B.S.
degree in mathematics from Manhattan College in New York
City, and was employed by the New York City Department of
Social Services as a caseworker. Gary began using drugs while
still in college, first marijuana, then LSD, and finally heroin,
to which he was introduced by a friend. He had been a heroin
addict for three years and had supported his habit by supplementing his salary as a caseworker with shoplifting. However,
he was poor at the game and was eventually arrested. Upon
being arraigned in Criminal Court he was recommended to and
accepted by Daytop Village.

Fourth case: Elsie R. is a thirty-one-year-old woman who came
from the Bedford-Stuyvesant area in Brooklyn. She is an only
child whose parents separated when she was three years old. Her
mother, a member of a Fundamentalist Protestant sect, attempted
to bring the girl up within the strict confines of this sect. During
her junior year in high school, Elsie became pregnant and was
forced to get an abortion by her mother, who felt ashamed of her.
When she returned to school, she began to use drugs and soon
became addicted to heroin. Also at this time, she met a young
male addict and began living with him in a common-law relation-

ship. Her common-law husband supplied her with drugs when he was able to steal, but when he was unable to, she worked as a prostitute. Elsie felt that prostitution was too emotionally strenuous and volunteered for and was accepted into the Daytop Village program.

Fifth case: Sheryl P. is a pretty twenty-year-old Negro girl from the Gowanus section of Brooklyn. She has been a heroin addict for the past five years, having first been introduced to drugs by her boyfriend at the age of fifteen. Previously Sheryl had spent a very lonely childhood. Her parents were from the West Indies and had the double stigma of being not only new immigrants but also Blacks. There were no relatives or friends in their new land, and both parents had to work to provide an adequate living for their two daughters. Sheryl was not encouraged to develop relationships with other boys and girls; she spent her time either watching television or engaging in private fantasies based on the material she had seen on television. When she finally met her boyfriend she was willing to do anything to keep his companionship, and began providing heroin with money earned by prostitution. Sheryl expressed her feelings about prostitution: "The first time I was scared as hell to try something like that but after that it was real easy because I knew I was pretty."

Eventually her parents realized that their daughter was addicted to heroin and immediately sought help. They were instrumental in getting her into the Daytop Village program. Sheryl reported that she had enjoyed her life as a drug addict because she never realized she was addicted. "I never thought I was hooked, but there I was every night with a cooker."

In the above information there is a configuration of patterns that the addict finds easy to accept. At first he is involved with the pleasurable experience of rebellion and being "different" from his peers. Then there is an acceptance of his new peer group—other addicts and the culture they are a part of. In the cases mentioned there seemed to follow a period of deterioration or fear of imminent disaster. During this last period

an episode of cure begins in the private thoughts of the addict rather than in his overt behavior. These deliberations develop as a result of experience in specific situations of interaction with important others that cause the addict to experience social stress, to develop some feeling of alienation from or dissatisfaction with his present identity, and to call into question and examine it in all of its implications and ramifications. In these situations the addict engages in private self-debate in which he juxtaposes the values and social relationships which have become immediate and concrete through his addiction with those that are sometimes only half remembered or only imperfectly perceived.[6]

Freddie G. describes this "as the worst period of my life. I found myself wandering around the streets of New York filthy all the time. I had no place to stay. I slept on rooftops, in hallways, in damp cellars, any available place and always with one eye open. I felt that everyone was my enemy, and I thought everybody was a stoolie. I was really low then, not eating, using dirty 'works,' and was cold all the time." It was at this time that Freddie got hepatitis and was finally taken to a hospital, where he made the decision to enter Daytop.

In the case of Charlie H. it was his ability to perceive that his relationship with heroin was becoming too much of a bond and was no longer a pleasurable experience. "I couldn't control it anymore. There wasn't any fun in it. . . . When I finally got caught I was happy."

Gary S. was never fully indoctrinated into the culture of the drug addict. He, too, expressed relief at being caught in the act of shoplifting and eventually being admitted to Daytop.

Elsie R. could not accept herself as a prostitute. "I was turning two dollar tricks and lost about sixty pounds. I was filthy, didn't have any teeth, my hair was falling out. I was no longer a person." Once Elsie recognized what she had become and could no longer accept herself or find other models to emulate, she had an emotional breakdown which subsequently allowed her to be admitted to Daytop.

In all of these cases the individuals developed a feeling of alienation from or dissatisfaction with their identity as addicts. They grew more aware of the world around them, and of the difference between themselves and non-addicts, and were able to accept the idea that the "square" world wasn't all that bad.

At this point, it is of interest to look at one more ex-addict and his introduction into Daytop Village. Vincent T. is an eighteen-year-old Puerto Rican who had been on heroin for four years. He was first introduced to drugs in junior high school and supported his habit by petty thievery, purse-snatching, and general hustling. A friend of Vincent's was a resident of Daytop Village and tried to interest him in the program, but he refused to listen, commenting that this was only for "squares." One evening his friend invited him to attend a party at a private house. The party would be a very swinging affair, he promised, and guaranteed that Vincent would have a "ball."

When they arrived, the party was on, the music was "groovy," the people were a "gas," and Vincent felt a strong empathy with all those present. He couldn't understand his feelings, or why at a party with so many "swinging" people there were no alcoholic beverages being served. A little later he noticed that his new friends had formed a group and were carrying on an earnest conversation. The music had been turned off; the party mood had changed into a very intensive, interpersonal experience. These people were all talking about their experiences with heroin and about their lives in general, and before he realized it he, too, was talking about his experiences and his life in general. What actually was occurring was the beginning of a marathon session which lasted a full twenty-four hours. When it was over, Vincent felt that his whole life had changed and that there were other "bags" to get into besides that of "H."

Here we have the case of an individual who was addicted but had not suffered any perceptible stress in his addictive process. However, his novel introduction into a Daytop marathon group therapy session presented him with new role models, even though they conflicted with the values he had previously accepted from the culture of drug addition.

The Role of the "Square" Community

The configuration of patterns that the addict finds easy to accept emanates from two sources—the addict himself and the community. The community supports the addict by buying stolen goods from him, thereby providing him with the funds to purchase his heroin. The stolen goods are purchased by private individuals and stores which sell these goods back to the community. The female addict in the lower-class area functions as a prostitute, and thus she, too, is supported by the community.

It is also a fact that very considerable profits are made by insurance companies in areas afflicted with large-scale addiction. Property insurance rates are high, although the individual storekeepers are not the victims of increased insurance premiums; the customers are the victims here because of increased retail prices. The storekeepers also make bogus claims about stolen or missing stock and collect indemnities for these false claims.

The police likewise have a role in this configuration of patterns. All the addicts interviewed reported that the police took bribes, and that some sold heroin. The biggest offenders are said to be members of the Narcotics Squad. As a rule, none of the important people involved in the manufacture and sale of drugs are ever arrested. Occasionally, however, if there is public pressure in the form of newspaper editorials, radio and television commentaries, and widespread complaints, there are large-scale arrests of addicts and even of big-time operators. Arrests are also made whenever addicts fail to cooperate with the police—such as refusing to inform or not sharing the profits received from selling drugs.

This information was substantiated unofficially by members of the New York State Narcotic Addiction Control Commission whom the writer interviewed. One member in charge of an information office reported the following: One day he saw a black limousine pull up and park in front of his office (on a crowded avenue). A man whom the official recognized as a known pusher stepped out of the car. He was carrying a transparent polyethylene bag inside of which were little white packets that looked suspiciously like ten-dollar bags of heroin. He entered a bar across the street and returned without the bag, then remained seated in his car until a policeman came along. The officer said a few words to the driver, who handed him an envelope—unquestionably his payoff. A policeman friend of the writer reports there are so many addicts on the street that "if all were arrested, there would be no room in jail for them." That is why most policemen ignore them, and some decide, with the silent acceptance of their colleagues, to make money on the addicts.

Drug addiction may be viewed as a system of human interaction. Addicts share the same *activity*—the use of and the means of obtaining drugs. They *interact* with each other in the exchange of drugs and the relationship involved with them. They share the same *sentiments:* every addict interviewed believed that all drug users are "hip" (acceptable) and non-users are "squares" (unacceptable). All "squares" are to be taken advantage of in the process of getting drugs. The last statement forms the basic norm for the system.

The adherence to the system emotionally alienates the addict from his community. He then becomes an exploitative instrument of certain forces in the community. By providing stolen goods at a reduced rate to impoverished members of the group, he helps to ameliorate their frustrations. (This is especially true of black urban communities.) He is also utilized by the economic forces in these communities as a means of exploiting black people— increased prices, bogus insurance claims, retail stores directly involved with the sale of stolen merchandise.

In general, the addict is an instrument utilized to impede social mobility. Most often he is not aware of this particular aspect of his role; if he saw how he was being used, he might no longer be an addict. As Finestone puts it:

"In an open class society where upward mobility is positively sanctioned, an awareness and sensitivity to the dominant values is the first stage in their eventual assimilation. Insofar as the social type of cat represents a reaction to a feeling of exclusion from access to the means toward the goals of our society all measures such as improve educational opportunities which put these means within his grasp will hasten the extinction of this social type. Just as the 'hoodlum' and 'gangster' types tend to disappear as the various more recently arrived ethnic groups tend to move up the status scale of the community, so it can confidently be expected that the cat as a social type will tend to disappear as such opportunity become more prevalent among the colored population."[7]

3

Birth of a Mini-Movement: *A Tenants' Grievance Committee*

John W. Ford

"Black bourgeoisie" is the name given to Afro-Americans who have made it. The torments of the parvenu have for some time provided a theme for popular literature and no doubt, we can soon look forward to the appearance of the black social climber in the novel and the mass media. The black middle class is small but growing, and so is the ethnic consciousness that nips at its heels. As in the case of other ethnic minorities, the middle-class black is plagued by conflicting life styles which make claims on his identity: on the one hand he resents the affront to his blackness; on the other, he wants to preserve the respectability and comforts of the middle-class life style that he shares with middle-class whites. For the most part, his conflicts will manifest themselves in a manner common to those caught in the spiraling upward skid—the pursuit of the stereotyped material and

*moral attributes of the straining set. However, as we witness
the early stages of black social mobility we shall also see examples of middle-class black activism such as are exemplified in the tenants' grievance committee. The following study
offers us a microcosm of the elements typifying the social
problem, and hence presents a unique opportunity to examine the interplay of social forces and interests as the
conflicting parties draw their ranks and seek preeminence
for their definition of the situation.*

*John W. Ford, instructor of sociology at Brooklyn College, is en-
gaged in administering the development of the Afro-American Institute at that college.*

Usually, the expression social movements conjures up images
of mass rallies, marches, violence, and revolution. It is
this kind of imagery, however, which can blind one to things
taking place in the world around him. Most social movements
arise out of a condition of perceived collective discontent. In
terms of the contemporary scene, the most noteworthy example
that comes to mind is that covered by the rubric "civil rights
movement." Nevertheless, there are many groupings of people
who act collectively to remedy some situation or other which,
while having ethnic or racial overtones, escape notice and are
not included under monolithic headings such as civil rights,
student power, the labor movement, and so on. One such movement, the tenants' association, is typical of small community
groups which have formed as a means of people trying to shape
their lives and actualize their ideals in the face of some situation
perceived as threatening or dissatisfying.

In the pages that follow we shall see how a group organized at
first with rather hazy aims and objectives propels itself into an
organization with specific goal-directed actions. We shall see
emerging the patterns of organization and leadership that are
recognized as typical of the social movement, and we shall also
witness the subtle interplay of factors involved in the middle-
class Negro's social predicament which lend shape and form to
his efforts to make his existence comfortable.

The name of the community involved in this study is the

Lancaster-Bennet Apartments. These are four nineteen-story buildings, erected and completed around the middle of 1963, when occupancy began. Located in the Soundview section of the East Bronx, the community is allegedly a middle-income development financed under the Mitchell-Lama Law, whereby the state finances 90 percent of the development and the remainder is financed by a private investor who attempts to realize a profit of 6 percent on his investment. It is not a city housing project.

The apartments were occupied by a large percentage of tenants who had previously considered other apartments nearby, but who were disappointed in the size of the rooms, the layouts, and the design of terraces. They had then walked a few blocks to the Lancaster-Bennet Apartments and looked at them. Most tenants to whom I spoke agreed that the Lancaster-Bennet Apartments offered the best value of all of the communities viewed. The rooms were attractively laid out and large, and the terraces were more esthetically pleasing. The prospective tenants were also told that a t.v. intercom system would eventually be installed. This promise of an intercom system which would enable tenants to view callers on their screens was apparently a major reason for many of the tenants' decisions to live at the apartments. Many of the tenants were Negroes, and most were rather favorable to the rigid screening procedures used, typically, "to keep the wrong class of people out."

Mountains and Molehills: The Stage of Social Unrest

Rumor plays an important part in any given social situation, and it began to influence the orientation and attitudes of many of the tenants soon after the first had moved in. Conversations could be heard on the buses, in the lobbies, in the laundry room, and in the elevators. It was rumored that "a large number of Negroes are moving in."

"Oh? Well, if they're the right kind they have just as much right to live here as anyone else." This last statement could just as easily come from a Negro resident of Lancaster as a white resident. The rumors continued.

"You know, studies have been shown to reveal that when a certain point is reached with Negroes moving in, the whites begin to move out."

"Is that a fact? Well, I'm for integration and all that, and as long as you know how to act, I don't care if you're brown, black, white, yellow, green."

"Yes, besides, they're doing a terrific job of screening. We won't have to worry about the wrong kind of people getting in *here*. Do you know that when I applied I had to tell them all about my . . . and it took so long for my application to come through . . . and they turned this couple down although they easily cleared $15,000 a year."

"We won't have to worry. That's for sure."

It was also rumored that the apartments were not being rented as rapidly as they should have been.

"I wonder why? Could it be that there're so many of *them* moving in. . . ."

"No. Of course not. First of all, next to food, shelter is the most essential necessity to a Negro, and you've got to admit that these are some of the best places to live for the money. Even if they didn't have a single white tenant there'd be enough Negroes and Puerto Ricans to rent these entire apartments."

"That's what I mean. There're so *many* of them moving in that . . ."

"They're doing a terrific job of screening, just remember that. They don't want another ghetto here. They could have all of these apartments rented by tomorrow if that's what they wanted. I don't think you have anything to worry about, honestly."

The tenants did worry, however. Their apprehension increased after hearing that the TV intercom system might not be installed because the cost would be too great. They heard that the manager, Mr. Bernstein, was not a "nice" man. They heard of neighbors' experiences in which they had informed Mr. Bernstein of a faulty ceiling or maladjusted refrigerator or a squeaking closet door, and had received an answer to their problems that was frequently unsatisfactory. They seemed to detect a change in the attitude of management from the time they spoke to the salesmen and the time they had moved in.

The tenants' fears were finally confirmed when they began to notice a large number of the "wrong kind of people" in the laundry rooms, in the recreational areas, and in the lobbies. If there had been any doubts previously, these were removed when an instance of major significance occurred. The benches located in front of the apartments had to be taken out because of the vulgar language used by the occupants. Complaints from the tenants on the lower floors made it apparent that the situation was intolerable. I checked with several of the guards and found that it was not teen-agers who were predominantly the guilty ones, but adults.

When the apartments became fully occupied, apparently by the "wrong kind of people," some tenants began talking about moving out. Others said: "Be damned if I'm going to move. I had a tough time trying to get in here and if I move now, the same thing will probably occur the next place I go. Besides, the white man can move to just about any place he wants. Me, I'm limited. That's why I'm going to stay and do something about it."

It was this type of person who remained to become a member of the action committee.

After the formation of the committee, it was discovered that many of the "wrong kind of people" did not live in the Lancaster apartments but would frequently wander in and use the community's facilities. This resulted in a more determined drive to obtain some sort of security system which would reduce the frequency of such occurrences to a minimum.

It is significant that many of the tenants were concerned about keeping the "wrong kind of people" out of the apartments. It is even more significant that they were less concerned about simply keeping the wrong *race or class* of people out than about keeping certain *lower-class racial* or ethnic groups, if not out, at least to a minimum. Specifically, they were concerned about the rumored large percentage of lower-class Negroes and Puerto Ricans who were apparently moving in.

These concerns were probably based upon previous experiences, either directly or indirectly, in which a majority of Negroes and Puerto Ricans were thought to have led to a deterioration of the community. It did not occur to many that perhaps the members of the minority groups who desired to live at the Lancaster-

Bennet Apartments would behave as other American middle-class people. They may have feared that the services of management would probably be influenced by the percentage of minority group tenants—that is, if the percentage of these were low, management's services would remain high; if the percentage were high, management's services would deteriorate. "Maybe it's because they're aware that so many Negroes and Puerto Ricans are already here and they don't care any longer. That's the way they work, y'know." Beyond this, the tenants were aware of a kind of manifested "guilt by association." They considered it important that the percentage of Negro and Puerto Rican tenants remain low lest it reflect on their image: a large percentage of the wrong kind of people seemed to imply that the other tenants would suffer the consequences of living in the same community.

Thus, rumors began to circulate as a result of such fears. Some were aware of the phenomenon of the "tipping point," whereby whites begin to depart as certain minority group members become numerous in a community. Others attempted to reassure the fearful tenants, and perhaps themselves as well, that there was no real need to worry since management was said to be "doing a terrific job of screening."

Another interesting aspect of the community atmosphere was the previously mentioned belief held by some minority group tenants that whites were unlimited in their ability to find ideal places of residence. Those holding this belief were unaware, however, that some white tenants had in fact looked for other places to live, but had frequently found that Lancaster offered the best value for their money; therefore they remained in the apartments—also promising themselves to "do something about it."

Murray Lenz, for example, a member of the action committee, is a clothes cutter in New York City's garment district who is attempting to save enough money to buy a cab. If he were to move from the apartments, he would either have to pay higher rents or sacrifice the larger rooms as well as the design and layout, which attracted him in the first place. Murray and his wife decided to remain and become active in the action committee. They said they hoped thereby to maintain the initial high standards of their dwelling and of the larger community as a whole, while paying less rent for their apartment than they would for a comparable place elsewhere.

It was not true, then, that the whites felt themselves unlimited in their ability to live anywhere they might desire. There are circumstances which preclude the movement of whites as well, even though these circumstances are not as restrictive as in the case of Negroes and Puerto Ricans. In certain areas of the North Bronx, for example, where private homes predominate, whites are discouraged from buying by the builders, who then sell the same homes to minority group members at a higher price.

This "immobility" factor proves an interesting one, for it implies a disparity of power in the landlord/manager-tenant relationship. As one study of the urban poor has shown, the tenant, "having an immediate and constant need for housing, is more dependent on the landlord for housing than the landlord is dependent on him for rent."[1] As a result, the landlord has more latitude in setting the terms of a contract as well as in complying with them. In addition, "the landlord ordinarily participates in many rental contracts. Whereas each tenant is dependent upon one landlord, the landlord diffuses his dependency among many tenants."[2]

The same study also indicated that the relative degree of tenant powerlessness and unwillingness to organize was contingent upon a fixed upper level of income and factors such as education.[3] At Lancaster, the group was middle income, more educated, aware of more prerogatives, and hence, less submissive. However, as we shall see, it was the lumping together of both lower- and middle-class blacks in the eyes of the management which served to induce action, since part of the tenants' struggle involved changing the prevailing definition of the situation which determined their status and treatment by others. Perhaps one of the most important factors impelling these people to act was that which lent body to the rumors—status insecurity.

This insecurity was most apparent among the middle-class Negro tenants, but, as in the case of Murray Lenz, it applied to some whites as well. In a certain sense, many of the people living in Lancaster-Bennet were marginal. On the one hand they considered themselves to be middle class and expected to be treated as such; on the other hand, there was another status dimension which applied to them, namely, the racial one, presenting them with an inconsistency which they strove to correct. The sociologist Gerhard Lenski, who has done a considerable amount of work in this area, has commented that "persons of inconsistent status are more likely to support liberal and radical movements . . . than are persons of consistent status."[4] Jewish merchants and professionals, of course, provide the classic case, but since, in terms of the history of ethnic succession in our society, the Jews "have made it," so to speak, other minorities such as the blacks are finding themselves the vanguard of reform.

The tenants who formed the nucleus of the action committee did not, however, start from scratch. They had been preceded by the L.R.A. (Lancaster Resident's Association), whose alleged inaction proved still another reason for the formation of the action committee. The L.R.A. was an association designed primarily to further the interests of the tenants, but since management made monetary contributions to such programs of the L.R.A. as the nursery school and the community newspaper, the association tended to favor the interests of the management.

"Besides, it's mainly run by women," exclaimed one member of the action committee. "We want someone who'll give management a little push to fix the elevators, put an intercom buzzer system in, clean the laundry room, and that sort of thing. All this jazz about 'cultural activities' is all right, but I don't have any children in nursery school. What I want around here is some service for my money." This remark was made by Ted Minnow, later to become the chairman of the action committee.

There were many tenants who felt this way, especially in regard to dissatisfaction with the manager, Mr. Bernstein, who would be ingratiating in the face of a complaint and at the same time "pass the buck" for a failure to rectify an already exacerbated situation. Gradually, as more tenants became frustrated in their dealings with management, their discontent grew until the realization dawned upon them that in terms of their common interests as tenants they were all in the same boat. In fact, as we shall see, the unrest fostered the growth of a collectivity similar to a social movement. So trenchant was the likeness that I decided to apply Herbert Blumer's scheme of the development of the typical social movement to the tenant's committee.

Blumer visualizes the social movement as progressing through four stages: social unrest, popular excitement, formalization, and finally, institutionalization.[5]

A typical social movement in its initial stages is organized loosely and characterized by impulsive behavior ("milling"). In attempting to cope with a problem situation, members of groups related to a specific social movement become organized, bring together a common body of customs and traditions, establish leadership, and focus upon a scheme of procedure. They are, as Karl Mannheim put it, somewhat "utopian" minded.[6] They will not be satisfied until conflict has been reduced to a minimum, which presupposes a substantial change within the old order or the status quo.

This "natural history" approach has apparently been extended by social scientists from the study of collective behavior, with modifications, to the realm of social problems in general, although students of social problems and deviant behavior have long subscribed to the natural history perspective.[7] Thus, when any social situation creates a conflict of interests between two or more groups and is surmised by these as calling for remedial action, the orbits of the two areas converge.

It may be argued that designating the action committee as a social movement overstates the case; but whether a movement is considered on a grand scale or a minor one, it has certain characteristics and patterns of development that are common to all. It is in terms of these common patterns that the conflict between the action committee and the management becomes interesting. Blumer's scheme will be used, then, as the general frame of reference in which the task-oriented action committee can be discussed. The first of the four stages of our social movement, social unrest, has already emerged clearly out of the circulation of rumors and the emergence of collective discontent.

Where the Action Is:
The Stage of Popular Excitement

The stage of popular excitement is marked by even more milling, but in a less random and aimless fashion than in the previous stage. There is a sharpening of objectives since notions emerge as to the causes of the conditions and possible solutions. In this stage one or more leaders appear who can play the role of either prophet or reformer.

In the case of the action committee, the behavior of some of the tenants was viewed as part of the adverse conditions, but the management was found most guilty. The most frequently alleged fault of management was a "lackadaisical attitude." From this apparent lack of interest emerged all of the evils, either apparent or real, perceived by the dissatisfied tenants. During the first general L.R.A. meeting between the tenants and management, the beliefs of the tenants were "confirmed" when the management proceeded to walk out. Following is an account of that meeting, which precipitated the formation of the action committee and was the focal stimulus for the stage of popular excitement.

Prior to the first general L.R.A. meeting, the management had distributed notices and posted them upon the bulletin boards in each building, informing the tenants that Mr. Bernstein would appear to discuss the community's problems. The meeting was held on September 3, 1964. The community room, which holds several hundred people, was filled to capacity, and even the adjoining hallways were filled.

The meeting was to begin at 8:30 P.M. I arrived at 8:40 and had to stand outside. From the doorway I could see and hear Mr. Bernstein speaking about the vandalism that was taking place. He said he was surprised to see the contrast between the beautifully furnished homes of the tenants and the external aspect of the apartments. He claimed rumors had been started that the developments was occupied by non-whites up to 90 percent, but that this was untrue; it was only about 60 percent. He asked the bearers of these rumors to cease and desist, and then stated that he had a man with him to explain the delicate mechanisms of the operating devices of the elevators so that the tenants could understand them better. The director of the security guards then spoke about the duties of the guards. Others were scheduled to speak upon different subjects, but the tenants appeared to interpret these scheduled speeches as delaying tactics. Murmuring among the tenants arose as they grew restless and anxious about their immediate problems, and questions were now put forward as to what was going to be done:

"We don't want to know how the elevators work, we just want them to work. I had to walk upstairs twice last week after returning home from work. Thank God, I don't live on the nineteenth floor."

"What about the buzzer system that you promised would be installed shortly after we moved in?"

"What about the shopping center? When the hell are we going to see the ground broken for that? I'm tired of going a mile to the supermarket when I need a lousy loaf of bread."

"When are you going to clean the walls?"

"I pay over one hundred and twenty dollars a month for a one-bedroom apartment. When are you going to fix the ceiling that's been broken since two weeks ago?"

Mr. Bernstein then became involved in a shouting match with a vociferous female tenant who claimed that things might be better with a change in management. It was then that Mr. Bernstein's secretary, apparently piqued at the criticisms directed toward the manager, spoke up: "Listen, I'm not going to stand here and allow you people to browbeat Mr. Bernstein like this. Now, I happen to know that he's a wonderful person, and he's doing an excellent job of managing these apartments. Furthermore . . . "

However, she did not get a chance to express any further opinions, for the obstreperous female tenant who had previously criticized Mr. Bernstein now launched an attack on the secretary: "Listen, honey, you may think he's wonderful; good. I happen to think he's a terrible manager. Besides, we're not interested in what you'd have to say anyway; you're only his secretary."

"And you're the type of tenant we don't want here," Mr. Bernstein said. "You're only a trouble-maker and if you don't like it here, then get out."

"I'm not going anywhere. You're the one who's going to leave."

Mr. Bernstein then told the woman to shut up, and the meeting began to deteriorate rapidly at that point. Management proceeded to walk out, and the meeting was "taken over" by the dissatisfied tenants. It was at this time that Ted Minnow came into prominence. He literally stood upon a table amidst the crowd and caught its attention.

"So management has walked out. So what? So now we can get down to business and finally try to solve some of these problems." (Much clapping and verbal agreement here.) It must have inspired him, because he took a deep breath, planted his feet more firmly, placed his arms akimbo, and continued: "Listen, you saw what management did. He treated you like children. Now I don't know how *you* feel, I consider myself an adult and expect to be treated like one. He made you feel as if you were the ones responsible for conditions around here, not the people who are actually responsible. Now, let's admit it: there are some pigs living in Lancaster. This point we will concede to management. But they are here only because of management's greed to obtain the rents from a fully-rented development. If these pigs had been as rigorously screened as you and I were, we wouldn't have these problems. But they are here, and now it's management's responsibility to clean up their mess, not ours." (Vigorous applause.) "And you've seen how the L.R.A. conducted itself. It's done nothing. I want something done. Now how about you?"

"Yes." (Collectively from the crowd, with even more vigorous clapping and murmurings of agreement.)

"Then let me have your names, or join up with the L.R.A. because we need your support. Even if you don't have money now, give your name; we'll collect the money later."

He got down and another person tried to conduct the signing up of new members of the Lancaster Resident's Association. This person also wanted to say something, but without much success. He, I was to learn later, was Greg Dixon.

Richie Danton had participated in the chaotic "discussion" and so had Stan Rubinstein—individuals who were to become members of the newly forming action committee. Stan was trying to get the attention of the crowd in order to speak, but without results. There were protests of, "It's time to act, later for talking," "Let's sign up. That's the only way we'll be able to do anything."

I asked Minnow what he had in mind. He replied, "Well, damn, man, you saw what happened. This man doesn't care if we get any satisfaction or not. I'm tired of talking for nothing. I say sign up, increase the membership of the L.R.A., and he's got to listen to our demands."

He told me later that he would call a special meeting of those who had expressed interest in forming a kind of "action" committee. It was a few days later when I called Ted to find out how things were going, and he told me that he would be seeing me shortly regarding the meeting to be called. He did show up later, at night, with a bag filled with mimeographed sheets that called for a meeting on September 25, 1964. I asked him if he wanted any help with all those sheets, and he said no; he would go and deliver them himself.

The most striking predictable phenomenon of the first general L.R.A. meeting was the emergence of a leader. Typically, there were several people who attempted to gain control of the situation. They competed against one another for the attention of the crowd. One lady assumed that parliamentary procedure was in order and commented: "After all, Ted Minnow had spoken, so why don't the people listen to Stan Rubinstein?" Under such emotional conditions, however, the only person who can gain attention is the one who is bold and daring enough to seize it. This Minnow did by standing atop a table and speaking, even yelling, louder than anyone else.

Agitation is of primary importance in a fledgling movement because it operates to arouse people and to make them potential recruits. When Minnow stood upon the table and declared that at last the tenants had a chance to solve some of their problems by signing up and joining the L.R.A., he was showing them a way to an ideal state of affairs which would substantially change the status quo. Such appeals as, "Personally, I'm tired of the weak inaction of the L.R.A., I want something done. How about you?" were designed to stir up the people and liberate them for movement in new directions. Those new directions would be manifested in the formation of the action committee.

The conflict between the tenants and management was emphasized even more by the walkout of management. The management appears to have been disposed to walking out in any case as a strategic move to disarm the tenants and to leave them with a feeling of helplessness. But the walkout had actually the opposite effect and provided a better opportunity for Minnow to emerge as the tenants' spokesman; he immediately filled the gap of bewilderment created by management's exit.

Minnow allayed the fears of the tenants by telling them in effect, "We don't need management. We can do a better job ourselves." He fulfilled the role of agitator as one whose:

... dynamic and energetic behavior attracts the attention of people to him; and the excitement and restlessness of his behavior tends to infect them. He is likely to act with dramatic gesture and to talk in terms of spectacular image.[8]

It is significant that many of the others who attempted to speak at the general L.R.A. meeting also became active within the newly formed action committee. I was hardly surprised, therefore, to see several of the militants at the L.R.A. meeting also present at the first action committee meeting. It is likely that if Minnow had not been present at that meeting, one of the other participants would have emerged as a leader, but possibly in a less dramatic manner.

Although Minnow expressed dissatisfaction with the "weak inaction" of the L.R.A., he realized the value of the relative legitimacy and respectability associated with it. Therefore, he did not advocate total abandonment of the L.R.A., but expressed dissatisfaction with the manner in which it was being run. I suspected that Minnow felt that the "weak inaction" of the L.R.A. was a result of its being run mainly by women, and if Minnow had anything to do with it, the women's role in the L.R.A. would be greatly diminished.

Another important factor was the widening conflict between management and tenants. There was decreasing room for doubt as to where the opposing parties stood in relation to each other. Management believed that some apartments were occupied by irresponsible tenants, and the tenants thought the buildings were being managed by an irresponsible manager. It was inevitable, then, that the conflict situation be expressed in such an overt, dramatic manner as a walkout.

In essence, the conflict between the members of the tenants' grievance committee and the management was manifested in the expression of opposing ideologies. Thus, the arguments of the members of the action committee included the following: the maintenance is below standard; the management is lackadaisical in handling tenants' problems; the managerial services are not commensurate with rent. Management, on the other hand, claimed that the accusations of the action committee were unfounded, its demands unjust, and finally that most of the community's problems were created by the tenants themselves. The crystallization of interests into energizing ideologies served to maintain group boundaries, strengthen group consciousness, and establish group identities.[9] As the sociologist Simmel asserted, a state of conflict pulls the members tightly together and subjects them to such uniform impulse that they must completely go along with or repel one another. "This is the reason why war with the outside is sometimes the last chance for a state ridden with inner antagonisms to overcome these antagonisms, or else break up indefinitely."[10]

Thus, the battle lines were drawn as a consequence of the walkout. War, at least symbolically, was declared between the two opposing parties. The next stage was formalization, in which the group's organization takes more definite shape, with rules, policies, tactics, and discipline.

Men and Boys Together: The Stage of Formalization

When I entered the meeting room of the action committee, the discussion centered upon "the redheaded secretary" (no one ever found out her name). This is significant; it kept her from becoming a real person, and therefore made her more of a potential enemy. It was more reassuring to think of her as Bernstein's secretary, a kind of appendage or lackey to the manager, rather than, for instance, Miss Smith, who might be another enemy with whom to contend.

Someone commented that it was a shame she was allied with Bernstein, because "she's really a good-looking gal."

"Yeah," someone else said, "I wish something like that would speak up for me the way she spoke up for Bernstein."

"What's wrong with your wife?"

"You kidding?"

"Say, who was that loud-mouth woman giving both Bernstein

and the redhead hell? Whoever she was, she really brought the secretary down: 'You're only the secretary.' Whew!"

"That's why when you get a bunch of women together, watch out."

The *esprit de corps* of the action committee evinced a kind of regression to an anti-feminine comradery common to lower-middle-class and upper-lower-class male peer groups, which plays a great role in liberating children, and later men, from the female-dominated family.[11] It provides the starch for groups such as the action committee, develops group consciousness and a sense of exclusiveness, and provides them with the gumption necessary to sustain them in their battles with outsiders and competing groups.

The preceding conversation about the redheaded secretary could only have taken place in the absence of women; this was one of the most noticeable and significant factors of the meeting. I then understood why Ted himself chose to distribute the notices: he wanted to make sure that no women should receive the sheets and thus become possible members of the action committee. A later check with Minnow confirmed my suspicions. A sense of solidarity had manifested itself in the general agreement that it was time for a change, that the tenants did not have to take this kind of treatment from management, that from now on things were going to be different, and that the action committee was going to be the cause of this radical change in the prevailing situation.

We were all formally introduced to each other by Minnow and then took our seats. Ted sat at the head of the table, Bobbie Remington was next to him, Hascal Benway sat at the end, and I was next to him. Greg Dixon sat in the middle. Donnie Jones and Steve Zeiger were next to each other near the head of the table. The committee was somewhat representative of the racial and ethnic backgrounds of the tenants, which included blacks, whites, and Latin-Americans.

Minnow suggested that we get immediately to the matter at hand. He stated that he was an engineering student and did not think he could chair the meetings. He asked for volunteers and got no responses. Then he started making suggestions.

"Steve, you've had some experience with the L.R.A. Why don't you take it?"

"No, I'm already a member of the L.R.A., and my wife is treasurer. I think it would be a bit too much."

"What about you, Donnie?"

"Sorry, my man. I'm always making it out of town for some conference or another. I wouldn't be able to make the meetings."

A few more when queried, including myself, turned down the assignment.

"Well, since it seems that no one wants the job, I'll take it," said Greg facetiously.

"Just let me say this," Minnow said. "I don't think anyone who thinks this is a joking matter should take the chair, since it's a responsible position. We are all here, not because we want to be here, but because we feel it's necessary in order to maintain a level of living that is presently threatened. Now Greg, if you want the chair, take it, but for crying out loud, man, don't kid around."

Steve Zeiger then spoke up: "Since Ted was the one to initiate this movement, I think he should take the chair. He doesn't have to do all the work; later on we could elect a co-chairman to help out." There were a number of voiced agreements to this, and Minnow accepted the position.

An agenda had been prepared, and only Item A was completed: "Enumerate the problems of the community in general." Some of the problems were: Security—when will the doors be locked and the intercom installed? Elevators—when will they be operating properly? Management—when and how can their lackadaisical attitude and multiple excuses be changed? The tone of this first meeting was one of seriousness and urgency. It was conducted on a businesslike basis. Its formal atmosphere was accented by Ted Minnow's domineering attitude. He frowned upon joking of any kind and constantly reminded the other members that there was a job to be done and time should not be wasted kidding around.

These comments were most often directed toward Greg, who considered himself a comedian and had a manner of behaving that made Ted angry. It was evident that they would have a serious confrontation before long. But the first meeting ended in an atmosphere of enthusiasm and conviviality; all were convinced that they were going to accomplish a great deal.

In reviewing the interaction of the members of the action committee, one is hardly surprised at the predictability of the behavior of its members, which is typical of individuals who have formed a group with reform as their goal. In their roles as social reformers the action committee felt it necessary that the business be conducted seriously and efficiently since mistakes would be taken advantage of by the opposition. It was imperative that their image be reassuring to the tenants who supported it, with the committee cast in the role of savior of deeply felt values. The members were thus knights in armor, and the best proof of this was the absence of women at meetings: the women had complete trust in the men and the men would not fail them. The L.R.A. had failed precisely because of *women* and men without courage—good mythic scapegoats—at the controls. But it would not happen in the action committee. It was not that kind of organization.

It appears that these dedicated members of the action committee had come to believe their own propaganda. It also appears that they were playacting, but playacting can be a serious enterprise. Minnow's reprimand to Greg Dixon clearly illustrated this point. Greg did not take the chair because he could not help but "kid around." His role as he saw it was that of a very clever fellow, and he probably laughed at Minnow's opinion that "we are all here, not because we want to be here but . . ." for some altruistic reason. Greg probably did *want* to be there, because it afforded him the opportunity to engage in a bit of fellowship. But this informality probably contributed to the group's solidarity.

Students of the small group have frequently commented upon the tempering effects of an "expressive" person such as Greg on the tension-producing actions of an "instrumental" leader like Ted.

The action committee had its informal aspects as well as its formal ones. There were certain members who interacted with each other more frequently than with certain other members of the committee. A number of in-groups and out-groups were visible. The criterion for determining whether a person was a member of an in-group was the frequency of his participation in the

informal operations of the action committee. A member of the
out-group might participate frequently in the formal operations
of the committee, but this was due to his "right" to do so. Many
members took advantage of this right and attempted too much,
often alienating themselves from the other members. For instance, Arnold Reynolds suggested during one of the meetings
that the members should wear buttons identifying themselves as
members of the action committee, so that other tenants could
easily recognize them. The answer to this suggestion was: "No
buttons, for crying out loud, this is no boy scout's group." Arnold
did not give up, however. He also suggested that the members
should socialize more "by going out together as a group on
picnics and things like that." This suggestion produced guffaws
and raised eyebrows from members who thought him a bit naïve.

On the other hand, there were members regarded with such
great esteem that they were frequently invited to participate in
the informal operations of the action committee. One of the
most esteemed was Donnie Jones. He had a Ph.D. in education,
was friendly to most of the members, and probably held more
social gatherings in his home than any other committee member.

These informal operations were a cohesive force even for the
formal functioning of the action committee. Although Ted
Minnow and Greg Dixon argued constantly during the formal
meetings, they were close friends on the outside. One would
suspect that the action committee served also as a safety valve
for their friendship; as long as they could argue within the
confines of the action committee, outside disagreements would
be minimized.

Tightening Up: The Stage of Institutionalization

In the fourth and final stage of the social movement, a fixed
organization with a definite personnel and structure crystallizes
in order to execute the purposes of the movement. In this stage,
the "tactics are evolved along three lines: gaining adherents,
holding adherents, and reaching objectives."[12]

One of the first indications of strategy was the division of the action committee into smaller subcommittees: a tenant subcommittee, a security subcommittee, and a maintenance subcommittee. It was suggested that a subcommittee dealing with management should be formed, but there was general agreement that this action could come later; besides, there were not enough members to form a fourth committee. It is hypothetically possible that a tacit agreement existed *not* to form a subcommittee to deal with management, for management was the enemy and it is easier to perceive someone as an enemy if no lines of communication are established between the opposing groups. Further, certain tactics could be successfully carried out only if management were imputed to be the primary cause of the conflict.

A meeting was called by Minnow in order to "get the ball rolling." After lengthy discussion, it was decided that the problems of the community should be outlined and possible solutions offered, also that influential groups should be made aware of these problems so that the action committee could seek help from them. This was done, and the findings were condensed into a form letter which was sent to the owners of the Lancaster-Bennet Apartments, the Board of Directors of the apartments, and the management. The State Division of Housing was to receive a copy only if a satisfactory reply was not forthcoming after fifteen days. Greg Dixon suggested the possibility of going to extremes, if necessary, and holding demonstrations, but most committee members agreed this might not be necessary.

"Then how's about getting written statements from the tenants concerning their problems?" (Greg)

"What do you mean?" (Ted)

"I mean," Greg continued with growing irritation, "that we would have a stronger case if we were to supplement the letter with written statements from the tenants saying: 'Mr. Bernstein lied to me. I now understand we are not going to get a buzzer system.' 'Mr. Bernstein is a cruel man.' 'He's a bastard': anything that will convince others that this man should be replaced as manager of these apartments."

There were some members who agreed with Greg; others expressed their doubts about the written statements, and then Ted spoke up.

"Well, it's a good idea, really, but I'd say it's too late to obtain written statements from the tenants."

"What do you mean, 'too late'?"

"I mean, we want to get some action, right? Well, if we keep on waiting until everything is just right, we'll never get anything done. Common sense should tell you that."

"Excuse me, maybe I don't have common sense."

"Don't feel badly, Greg, lots of people don't have common sense. Why, some of my best friends are just like you."

That did it. Ted and Greg consumed approximately ten minutes arguing before they were finally quieted down.

The results were that the owners, the Board of Directors, and management received a copy of the letter, and a potential letter to the State Division of Housing was agreed upon. After certain officers of the L.R.A. found out about the actions of the committee, they expressed resentment at the committee's having acted without the L.R.A.'s approval. Although the L.R.A. had reluctantly tolerated the "radicalism" of the action committee, hostility developed between those officers of the L.R.A. who thought that Bernstein was doing a fine job and those members of the action committee who felt that he was not doing a satisfactory job at all.

It would appear that not only did the action committee foresee the necessity of employing strategy to gain its particular ends, but the opposition, management, also foresaw the necessity of behaving in a strategic manner. The management's contributions to the cultural programs of the L.R.A. were instrumental in bringing the L.R.A. officers into its camp, so that when open conflict ensued between the action committee and management, the L.R.A. found it imperative to side with management. Furthermore, the L.R.A. had to oppose the behavior of the action committee in the light of its own interests: the committee was usurping the power and authority of the L.R.A. by taking the initiative on such "radical" matters as accusing management by letter of neglect in its duties. For all the L.R.A. knew, the action committee could be planning to "take over" the larger group.

The L.R.A. found itself in a dilemma. Since it was supposed to represent the interests of the tenants as a whole, it could not openly express its affinity for management without further alienating those tenants convinced by the propaganda of the action committee that the L.R.A. "was doing nothing."

No answer from management regarding the letter of the action committee had been received by the fifteenth day. Therefore, it was decided to send a copy, enumerating the problems of the community and some possible solutions, to the State Division of Housing. Unfortunately, I was not able to attend this meeting, and I was told by Donnie Jones that Ted and Greg had again become entangled in arguments and Ted had "resigned" by walking out. Bobbie Remington then took over as chairman, and the letter that was supposed to be sent to the State was delayed.

When management finally answered the letter, it was after the fifteenth day, and it was not directed to the action committee, which had by this time been recognized as spokesman for the tenants, but to the tenants as a whole and distributed as a memorandom.

Greg said to Ted: "I told you so." He meant that we should have taken his suggestion of having the tenants submit written statements about the conditions of the apartments prior to sending the letter to the State. "As a result of not taking this action," Greg continued, "Bernstein outmaneuvered us by addressing his reply to the L.R.A. instead of the action committee." Another argument followed and resulted in a further split between Ted and Greg.

It was decided that hereafter it would be wiser to obtain documentation from the tenants. A number of members distributed the letter that was sent to management, plus a separate questionnaire, which asked whether they agreed or disagreed with the tactics of the action committee.

The sheets were delivered and picked up several days later. Only a small percentage were returned, mainly because the letters did not include a pick-up date (so the members of the committee believed), and people just did not get around to writing.

All of the above occurred before the Christmas holidays. The members voted to cease activity until the beginning of the new year, but only after they had instituted a network of floor representatives. This was a tactic suggested by Ed Murray, who had had previous experience with a development in Brooklyn (managed by Bernstein). There were to be representatives on each floor to respond to the grievances of the tenants. The representatives were to report to the building captain, and the four building captains were to report to the action committee. Thus, the tenants would be able to express their grievances to the floor representative as an extension of the action committee. Theoretically, this communications network would facilitate more effective contact with the tenants than either management or the L.R.A. had.

The Strength To Be Heard

The action committee realized that it had finally gained recognition, status, and prestige when it held four important meetings with individuals directly concerned with the problems of the community. One of these individuals was Bernstein, the manager of the Lancaster-Bennet Apartments.

The first meeting was held before Christmas, 1964, with Mr. Hingle, the superintendent at Lancaster, and his assistant, Bernard. They had requested a meeting with the committee in order to clarify their positions in the existing conflict. Mr. Hingle wanted it clearly understood that he did not agree with most of Bernstein's policies. He wanted to do a good job, and he did not want his reputation as a competent superintendent maligned. He thought that it was Bernstein's attitude not only toward the tenants but also toward his own staff that created most of the tension. Hingle said that he would cooperate in order to ease some of the tensions between management and the action committee.

The second meeting with Bernstein and his secretary was held around the last day of January in one of the clubrooms of the community center. Mr. Bernstein was agreeable and willing to work along with the members of the committee. His ultimate goal was to create a desirable community in which to live, he said. We questioned him thoroughly about the grievances as contained in the letter to management of October 28, 1964.

Bernstein said that he would be willing to try locking the

doors in one of the buildings for a reasonable period of time in order to minimize the frequency of vandalism. He would first have to see a locksmith to change the lock so that the tenants' keys could fit it. This whole process would take about ten weeks, he promised. Actually, the process took more than twice as long as he had promised.

The third meeting was held in the middle of March with Commissioner Perry of the State Division of Housing and several other figures of the State. Bernstein was present, although he was not invited by the members of the action committee. This was a general L.R.A. meeting with other tenants present.

The meeting immediately developed into an antagonistic affair between Bernstein and the tenants, with each hurling accusations against the other. Perry tried to defend the previous actions of management, but when it became apparent to him that there were deep underlying feelings on the tenants' part toward Bernstein, he called for an adjournment of the meeting. Nothing could be solved under the prevailing conditions, he stated, and he suggested to the members of the committee that they meet with him at his office. This was arranged immediately after the meeting had adjourned.

The fourth meeting was held with Perry on April 12, 1965. I was unable to attend because of a prior commitment, but I spoke with each member later: Donnie, Richie, Joe, Bobbie, Calvin, and Murray. They all told me nearly the same thing, but Calvin provided a more complete report. He stated that Perry had realized that something was wrong at the previous meeting, and further investigation had revealed that promises were made by Bernstein which were not kept. The buzzer system was not going to be installed by the date promised by Bernstein. The entire halls were supposed to be painted rather than just the sections in front of the elevators. The most significant statement from Perry concerned the possibility of converting the apartments into cooperatives. Most of the members were enthusiastic about the idea. Richie Danton, however, felt that Bernstein would leave a number of things unfinished if the cooperatives became a reality. "For instance, he wouldn't finish putting up the chains around the lawns. He wouldn't see to it that the crosswalks are completed. There're a number of things he'd leave unfinished.

And we'd have to pay for them," he emphasized, pushing his face closer to mine to make sure I got the point.

After these four meetings, the members of the action committee appeared to relax in their activities. They had not yet obtained their ultimate goal, the removal of Bernstein as manager, but they had been recognized by a sufficient number of important people to feel less anxiety-ridden than they had felt initially.

This "slowing down" process resulted from the routinization that inevitably results from organization. In other words, Ted led the action committee until it came to be governed by rules rather than the dramatic personal qualities of a leader. Hence the routinization of the action committee reached the point where it "crystallized into a fixed organization with a definite personnel and structure to carry into execution the purposes of the movement."[13]

Thus, we have traced from its beginning the several stages of a task-oriented group to the final stage of institutionalization, and have discussed some of the means and mechanisms by which the action committee grew and became organized.

The formation of the committee, however, can also be partly explained by examining the predicament of middle-class Negro tenants, indeed, of middle-class Negroes in general. A middle-class Negro, in an attempt to correct some "misbehavior" or disturbance created by a lower-class black, anticipates a negative reaction. From his past experiences he knows that more often than not his attempts, no matter how diplomatically or tactfully handled, will probably be answered with "Who in the hell do you think you are? You ain't white, man, you're just as black as I am, *and don't you forget it.*" Rather than place himself in such an embarrassing position, the middle-class Negro avoids the situation, just as the middle-class white so frequently does. Thus, the Watts riots in California occurred, for one reason, because of a lack of black middle-class leadership.

One method of ensuring one's tenuous social position is through the ostentatious display of status symbols.[14] However, conspicuous consumption is often insufficient as a means of securing status security; hence other indicators of higher socioeconomic positions are necessary. One of these indices is place of residence.

Since all Negroes are not qualified economically to live in certain areas, residence in a higher-rent community as Lancaster-Bennet is an indicator of affluence. To many Negroes the apartments were a "utopia." They could finally relax, assured that the nemesis of their existence—the lower-class Negro—could no longer pursue them. They failed to take into consideration, however, the counterpart of the lower-class Negro: the white man of power and influence who makes no distinction between the lower-class and the middle-class Negro. A person such as this will inevitably reveal himself as one who has "the wrong attitude." This is the reason Bernstein drew the dire criticism mainly from the Negro members of the action committee. His comment, "I am surprised to see the contrast between the beautifully furnished homes of the tenants and the external aspect of the apartments," was interpreted by many of the tenants as implying that he did not expect to find the homes so tastefully furnished. The roots of their resentment at this lie in the interpersonal dynamics of status inconsistency, wherein the person manifesting inconsistent status will attempt to establish his identity in terms of one of his superior roles—in this case, class—as opposed to one of his inferior roles—in this case, race—in the face of contrary claims made by his alter ego, i.e., the "looking-glass" of his self.[15]

In reply to my questioning Bernstein's comment, Donnie Jones said: "Hell, he probably thinks all Negroes are like his sixty-year-old 'girl' who cleans his home every week. He *knows* she's lower class, and since we all look alike . . ."

In their study, "Social Class and Color Differences in Child Rearing," Davis and Havighurst concluded: "The *striking* thing about this study is that Negro and white middle-class families are so much alike, and that white and Negro lower-class families are so much alike. . . . There are significant differences in child-rearing practices between the middle and lower social classes in a large city. The same type of differences exist between middle and lower-class Negroes as between middle and lower-class whites."[16] We have seen how when the races meet, they shift gears from a class to a caste frame of reference. Middle-class Negroes discriminate against their lower-class brethren on a class basis but are resentful of being discriminated against on the basis of race.

As a result of this general situation, the members of the action committee viewed themselves as struggling against two opposing forces. The first was the lower-class element, who, in the eyes of the committee, were seeking the same material comforts as the middle class, but who had not demonstrated that they were socially and culturally capable of combining these comforts with the same middle-class values. Thus the middle-class-oriented action committee felt it was imperative that this lower-class element be kept out of their utopia. This, plus the invidious racial distinction, placed them in a double bind from which they sought liberation.

Second, there was the man, or group of men, in power, who demonstrated an ideology or belief system that was detrimental to the interests of the members of the action committee, as shown by behavior interpreted as coming from the "wrong attitude." In the case of the action committee, it was Bernstein and "management" who, in the belief of the members of the committee, were most responsible for allowing their utopia to deteriorate by letting in an irresponsible element, and to blame for not honoring their implicit commitment to maintain the premises. Furthermore, although it proved unsatisfactory, a precedent of sorts had been established to ameliorate the situation (the L.R.A.), and this provided a contrasting definition of how they were going to shape their identity as a group, thereby setting the stage for the action committee.

If my interpretations are valid, then it would appear imperative that a better line of communication be established between the managements of high-rise developments and the tenants they are obliged to serve. This aspect of "applied" sociology is a field of growing importance as the number of persons living in these developments increases.

Since the manager of a development plays such an important role in dealing with a diverse assortment of people with different living problems, either real or fancied, he should be carefully selected for those traits of intelligence and consideration which ensure an optimum of harmonious community living. The tenants also have an obligation to maintain the standards set by the community, and if deemed necessary, an educational program or open hearings upon community problems should be conducted before these social problems become so acute that they result in conflicts such as those described here.

The sociologist Lewis Coser concludes that conflict can only be "dysfunctional" when a social structure does not allow for toleration or institutionalized channels for the expression of conflict.[17] It is not the existence of conflict per se that threatens to "tear apart" a given social structure, but the rigidity of that structure which permits hostilities to accumulate and become so intense in their manifestations that a major line of cleavage is established.

Last, participation in such tenants' grievance committees presents excellent opportunities for empirical data to the student of small group theory. These data may then be utilized for analysis from a number of orientations. For instance, leadership as a social phenomenon may be studied in its natural setting. There is the disadvantage of having virtually no control over the quality of interaction, but the advantages of being able to observe human interaction in its natural setting, as it is lived from day to day, are inestimable.

4

The Gilded Asylum

Corrine Huesler

The conventional image of the insane asylum smacks of the horrors of a medieval torture chamber. Recent sociological studies of public mental institutions indicate that while these places are not snake pits, neither are they nests of happiness. Unlike the usual explanations about lack of funds and staff, sociological analyses of these institutions tend to stress more the basic social properties which lend them their demoralizing aspects. It should be no shock, therefore, to find some of the very same qualities woven into the fabric of the $1,000-a-month private "progressive" mental hospital. As the following study illustrates, getting the "best" of care, while it alleviates some of the grosser indignities of total institutional life, in some ways only diversifies the characteristics endemic to such places.
Corrine Huesler, who has won prizes for her painting and graphic work in several shows, is living in West Germany with her husband and children.

With vivid clarity I recall the day: January 29, 1964. I woke up to the noise of a massive diesel engine racing through my head, choking out the hospital sounds around me. As I remembered why I was lying there, why the intravenous needles were plugged into my veins, I cried because I had failed, just as I had failed in every other thing I had tried in living; I had failed to die. The green slime I vomited was the last vestige of my body's rejection of the poison. Over and over again I repeated to myself, "and now what, now what?"

It was hardly a question, only a vague request for help. I understood it only as a resignation to the hopelessness that I felt. As the days progressed and I spoke to my psychiatrist, it became apparent to both of us that I could not return home. He told me of a private hospital two hundred miles south. Though he had never seen it and knew no details, he said he had heard it was "a good one." I agreed, without hesitation, to go; the shame of my actions and my failures made anything more welcome than facing my family.

It was arranged, and within one week after my suicide attempt, I was taken to this hospital. The drive was four hours long—and yet frighteningly short. I had built up a fantasy of what the place would be like, based on my knowledge of the 1864-built edifice in our town. As a child, I recalled, we had sneered, "Nut house! Looney bin!" I thought that even a "good one" might be a four-story, red-brick building with small, barred windows, shrouded in the gloom of gothic-ornate iron fences and willow trees. Naturally it would be at the end of a long dead-end road . . . dead-end in more than one respect.

We arrived at the locale of my imprisonment, a city with a population of 500,000, and looked for the suburban area of our destination on a road map. When we were within the immediate vicinity, I saw a sign, "TO HOSPITAL EMERGENCY EN-TRANCE." My eyes jerked over a vast complex of multistory, cold, boxlike buildings—with barred windows. I fell momentarily silent, my stomach turned sick with dread, and my mind cried out that it was worse than I had expected. We followed the entrance sign onto the grounds. At least there was no locked gate. Seeing a white-coated attendant walking briskly in the winter cold, we stopped to ask him if this was the Private Psychiatric Hospital. "No," he said, "you're about six blocks too far west. This is the County Public Mental Hospital."

I stopped thinking. It seemed hopeless to imagine that my fate could be any better than that. We found the street and turned into a narrow drive flanked by two prosperous-looking churches and surrounded by quiet upper-middle-class houses, and drove to the top of a knoll. There a small white sign told us that we had arrived at the hospital. Beyond the sign was an arbor of trees with not a willow among them; skirting them below was a low wall, perhaps two feet high, made of rough stone. The gateless entrance was wide, and in summer was obviously surrounded by rich flower beds. Dotted among the great old trees were Tudor cottages of white stucco and brown wood, and in the center of a circular drive stood a magnificent two-story frame building with high white pillars around an open porch that ran the length of the façade. People walked unhurriedly, well dressed and apparently normal. It puzzled me: were they guests or staff? We stopped at the Admissions Building, and were greeted with, "Oh yes, Mrs. Huesler. We've been expecting you!"

I was escorted to the Diagnostic Unit and shown to my room: soft green rug, sunny yellow walls, warm maple furniture—not unlike my own home. The pictures on the walls were Audubon prints, the draperies toile prints that contrasted nicely with the shape of glass-paned, barless windows; the snow-white ground beyond them was beautiful against the brown-black tallness of winter trees.

I was left alone for a time after I said good-bye to my driver. I sat on the bed and tried to believe what I was seeing. Still stunned, I got up and opened a door. It was a closet. Another door next to it led through a short green-carpeted hallway to my semiprivate bath of yellow ceramic tile. I was overcome by that same feeling I have when entering a hotel room for the first time—of being grateful that someone has taken the time and effort to make me comfortable in a strange atmosphere.

When the nurse came in to brief me on hospital procedure, my first question was, "Who are the people I see walking on the grounds?" She told me that they were my fellow patients. I thought to myself, they don't *look* crazy! The dread inside me was quickly turning to other emotions, distracting and thought-provoking.

Such was my introduction to the closed world which was to be my home for seventeen months. Three years have passed now since the termination of my intensive therapy, during which time I have found it important to objectify and interpret this experience. My psychotherapy has netted fine results: I am now functioning more successfully as wife and mother, and am capable as well of pursuing my individual goals as an artist, with less frustration and more awareness of myself and my surroundings.

My feelings toward having been an inmate of an institution closed off from the outside world are fully as significant to me, however, as my response to my present life. Was this experience a pleasant or rewarding one? What kind of a place was, in fact, this "good" hospital to which my doctor sent me?

Answering these questions has not been simple. Other researchers have dealt with life in a mental institution from the standpoint of outsiders looking in, but I was an inmate, emotionally involved, with ambiguous feelings toward the many aspects of institutional life. This has, no doubt, made my task somewhat more difficult, but I think I have allowed myself time for the emotionality natural from such an encompassing situation to settle down and come into objective focus.

Much of what follows has to do with my experiences as a patient in a private hospital. In appraising life in this kind of hospital, I have found Erving Goffman's book, *Asylums,* which deals with life in a mental institution, to be of great value. While this book focuses on the mental hospital as a social establishment, it attempts to shed light on other establishments called "total institutions";[1] that is, places of residence and work where the inmates, cut off from the outside world, "together lead an enclosed, formally administered round of life." Goffman's experience with mental hospitals derives from his study of the public hospital. Unfortunately (despite the fact that the private hospital provides its patients with greater physical comfort and better psychotherapy facilities), I find I must agree with Goffman's statement below. The depressing fact is that the "good" private hospital does not differ basically from the public hospital; indeed, inmates of both appear to struggle under the same oppressive and inflexible system of total care he describes so aptly:

Mental patients can find themselves in a special bind. To get out of the hospital, or to ease life within it, they must show an acceptance of the place accorded them, and the place accorded them is to support the occupational role of those who appear to foresee this bargain. This self-alienating moral servitude, which perhaps helps to account for some inmates becoming mentally confused, is achieved by invoking the great tradition of the expert servicing relationship, especially its medical variety. Mental patients can find themselves crushed by the weight of a service ideal that eases life for the rest of us.[2]

Although my personal gains as the recipient of psychotherapy were valuable, the experience of being a mental patient was far from pleasant and often painful. Some of the pain I experienced was to be expected, but several aspects of the environment demand closer study.

Birds in a Gilded Cage: Public and Private Hospital Settings Compared

To dispel any remaining images of the "snake pit," it is necessary to go back for a moment to the physical description of the private hospital. This institution, which I will refer to as hereafter as PPH (private psychiatric hospital), is set on a thirty-nine-acre plot of wooded land. Spread on a gentle hill in the heart of a semiexclusive suburb, PPH is only two blocks from this suburb's shopping area, and a few miles' bus ride from the central city.

Included in the hospital complex are seventeen buildings; one of them is "S" Hall, the only "unlocked" patient sleeping area, housing about thirty people in three separate units, and also containing the hospital kitchen, staff dining rooms and lounges, conference rooms, laundry facilities, and an elegant patient dining room, lounge, and library. A second large colonial-style building holds two units of twelve patients each, plus the hospital's only maximum security ward, with private rooms for five patients. Several smaller cottages house eight to twelve people, including the custodial care inmates, many of whom have lived at PPH since the days when it was a sanitorium for "rich eccentrics." Other hospital buildings provide a gymnasium, a patient recreation center, occupational therapy area, an activities center, a diagnostic unit, a small high school, a "Halfway House,"[3] and a variety of administration activities.

Several gardeners tend the extensive areas of flower beds, lawns, shrubs, and trees, and keep the tennis court and archery range in good condition. Much of the acreage is in its natural state, with paths leading through the trees to a cook-out area, behind which is a steep embankment, and below it, a broad area of public park.

Patients throughout the hospital, with the exception of one unit exclusively for women, are mixed with respect to sex, age, and interests. Placement in one unit or another, then, is based on the individual's behavior.

While Goffman reports of the public hospital that private rooms were to be had by only 5 to 10 percent of the patients,[4] at PPH nothing other than private rooms exist; furthermore, for those who request it, rooms with private baths are also available. In addition, where the average public institution has thirty staff members to every one hundred patients, the ratio of total staff to patients at PPH is better than two to one, with an average of one nurse for three or four patients.[5] Furthermore, the average daily expenditure per patient in a public hospital is about five dollars.[6] Goffman states that at St. Elizabeth's only 100 out of 7,000 patients received individual psychotherapy of any kind.[7] The situation is the reverse at PPH; the care it offers is vast in quantity, and, as in a good hotel, this kind of attention costs the guest greatly. The monthly base rate in 1964 and 1965, without private bath, for room, board, and normal nursing service was $1,000 a month. Added to this were two to five one-hour sessions with a psychiatrist each week at $25 per hour, plus any medical care or medication necessary, special nurses, laundry and cleaning, and the initial three to five days of medical examinations and psychological testing in the diagnostic period. Of course, the patient was expected also to have a weekly allowance of spending money, generally a minimum amount of ten dollars.

Life Styles

While the majority of patients at PPH come from upper- or upper-middle-class families, often with unlimited funds to support their hospitalization, I came originally from a mobile lower-middle-class family. My grandparents emigrated from Finland in the early 1900's, and settled in a poor farming area of one of our northern states. My parents had no schooling beyond the eighth grade, and spoke English only as a second language. They moved out of their Finnish community when they married, and after years of being proud but penniless, started a business in a midwestern town that was moderately prosperous. My life, until I met my husband, was always threatened with the prospect of the business folding, and the *nouveau riches* again becoming paupers. For this reason, among others, an early marriage to a stable man was attractive. When I met my husband he had only been in this country for two years. A native of Switzerland, his home life had been far more cosmopolitan, civilized, and stable than mine. When I met him, he was one of two research engineers in a small but promising company. By the time I was hospitalized, his position had advanced to chief engineer, and his staff included more than a score of technical people. By then, we had collected comforts that I had wanted all my life, yet I could never quite forget my poor beginnings, or the need to conserve and work to keep life going. These things were obviously a part of me even as a mental patient, and my resistance to the gilded, endless quantity of services forced upon me at PPH was real, and often caused significant difficulties in my progress in psychotherapy. It was, I believe, quite unnatural for me, as for many of the growing number of other middle-class patients at PPH, to accept the hospital's policies without questioning their effect on the family budget, or on our morale.

Food for Thought

The great quantity of services was, for example, startlingly evident at PPH in the dining room and almost an unbelievable contrast to Goffman's statement concerning a public hospital:

On days when bananas were made available, a few of the patients would spirit away a cup of milk from the jug meant for those who required milk on their diets, and would cut their bananas up in slices, put on some sugar, and expansively eat a "proper" dessert.[8]

For me, as for most of my fellow patients at PPH, it was a constant struggle not to gain weight. The menu often included delicacies I had never eaten before, with many of my favorites—fresh lake trout, various kinds of steak done to my taste, shrimp or crab cocktail, beef au jus, and—in contrast to the milk and bananas—banana cream pie (so good it would almost be worth going back for!). At each meal we were given a menu with several choices of soup or juice, entrees, breads, and desserts, the latter always including fine imported cheeses. The tables were set at each meal, including breakfast, with fresh white tablecloths and napkins, numerous forks, spoons, and knives for the many courses, and sparkling clean plates that were whisked away when the hot food, under silver covers and on heated plates, was served. A waitress was provided for each five or six tables.

Goffman suggests that in the public hospital the meals that were provided on open house or inspection days were especially prepared to impress the outside guests.[9] Hardly the case at PPH —there was nothing to be improved. I often took my guests to dinner in the patient dining room with as much pride as I would have served them in my home, knowing that this opulence was part of my daily life at the hospital.

The quality of service was evident in other ways as well. In the public institution, "the complaints about unclean food, messy quarters, soiled towels, shoes and clothing impregnated with the previous users' sweat, toilets without seats, and dirty bath facilities"[10] are common. On the other hand, at PPH I began to resent the amount of work that was being done around and for me: clean towels were supplied when the former ones were not soiled; a daily maid cleaned my room when I was capable and eager to do it myself; the elegance of the dining room service seemed an unnecessary frill; laundry men shuffled in and out constantly with patients' clothing, while we sat by chatting and smoking. I never took advantage of the laundry service, often irritating the staff with my "wash days," when I had damp clothes on hangers all over the ladies' bathroom. Shortly after my arrival, however, other women began to do their own laundry too, and by the time I left, a washer and dryer had been installed for patient use because of the widespread patient insistence on being provided this facility.

The Uniform

The question of clothing was a particular sore spot with me at PPH. As a housewife, before I was hospitalized I was accustomed to wearing neat slacks and a blouse much of the time. Though I had no particular objection to complying with the hospital rule of women wearing dresses, I had naïvely brought along several pairs of knee-high socks and tights—to wear for comfort and economy, since I am particularly hard on nylons. I was immediately told that the hospital did not consider knee-highs or tights appropriate dress for mature women. I was twenty-nine years old, with a trim figure, and saw no reason for accepting their decision as final. On this account I was well supported by the growing number of women patients of my age and inclination. We wrote a petition, had it signed by every woman patient of our standing, and attached to it a variety of high fashion photographs from popular fashion magazines—proving that this practice was, indeed, perfectly acceptable in our age bracket—and submitted it to the hospital staff for approval. Several weeks later, their decision was announced: "Due to the cold weather, the rule on proper dress has been changed. Women may wear knee-highs and tights during the day. Women eating their evening meal in the main dining room and using any hospital facility outside of their own unit during the evenings must wear nylon stockings at these times, as well as during sessions with their doctors." We were to wear nylon stockings during our doctors sessions, obviously to show the proper respect and veneration for the staff.

If we were not forced to wear someone else's sweaty uniform, we were expected to wear the uniform of the "proper society woman." This high status uniform is as dogmatically prescribed as that of the low status public hospital patient who is forced to wear someone's castoffs. The underlying principle serves to illuminate the similarity of the ridiculous and the sublime. By the use of force, the public and private hospitals both imply the same attitudes, even though they are at opposite ends of the status scale. The staff's public image is all important, with its doctors commanding the most esteem.

The quantity of ministrations, then, at PPH was both a luxury to be enjoyed and a headache to be tolerated. In the areas I have discussed, the staff was both confident and rigid in its actions.

Divide and Conquer: Limitations on Patient Autonomy

Perhaps less tangible, but just as real as examples of the pressure brought to bear on inmates of total institutions, are the attitudes of the staff toward the patient's behavior. As my long period of hospitalization progressed, I sensed that PPH had already undergone many changes to liberalize the life of its inmates. Yet it was clear that the staff was unable to shake the tradition of being infallible, and therefore was able to give little more than token privileges to the patients, and even then only with an underlying attitude of ambivalence and mistrust. One may here agree with Brewster Smith in saying that present-day hospitals have not, indeed, succeeded in a revolution against their outmoded methods, but are, rather, "confined to existing models while lip-service is given to new ideas."[11]

For example, unlike the public hospital, at PPH I was permitted to write letters to whom I pleased, and as often as I pleased. There were no restrictions of any kind placed on the contents of my correspondence. Since I posted my letters personally, or asked the staff to do so after I had sealed the envelopes, they had no way of knowing if I had written anything negative about the institution. As far as I could tell, this was a general condition with all patients, except in special cases where a patient was known to be writing legally damaging material.[12] To be sure, this kind of permissiveness can be interpreted as a desirable action on the part of the staff, helping to maintain the patient's extramural ties and build his sense of self-confidence. But such liberal action can also be seen as a staff expedience, indicating just how far the staff will go to protect its image with wealthy clients. At PPH, the affluent relative pays handsomely for the comforts provided his mentally ill loved one, and frequently expects even more service. Often enough a situation would occur in which a patient was removed from the hospital by irate relatives who felt that the physical situation was inadequate. But complaints would have gotten to the relative during a visit, even had the patient been forbidden to write about his displeasures. Since the repercussions of the relatives are a threat, the staff is intimidated in this way into giving the patient the freedom to write what he wishes.

Similarly, at PPH there is no specific time or place reserved for visiting. Since "party manners" are always required of patients, and their whole domain may be considered a "proper parlor," the need for restrictions is unnecessary.[13]

Goffman states that in the public hospital patients must ask endless permission to carry out the simplest of daily executions, such as "smoking, shaving, going to the toilet, telephoning, spending money."[14] Although not all the units in PPH are as liberal as the one in which I spent the greatest portion of my stay, almost all units allow both men and women to keep their grooming supplies in their rooms. I also had a sewing machine, scissors, guitar, razor blades, matches, cigarettes, and a massive quantity of art supplies. I was never asked how I spent my money. The bathrooms—separate in each unit for men and women—were always well-equipped and available for use at any time. I had to ask my doctor for "telephone privileges," but they were granted without hesitation.

On the surface it appears that PPH gives its patients a great deal of trust, since it does not restrict daily activity anywhere near as much as does the public hospital, and to some degree this is true. As long as all goes well in therapy sessions, and the patient's general attitudes seem to be compliant and nonrebellious, he is permitted the freedom of managing his own possessions. But should he "act out," become depressed, refuse to communicate during sessions with his doctor, he is quite aware what the consequences will be: if he makes a phone call, the nursing staff will stand next to him and audit, and later chart, his entire conversation. Or worse, he will have to forego the privilege of using the phone. Furthermore, his activity may be limited for a time (indefinitely stated, but understood by all to mean that the patient must resume cooperating with the staff). Thus he will not be able to manage spending his own money. As a precaution against serious rebellion from the patient, the staff is likely to assume possession of his grooming supplies, sharp objects, and matches. He may also be asked specific questions about his bowel movements, since their frequency may have some bearing on his state of mind. Thus, although the PPH patient enjoys his privileges, he knows he is treading on thin ice, and the staff may see fit to remove them at any time.

In yet another area the ambivalence of the staff at PPH may be seen according to the status of the client. Goffman puts it nicely: "Some establishments, like Grand Central Station, are open to everyone who is decently behaved; others, like the Union League Club of New York . . . are felt to be somewhat snippy about who is let in."[15] PPH was surely the latter. There were no Negro, Puerto Rican, or Mexican inmates. When I asked a staff member why there were only white patients, my question was evaded.

A few Negro attendants were, however, hired for the first time on an experimental basis during my stay. It became obvious, through subtle comments made by the nurses, that the placement of these attendants was being carefully controlled to see how the patients would react to authority figures who, for the most part, would be of far lower social standing on the outside than they themselves. It was, in fact, a major adjustment for many patients, although no one cared much that most of the hospital's kitchen and cleaning help were Negroes.

I recall one incident in which a good-looking, well-mannered Negro attendant was insulted by an irate patient after the attendant had made a polite request of him. The Negro had only worked on our unit for two weeks, yet one week after the incident, he was transferred to a ward of "sicker" patients. The PPH patient, unable to get away with such insolence with a white attendant, had won a point against authority in the refined manner that was permissible. Goffman points out that

". . . mixing age, ethnic, and racial groups in . . . mental hospitals can lead the inmate to feel he is being contaminated by
contact with undesirable fellow inmates."[16] It appears that at
PPH this factor has been well controlled through the admission
of white patients only, and manipulated through the hiring of,
for example, Negro attendants, to foster the superiority feelings
of rich clients.

During my stay at PPH I amassed enough art supplies in my
room to fill a station wagon. Although there was a well-equipped
arts and crafts area on the grounds, I was permitted to paint in
my room, and often caused the unit to smell of turpentine from
one end to the other. No one on the staff bothered me or asked
me to show my work. In fact, I had far less pressure put on me in
this respect than one has outside of the total institution. This
permissiveness toward creative experimentation even induced
me to take up the guitar, with happy results. I saw many other
patients also involve themselves in developing talents they were
not aware they possessed. The staff encouraged this kind of
activity, I believe, with a genuine desire to help the patient find
his areas of personal strength. Yet, even in this concern they
were often bogged down by their dedication to hospital rulings,
aside from any real consideration of their effect on the patient.

Ironically, for example, I was often thoroughly engrossed in
an activity which was interesting and meaningful—painting,
or sewing a dress for my daughter, or learning a new chord
progression on my guitar—when one of the nurses would inter-
rupt me, saying, "Mrs. Huesler, you have arts and crafts
scheduled for ten o'clock this morning. Don't you think you
should get ready?" On such occasions as this I would silently
curse, put my work away, and go to arts and crafts to spend
what I considered wasted time making an ashtray that I didn't
need or want, and for whose materials my financially over-
burdened husband received an additional bill. Only once did I
become angry enough over this forced attendance of activities
to refuse to go. I was promptly restricted to my unit and told that
my behavior showed withdrawal from responsibility and social
contact. The restriction, however, for me was like throwing
Brer Rabbit into the briar patch; I was free to indulge in my own
activities with no more interruption than three daily meals, coffee

hours, and doctor's sessions—until the staff caught on to my little game, that is, and paradoxically penalized me by making me go to scheduled activities again!

I was also involved in writing and illustrating the hospital patient newspaper. The staff's overt attitude toward the presented material was of extreme permissiveness. A young boy, for example, often wrote stories for the paper that were openly homosexual in nature; yet the staff "screening" committee permitted them to be published. Similarly, I was amazed when my poem below was passed for publication:[17]

> Love in the San
> Is sandwiched
> Between other
> More scheduled activities
> —Sans moonlight
> —Sans music
> —Sans mayonnaise
> Under garnished
> Over garmented
> Grossly overrated
> Strictly sterilized
> Sanitary
> And very
> Unfortunately, therefore, in
> Sane

The obvious reference to romantic attachment, completely taboo at PPH, was not censored. On the other hand, I once submitted a sketch for publication that was flatly rejected, and I was, furthermore, questioned at length about its none-too-subtle meanings. The sketch showed a pair of fat clowns in the center with bewildered faces; dangling from their limp hands were several puppets, whose stuffing was pushing through tattered clothing. Behind this grouping were numerous shadowy faces, some with hopeless expressions, others looking anxious or controlled. The staff had little difficulty determining that, in my sketch, they were the clowns. I was accused of trying to openly damage my own reputation, and told that in the future I should attempt to control my personal problems in the public view. Yet my poem was found acceptable, not to mention the homosexual love stories of our young writer; were these not, also, and even more so, damaging to our reputations? It seems that the staff was able to be permissive when, and only if, the material to be published did not threaten to damage *their* reputations, or perhaps threaten to undermine their authority over the patients.

The Patient Council

A few years before my inmate career began, a patient council had been organized at PPH. Made up of one patient representative from each unit, this group met once a week with several staff members, including a psychiatrist. Although in most respects the council is only a timid mock-government, ignorant of and afraid to ask for those rights which should be self-evident, it does occasionally manage to effect small changes in hospital procedure that benefit the inmates. The practical alterations in clothing and laundry rules which I mentioned earlier were effected through this group.

In addition, during my stay, one of the Patient Council's accomplishments was the organization of a "visiting committee," the members of which visit incoming patients at the Diagnostic Unit several times a week. We had all gone through the probing and totally encompassing initial environment of the diagnostic period, and felt that a new patient would be reassured by talking to someone whom he might trust more at the time than a staff member. The staff agreed that it was a good idea, and we began our visits on a voluntary basis.

The membership of this committee grew rapidly; we found many patients asking to serve immediately after their diagnostic period was over, so grateful were they for the comfort these conversations had given them. The contrast is vivid between this kind of constructive action on the part of hospital authority and the following account by Goffman:

> . . . in Central Hospital, as in prisons, there is a desire on the part of the staff to keep new inmates away from old ones, lest the new, through friendship or economic exchange, learn the tricks of the trade.[18]

It is obvious that the PPH staff has tried in several ways to encourage its patients to accept responsibility, and with some success. But even here I must qualify my account of the staff's attitude toward the visiting committee. When we, as visitors, arrived at the Diagnostic Unit, we were instructed not to say anything to the neophytes that might upset them. We were, furthermore, asked to leave the door to the patient's room open during our visit. The members of the committee were also screened before they were allowed to participate—not by other members of the committee, but by the staff. The reason we were given for the necessity for such screening was that a particular patient visitor might, during a conversation, upset the new inmate, rather than give him reassurance. We frequently joked about this among ourselves, knowing full well that what the staff worried about was that one of us might say something to the new patient that was directed against the staff or the hospital in general.

The Patient Council's efforts often ended in failure, as, for example, when the group tried to have the PPH dining room seating rules changed. If a patient had "dining room privileges" when he left the Diagnostic Unit, he was assigned to a specific table, usually of four persons. He was to sit only at this table at all three meals of the day. Each table was exclusively either for men or women, never both at one table, and the patient had to have the written permission of his doctor before requesting a transfer to another table.[19] The council attempted to change this ruling to allow both sexes to be seated at the same table. This request was denied by the staff with the intensity of utter finality. It may be assumed that their decision was based on their experience with anxiety-ridden male-female pairs, often separately married, who developed romantic attachments. Their decision seemed rather ridiculous, however, since we were not only permitted but actually required to socialize with both sexes all evening in the lounge after dinner, and in our units three times a day during coffee hours.

As I have said, we were, with the exception of one unit exclusively for women, a heterogeneous group. The staff obviously saw advantages in this kind of a small, intimate unit arrangement as a substitute in hospital life for close family ties. However, the arrangement often fulfilled their expectations to a greater extent than they planned for; they were uncomfortable about the patient's need to find a substitute husband or wife, boyfriend or girlfriend, yet perfectly content that in the family unit other love objects were represented: fathers, mothers, grandparents, siblings. Therefore, the interchange between patients was carefuly watched and often restricted: going beyond the stereotyped family pattern was tantamount to incest.

Love: a Four-Letter Word

The taboo on romantic attachment is probably the most frustrating concern of the PPH staff; it is a situation in which they appear to feel damned no matter how they handle it. This attitude is made apparent to the patients by the staff's inconsistency and the constant visible uneasiness of the nurses, in particular, in verbalizing their orders to the patients.

Two personal incidents will show just how far the staff's lack of trust of the patient, as well as of their own feelings, can go. For almost a year, my room was directly across the hall from that of a nineteen-year-old boy; he and I quickly became friends, since I was able to teach him something about painting, and he taught me many things about playing the guitar. One day he asked me to listen to a record which had some interesting chord work. Of course I knew I was not allowed to go into a male patient's room, so I stood in the doorway to his room and listened. Soon the head nurse came past, stopped next to me, nervously looked for an excuse to end what looked to her like an unhealthy situation, pointed her finger at my foot, and said, "Please move your foot to the hall side of Mr. B's threshold. You know very well that ladies are not allowed in gentlemen's rooms!" After several additional listening sessions, during which I was careful to keep both of my feet solidly outside of my friend's room, the matter was reported to our doctors. We were ordered to refrain from all "one-to-one" contact with each other. It was explained to me that "such conduct" (referring to my standing in a man's doorway) was undignified for a lady, although I am sure they feared a romantic attachment.

In another case, a woman patient walked into the lounge

after she had just come back from a two-week visit at home. Pauline had obviously lost a good deal of weight, and we all knew that she was pleased about it, so we wanted to compliment her by way of mild teasing. When she walked in, another patient remarked that Pauline was now so thin, she was a mere shadow of her former self. A third, and male, patient, picked up the cue, looked in the direction opposite Pauline, and said, "Where's Pauline? My God, she's gotten so thin, I don't even see her!" Karen got up from her chair, went over to the man, put her hands on his temples, and gently turned his head in Pauline's direction. At that, the head nurse interrupted this innocent and friendly fun with, "Miss S, please take your hands off of Mr. A! You know the rules: no one-to-one contact between patients!" Though this woman was far harsher than most staff members in enforcing such rules, she was highly respected by the psychiatrists at PPH, and no number of patients' complaints changed the opinion of the doctors. Her actions made us all aware of how powerless we were.

How little confidence the staff in general had in our ability to deal warmly, lovingly, and capably with even the simplest of human relationships.

This taboo on romantic attachments is heavily sanctioned throughout the hospital. The nursing staff is carefully coached to watch for such developments.[20] If they are prone to overreact, it is only a sign that, should they fail to report such dangerous patient behavior, they face dismissal. Since each patient's individual psychotherapist visits his unit every day, the nursing staff must be ready with a daily progress report. One can easily believe that the nursing staff looks for any snatch of emotionally-charged material it can report on a patient, thereby fulfilling what is required of them as warders of emotionally "sick" people.

The overall no "one-to-one" rule implies that there is to be no physical contact between any patients, except in supervised areas, such as during the weekly dances or in gym classes. When specifically imposed upon two patients, it further implies that there is to be no conversation between the two unless "others" are present. In the first place, such a rule is bound to make the relationship under question even more enticing; secondly, since the number and gender of the "others" is not specified, a sympathetic third patient can always be found who will go on walks with the couple or generally act as a smokescreen in the ever-present milieu of the watchful and suspicious staff. Often two couples, both under the sanction of no "one-to-one," will band together and exchange platonic partners in order to confuse the staff. Furthermore, since the large patient lounge is the after-dinner gathering place of most of the patients, and since most inmates are aware of interpatient affairs, all respect and deference are shown—that the couple, for instance, has a close proximity on a couch while watching TV, or that one or more other patients alert the couple when a member of the staff appears.

This conspiracy to outwit the staff is natural, since each patient empathically understands that the helplessness of his situation can only be alleviated—and only partially, at that—through the semieffective measures of the Patient Council, or by his banding together with other patients in quasi-conspiratorial behavior. It is unfortunate that this is necessary, for the whole vicious circle operates only to infect the inmate with further anxiety and resistance to therapy. It is my feeling that were these couple relationships permitted to exist freely, they could provide a wealth of material for the psychotherapist to work through with his patient, helping him to understand what need such a romantic attachment fulfills. Since they are negatively sanctioned by the doctor, the patient is put in a position where he must hold back reports of his feelings for another patient, for fear he will be rigidly physically restricted if he confesses. Hence, he will avoid the subject which is most poignantly revealing, and may lead the therapist away from the immediate anxiety-producing situation.

The patient's failure to comply with the no "one-to-one" rule to the satisfaction of the psychiatrist, as I have said before, leads to physical restrictions. He may, if the couple lives on the same unit, be transferred to another unit. Or he may be forced to forego the after-dinner social interchange in the main lounge, and to return to his unit immediately after dinner. He may be restricted from attending the weekly movie or dance in the gym, or from going to the patient recreation area (the one social area in the hospital, outside of the woods, which is unsupervised by staff). Or he may be confined totally to his unit, or even his room, where he would also have to take his meals. The lifting of the restriction comes only after both nursing staff and the patient's doctor are satisfied that the patient has repented, that he has seen the error of his ways, and intends to reform and conform.

Since the hospital authorities assume, in the eyes of both the larger society and the patient's immediate family, a good deal of responsibility for the actions of the patient, who is considered incapable of handling his own life situations, they are bound to be at a loss to know what to do when a romantic attachment develops. Often this occurs with married people, whose mates at home are paying the hospital bills and anxiously awaiting the return of their spouses, healthy and adjusted to marriage and family. In the case of unmarried individuals, the parents paying their bills do not want their offspring "messed up" with some "neurotic" individual, even though he may come from another wealthy and respectable family. The staff must please those who are financially involved. Furthermore, the hospital can hardly afford the bad publicity, the social disgrace that transpires when a couple, as happens occasionally, "escapes" together,[21] and may not be found until the situation has gotten out of hand. However, their overt reasoning is not gauged to this image protection, but to the patient's progress; the popular reason at PPH for why romantic attachments are not permitted to go unrestricted is that they provide the patient with a displacement for the reactions he should be directing toward his therapist, particularly in psychoanalytic-oriented psychotherapy. I do not deny that in many cases this may be true, but one may doubt if, given the persistent existence of such complications, analytic-oriented therapy will work anyway with such patients. Why not, then, provide them with a more permissive atmosphere, in which the patient could accept responsibility for his actions? It was my observation that these romantic attachments were never successfully dissolved by authoritative sanctions alone; several of them, indeed, ended in marriage, or, at least in full-blown courtships, once the couple had been discharged. It appears that only the individual himself, even though he has been tagged "mentally ill," can decide how he will handle his future.

Beyond Therapy

Despite the attempt, then, of the PPH staff to provide a living
arrangement that simulates a small family group, the situation
lacks the freedom necessary for a patient to develop spontaneously and maintain primary ties. In fact, when such attachments
develop, even between members of the same sex, they must often
be carried on at least in part clandestinely. I, for example, felt a
great loneliness for my children when I was at PPH. Many of the
friendships I had as a patient were, therefore, with young people.
It was generally and frequently requested of the patients that we
should not discuss our therapy material with anyone other than
staff members. I was exceptionally careful during conversations
with my young friends to remind them—if they became over-
talkative—to save their emotions for their doctor's sessions.
These friendships were many times the one thing that kept me
from languishing completely over the long-term loss of my own
children. Without doubt, my young friends felt the same, not
only toward me but toward other parent substitutes. Yet, here too,
where we mutually needed each other's warmth and comforting
words, the amount of time we spent together was carefully restricted by the staff. I was, at times, accused of trying to take over
the therapist's role with a young friend if I questioned a staff
member about why a restriction had been placed on our contact.
Perhaps I was inadvertently contributing to the patient's failure
to communicate in therapy, but here I must again question the
wisdom of the restriction: would it not be better to allow the
friendship to exist, and provide a therapy situation in which
both persons could air their feelings mutually, with a qualified
person helping them to understand what needs the friendship
is fulfilling? Instead, the staff forces the friendship to come to a
frustrating and empty end, or causes the two persons to carry
on clandestinely, with new anxieties churning up as a result of
their having disobeyed a regulation.

At PPH the group therapy sessions, which most units hold
once a week, are the official times set aside for discussing inter-

unit patient action. It frequently happened that we were, all of us, under separate restrictions for having become too friendly with another patient either in our unit or somewhere else in the hospital. We were mutually in sympathy with one another, without ever verbalizing this unity; none of us wanted the staff to find out that these friendships still existed surreptitiously, and so we would sit for the whole hour in tense silence, or else deal superficially with the first idea that came into our heads. Perhaps this is the finest example I can give, conversely, of the *real existence* of family life at PPH, which is in no way to the staff's credit or according to their plans, since our reason for banding together was to accomplish the same end that they simultaneously endorsed and condemned.

The group therapy sessions were something that I always looked forward to, however tense they may have been. I often felt that I learned as much, if not more, about how to handle my problems from the practical and jargonless remarks of my fellow inmates than from individual psychotherapy. The sessions were attended by all the patients and staff members of the unit, although the staff took part only as observers, usually taking notes, and always sitting silently at the side of the active circle. A psychiatrist sat in the circle with us, but seldom contributed more than a short remark to start the flow of communication or a few closing words of analysis. The hour was valuable to us as the one official chance we had to air our collective complaints against the nursing staff in the presence of a doctor. However, it could have been more successful had the unit staff also taken an active part. Although we did feel some release of tension and frustration in the simple verbalization of our feelings toward authority, the staff was still beyond our emotional reach, sitting outside of our circle and away from direct eye contact, in uniforms, with pencils in hand.

In fact, by the time I left PPH, this gap between staff and patients in the group therapy situation had been widened still further: the session room for our group was remodeled, with a wall of one-way glass installed (behind which we could no longer see or hear the staff) and an amplifier system in operation that carried our conversations to them. It was then less effective for us to discuss staff members, since none of us was able to see even a change in their facial expressions or postures as a result of our criticism. This change had undertones of authoritative insecurity, as though staff needed to barricade itself against popular assault, yet the reason we were given for the alteration was that it would cause less inhibition to the patients' verbalization of their feelings! It was a hapless situation at best; we lived twenty-four hours a day with these authority figures (and we certainly knew they were there behind the glass listening to us): were we not to think of them as part of the unit family as well?

To be sure, as Goffman also points out in reference to total institutions in general,[22] family life is an artificially contrived situation at PPH. However, the PPH staff does make a particular attempt to maintain the patient's contacts with his real family. All patients are encouraged to spend time on the grounds visiting with their families, to go out for social hours with them, and to have weekends or whole weeks at home in an effort to keep the family ties in existence.[23] The hospital staff of PPH, furthermore, encourages and often insists that the patient's family also be involved in therapy, either at the hospital or elsewhere. Numerous psychiatrists, psychologists, and social workers are available to work individually with the patient's family members, and also in family group therapy sessions. This is an admirable step in the right direction. However, it is obvious that the problem of meaningful family existence is not going to be successfully dealt with under the present approach to the treatment of mental patients, which is devoted to the orientation of the total institution.

I have already made several references to the preferential status given psychotherapy at PPH, a situation quite the reverse of the cheerless findings that Goffman reports: "A very standard complaint is: 'Nothing is being done with me—I'm just left to sit.' "[24] If, on the other hand, the PPH patient has any complaint, it is that too much is being done for him, not only physically, but mentally as well. Every patient has a minimum of two fifty-minute sessions of individual psychotherapy each week. If his benefactors request it, he can see either or both a doctor and analyst every day. In addition, as I have already indicated elsewhere, most patients have group therapy sessions once a week, and almost all are involved in some kind of family therapy program.

This emphasis on the availability of psychotherapy at PPH is, I believe, the single most important advantage that the private hospital offers in comparison to the public hospital. Speaking once again from my own experience, had I not been fortunate enough to afford the excellent therapy that I received, I doubt very much that I would be functioning with anywhere near the emotional well-being that I feel today. One may, of course, argue that my group therapy and individual psychotherapy learning was "brainwashing."[25] I heartily agree. I will admit also that, unlike many of my less fortunate fellow inmates, I arrived at PPH a willing subject; willing to put my faith in psychiatry because I knew no better solution to the extremely serious, self-destructive problems I had created for myself. I wanted help, and I got it.

I am not trying to suggest, however, that what worked for me must work for everyone, for at the same time that I felt myself to be benefiting from the methods of psychotherapy, it was poignantly evident that vast numbers of my fellow inmates were making little or no gain in understanding their problems as a result of the same methods. They could probably have benefited more from some other kind of treatment, had there been any other kinds available in the community. Many patients, especially the younger ones, seemed completely unable to respond to psychotherapy mainly because they found the institutional controls and general life of the hospital unbearable. Others were too impatient to wait out the slow pace of therapy. Still others had been forced to undergo therapy when they had no real desire to change themselves.

Moreover, enough general evidence has been collected in the past several years to prove that psychotherapy alone cannot be considered a cure-all for the mental problems of individuals in our society. Some research has, for example, suggested that spontaneous recovery occurs in emotional disturbances with as much frequency as those recoveries brought about by psychiatric methods.[26] Furthermore, regarding the assessment of degrees of mental well-being and aberration, some writers have found that psychiatric and psychoanalytic diagnoses are often unreliable and inconsistent. This becomes even more significant when these perspectives and methods are applied to other forms of deviant behavior.[27] In addition, psychiatrists' medical training forces them to fit their actions to the medical model paradigm of observation, diagnosis, and treatment. This prevents them from seeing "mental illness" as problems in living or as deviant behavior, as some writers have suggested.[28] This is not to mention the voluminous literature on socio-cultural factors that play a role in the development of functional mental disorders, and to which the psychiatric staff is too often blinded.[29]

I am not suggesting, of course, that we throw out the fine collection of knowledge, skill, or record of successes that psychiatry has given us in its short existence as an acknowledged healer of minds. Yet, neither do I believe that it should remain the undisputed God of self-knowledge. Would it not be advisable now to undertake as many new kinds of therapy as possible in the light of increasing doubts that psychiatry alone can answer the present need? Would it not be more just to begin to see the "mentally ill" as individuals responding to life situations, and with personal histories that sometimes are not conducive to the psychiatrist's couch?[30] In this spirit I should like to attempt to shed some light on the major source of error in the therapeutic means and goals at PPH and other mental institutions; and the further challenge of suggesting a different approach to the treatment of emotionally disturbed individuals—of all classes of people who care to avail themselves of such facilities.

Sanity and Work

Although our definition of work is changing with the addition of more leisure time, it is my belief that for some decades to come we will continue to equate our personal usefulness—and its corresponding degree of self-esteem—with the products of our labor. As I see it, and many of my inmate companions agreed, one of the primary failings of the mental institution is that its inmates are workless; and because they are workless, they are burdened with additional guilt and anxiety, which may hamper or halt altogether the progress of therapy. It may be a sad comment on our collective values to say that one *must* justify his existence by making money or, in the case of a housewife, helping her husband to do so, but it is nonetheless true. The person who is hospitalized, then, with this crucial element lacking in his life, feels himself a parasite on both his family and society.

I am quite sure, for example, that my progress in therapy was slowed by the constant anxiety I felt over draining the family funds—money my husband had worked hard to put away for other purposes. My doctor often suggested that I was avoiding the painfulness of therapeutic probing by using the issue of money as a red herring. There were times when she was no doubt right, but since I still feel with all clarity and certainty that this feeling of usefulness is an important issue, I am convinced that the individual's need to find meaning through productive work is as enmeshed in his feeling of self-esteem as is his awareness, through introspection, of other facets of his nature.

Certainly it is true that the individual *should* be able to consider his therapy experience productive work; he *should* realize that by going through the intense process of learning to verbalize his feelings and learning how to love himself and others, he is, indeed, adding a great deal to his family's and society's welfare. However, my observation at PPH was that this is not the case. Those people, in fact, who remained hospitalized through the entire period of intensive therapy were almost always married women, particularly those whose husbands had salaries well above average income levels. The men patients, on the other hand, no matter how financially able they appeared, frequently left PPH (against medical advice) in an anxiety-fraught steam over their jobs or businesses, in short, because they were concerned that they would lose their ability to sustain work contacts that they had put effort into building.

I am aware, of course, as I have indicated before, that there is sometimes a strong desire to run from therapy when the deepest wounds threaten to reach the surface. With men, who are trained early to hide their emotions, this may be even more true than with women. But just as important is the well-known fact that there are more men in our midst with serious mental difficulties than there are women; the suicide rate for men is higher also. Why is this true? Is it perhaps because men cannot feel free to indulge themselves in the financial luxury of a mental breakdown? Do they literally worry themselves to death with the conflict of personal and family responsibility? Are they ashamed to register themselves as mental patients in an institution for fear this will mark them for life—as Goffman puts it:

> Once he has a record of having been in a mental hospital, the public at large, both formally in terms of employment restrictions, and informally, in terms of day-to-day social treatment, considers him to be set apart; they place a stigma on him. Even the hospital itself tacitly acknowledges that mental disorder is shameful.[31]

Especially for men is this true. Not even a first-rate hospital can keep a man in therapy long enough to complete treatment, which would keep him from the pride of his work. No man can go to an employer, unless he is a first-rate self-salesman, and frankly admit that he has just spent two years in a mental institution!

Furthermore, few women can do it either. For those who are unmarried, their life's work is as financially necessary to them as it is to a man. Several unmarried women patients at PPH had elderly parents at home who depended on their support, or employers who would not keep them "on salary" longer than six months for hospital leave. The majority of us, however, were wives and mothers, and although we were not accustomed to working for a monthly pay check, we felt strongly—or wanted to feel—that our work at home was needed. In fact, and I cannot emphasize my point more stoutly than this: those women at PPH who came from very wealthy families often experienced their personal difficulties *because their lives lacked this feeling of usefulness*. They themselves often admitted, "What's the use of living? I have no work to do."

And so, whether it is applied to the rich or the poor, to men or women, Goffman's statement *does* fit: ". . . the individual who was work-oriented on the outside tends to become demoralized by the work system of the total institution."[32] The gravity of this becomes more apparent when we realize that several studies have shown that the prevalence of symptoms of mental illness is high among the unemployed and is closely related to occupational status.[33] While many of these studies naturally find negative variations between mental illness and social class, and while most of the patients at PPH are upper-middle-class, nevertheless the connection between work and sanity is clear. In some sense, then, many a patient's sojourn in PPH may be viewed in his eyes as a case of downward social mobility.

Goffman reports that in the public hospital patients are involved in "work therapy" or "industrial therapy" and are "put to tasks, typically mean ones, such as raking leaves, waiting on tables, working in the laundry and washing floors." He states that the hospital staff indicates to the patient that his participation will "help him to relearn to live in society and that his capacity and willingness to handle them will be taken as diagnostic evidence of progress."[34]

At PPH there is no "work" or "industrial therapy." In this respect, as demeaning as the work is, it is possible that the public hospital patient may be more fortunate than the patient at PPH. I was not accustomed to having so much done for me; I was eager to do some work in the hospital and lower my monthly fee for room and board by doing so. But even if my work had not lowered the fee, I would willingly have cleaned my room or raked leaves. Instead I was frowned upon for even wanting to do my own laundry! In the dining room, for instance, how often I thought that the many maid-waitresses who served us could have been sacrificed, to my family's financial benefit, if we had simply passed through a cafeteria line and served ourselves—with no less quality in the food. How often, before the chambermaid came into my room on her daily route, as I cleaned up my clutter, I wished the vacuum cleaner were in my hands instead of hers! How frequently I knew that I could have *thought* just as constructively, and maybe even more so, about my therapy material if I were pulling weeds from a flower bed; instead, part of my family's money went into paying gardeners to do this work.

To the PPH patient all is given, and he *must* take. Here is an ironic variation on Goffman's observation of the public hospital: the PPH patient who learns to accept these services graciously supposedly is being helped to relearn to live in his society, and his acquiescence will be taken as diagnostic evidence of his progress; yet what is really happening is that he is acquiring a trained incapacity to function in daily life.

This is not to say, however, that the PPH patient merely sits and drinks coffee all day. Early in his diagnostic period he is told of the many activities available to him. Within one or two weeks he is paid an official visit by an activity director, with whom he makes out a schedule of daily activities, much as one does in high school. All of these activities are optional, except for physical exercise in the gym, which must be scheduled at least twice weekly. A program must include, however, at least two activities a day and not more than five. Those patients who do not want to sign up for or attend activities are forced to do so; not wanting to attend is considered a symptom of withdrawal. The activities offered include chorus and musical instrument lessons; indoor and outdoor sports (including badminton, volley-ball, acrobatics, archery, basketball, and practice-range golf); arts and crafts of a wide variety; bridge and bridge lessons; dramatic workshop; nature study groups; hospital newspaper; Patient Council meetings and arranged events; and discussion-study groups. The one scheduled activity that contributed something to my enrichment was a series of discussion-study group sessions that were held once a week. The staff member in charge of these meetings was a deeply understanding teacher. We discussed Goldschmidt's book *Exploring the Ways of Mankind*, and later went on to use the material of the Great Decisions series. At the time of my discharge from PPH, a state university three-credit course in Introductory Sociology was being given on the hospital grounds, taught by an instructor who came from the nearby university center.

It is, of course, to be assumed that selected scheduled activities have value in various ways for all patients; developing latent talents in art or music, for example, helps greatly to build one's sense of self-confidence. But although these activities should be given a relevant place in the total treatment picture, they cannot and must not be considered a substitute for work:

. . . to say that inmates of total institutions have their full day scheduled for them is to say that all their essential needs will have to be planned for. Whatever the incentive to work, then, this incentive will not have the structural significance it has on the outside.

tudes towards it. This is the basic adjustment required of the inmates
and of those who must induce them to work.[35]

The trite but still applicable saying, "busy hands make happy
hearts," is an integral part of the American character. Yet when
many "normal" people stop to consider what they are doing in
their busyness, they may well see that too large a share of the
time and energy being expended is worthless. This shocking
awareness can, indeed, be reason enough for a mental breakdown, particularly during the middle years of life when one's
patterns of action have become rather rigid, and one is beginning
mentally to list the accomplishments of his lifetime. When such
a problem leads the person into a mental hospital, it is not difficult to see how his being forced to take part in activities—more
"busy work" or "make work"—will only frustrate him further
and make him feel more worthless and depressed. It is not only
the middle-age patient who experiences this, however; at PPH
the rapidly growing number of teen-agers asked the touchy question loudly: "What is my life worth? And why am I sitting here
making ashtrays?" They as well as their older fellow inmates
were seriously in need of an immediate feeling of usefulness
to make the slow progress of psychotherapy more tolerable and
meaningful.

Of course, for the person who is not work-oriented, the secure
life of the total institution is desirably free from real responsibility, and for this reason, coveted. A few patients at PPH still
had many potentially fruitful years ahead of them. They had
been hospitalized for as long as five years, but could function
well socially and showed no signs of psychotic behavior. They
were all from wealthy families who could afford to keep them
hospitalized indefinitely. But their doctors and the general staff
seemed uncomfortable about their presence. If one of these
patients was forced to look for a job in the community, he invariably sabotaged his chances for employment and fell back
into the comfortable and childlike existence of hospital activities.
The doctors seemed to be at a loss to know what to do with such
"institutionalized" cases.[36]

ii

THE PURSUIT OF
LEISURE

5

Time and Cool People[*]

John Horton

*Like every other aspect of social reality, time is taken for granted.
The linear, segmented conception of time characterizes our
Western civilization. From the cradle to the deathbed our
activity is coordinated according to a stylized time sense—
clock time. Anthropological cross-cultural studies have
demonstrated that the conception of time is culturally relative. Yet, even within our own scheduled society there are
those for whom clock time is suspended and for whom the
sense of time is contingent upon the pulse of daily activity.
This study utilizing a combination of methods, uses the concept of time as a lever for understanding the world of the
Afro-American "street set," where personal as opposed to
standard time "is a positive adaptation to generations of
living whenever and wherever possible outside the sound
and control of the white man's clock."*

*John Horton, associate professor of sociology at San Francisco
State University, is working on a book on ideological assumptions in current studies of social problems.*

[*] John Horton, "Of Time and Cool People," *Trans-action*, Vol. 4 (April,
1967).

Street culture exists in every low income ghetto. It is shared by
the hustling elements of the poor, whatever their nationality
or color. In Los Angeles, members of such street groups sometimes call themselves "street people," "cool people," or simply
"regulars." Whatever the label, they are known the world over
by outsiders as hoods or hoodlums, persons who live on and off
the street. They are recognizable by their own fashions in dress,
hair, gestures, and speech. The particular fashion varies with
time, place, and nationality. For example, in 1963 a really sharp
Los Angeles street Negro would be "conked to the bone" (have
processed hair) and "togged-out" in "continentals." Today "natural" hair and variations of mod clothes are coming in style.

Street people are known also by their activities—"duking"
(fighting or at least looking tough), "hustling" (any way of making money outside the "legitimate" world of work), "gigging"
(partying)—and by their apparent nonactivity, "hanging" on
the corner. Their individual roles are defined concretely by their
success or failure in these activities. One either knows "what's
happening" on the street, or he is a "lame," "out of it," "not
ready" (lacks his diploma in street knowledge), a "square."

There are, of course, many variations. Negroes, in particular,
have contributed much to the street tongue which has diffused
into both the more hip areas of the middle class and the broader
society. Such expressions as "a lame," "taking care of righteous
business," "getting down to the nitty-gritty," and "soul" can be
retraced to Negro street life.

The more or less organized center of street life is the "set"—
meaning both the peer group and the places where it hangs out.
It is the stage and central market place for activity, where to
find out what's happening. My set of Negro street types contained
a revolving and sometimes disappearing (when the "heat," or
police pressure, was on) population of about forty-five members
ranging in age from eighteen to twenty-five. These were the
local "dudes," their term meaning not the fancy city slickers but
simply "the boys," "fellas," the "cool people." They represented
the hard core of street culture, the role models for younger teen-
agers. The dudes could be found when they were "laying dead"
—hanging on the corner, or shooting pool and "jiving" ("goofing"
or kidding around) in a local community project. Isolated from

"the man" (in this context the man in power—the police, and by extension, the white man), they lived in a small section of Venice outside the central Los Angeles ghetto and were surrounded by a predominantly Mexican and Anglo population. They called their black "turf" "Ghost-town"—home of the "Ghostmen," their former gang. Whatever the origin of the word, Ghost-town was certainly the home of socially "invisible" men.

The Street Set

In 1965 and 1966 I had intensive interviews with twenty-five set members. My methods emerged in day-to-day observations. Identified as white, a lame, and square, I had to build up an image of being at least "legit" (not working for police). Without actually living in the area, this would have been impossible without the aid of a key field worker, in this case an outsider who could be accepted inside. This field worker, Cowboy, was a white dude of twenty-five. He had run with "Paddy" (white), "Chicano" (Mexican), and "Blood" (Negro) sets since the age of twelve and was highly respected for having been president of a tough gang. He knew the street, how to duke, move with style, and speak the tongue. He made my entry possible. I was the underprivileged child who had to be taught slowly and sympathetically the common-sense features of street life.

Cowboy had the respect and I the toleration of several set leaders. After that, we simply waited for the opportunity to "rap." Although sometimes used synonymously with street conversation, "rap" is really a special way of talking—repartee. Street repartee at its best is a lively way of "running it down," or of "jiving" (attempting to put someone on), of trying "to blow another person's mind," forcing him "to lose his cool," to give in or give up something. For example, one needs to throw a lively rap when he is "putting the make on a broad."

Sometimes we taped individuals, sometimes "soul sessions." We asked for life histories, especially stories about school, job, and family. We watched and asked about the details of daily survival and attempted to construct street time schedules. We probed beyond the past and present into the future in two directions—individual plans for tomorrow and a lifetime, and individual dreams of a more decent world for whites and Negroes.

The set can be described by the social and attitudinal characteristics of its members. To the observer, these are expressed in certain realities of day-to-day living: not enough skill for good jobs, and the inevitable trouble brought by the problem of surviving. Of the twenty-five interviewed, only four had graduated from high school. Except for a younger set member who was still in school, all were dropouts, or perhaps more accurately kicked-outs. None was really able to use or write formal language. However, many were highly verbal, both facile and effective in their use of the street tongue. Perhaps the art of conversation is most highly developed here where there is much time to talk, perhaps too much—an advantage of the lumpen-leisure class.

Their incomes were difficult to estimate, as "bread" or "coins" (money) came in on a very irregular basis. Of the seventeen for whom I have figures, half reported that they made less than $1,400 in the last year, and the rest claimed incomes from $2,000 to $4,000 annually. Two-thirds were living with and partially dependent on their parents, often a mother. The financial strain was intensified by the fact that although fifteen out of seventeen were single, eight had one or more children living in the area. (Having children, legitimate or not, was not a stigma but proof of masculinity.)

At the time of the interview, two-thirds of them had some full- or part-time employment—unskilled and low-paid jobs. The overall pattern was one of sporadic and—from their viewpoint—often unsatisfactory work, followed by a period of unemployment compensation, and petty hustling whenever necessary.

When I asked the question, "When a dude needs bread, how does he get it?" the universal response was "the hustle." Hustling is, of course, illegitimate from society's viewpoint. Street people know it is illegal, but they view it in no way as immoral or wrong. It is justified by the necessity of survival. As might be expected, the unemployed admitted that they hustled and went so far as to say that a dude could make it better on the street than on the job: "There is a lot of money on the street, and there are many ways of getting it," or simply, "This has always been my way of life." On the other hand, the employed, the part-time hustlers, usually said, "A dude could make it better on the job than on the street." Their reasons for disapproving of hustling were not moral. Hustling meant trouble. "I don't hustle because there's no security. You eventually get busted." Others said there was not enough money on the street or that it was too difficult to "run a game" on people.

Nevertheless, hustling is the central street activity. It is the economic foundation for everyday life. Hustling and the fruit of hustling set the rhythm of social activities.

What are the major forms of hustling in Ghost-town? The best hustles were conning, stealing, gambling, and selling dope. By gambling, these street people meant dice; by dope, peddling "pills" and "pot." Pills are "reds" and "whites"—barbiturates and Benzedrine or Dexedrine. Pot is, of course, marijuana—"grass" or "weed." To "con" means to put "the bump" on a "cat," to "run a game" on somebody, to work on his mind for goods and services.

The "woman game" was common. As one dude put it, "If I have a good lady and she's on County, there's always some money to get." In fact, there is a local expression for getting county money. When the checks come in for child support, it's "mother's day." So the hustler "burns" people for money, but he also "rips off" goods for money; he thieves, and petty thieving is always a familiar hustle. Pimping is often the hustler's dream of the good life, but it was almost unknown here among the small-time hustlers. That was the game of the real professional and required a higher level of organization and wealth.

Hustling means bread and security but also trouble, and trouble is a major theme in street life. The dudes had a "world of trouble" (a popular song about a hustler is "I'm in a World of Trouble")—with school, jobs, women, and the police. The intensity of street life could be gauged in part by the intensity of the "heat" (police trouble). The hotter the street, the fewer the people visible on the street. On some days the set was empty. One would soon learn that there had been a "bust" (an arrest). Freddy had run amuck and thrown rocks at a police car. There had been a leadership struggle; "Big Moe" had been cut up, and the "fuzz" had descended. Life was a succession of being picked up on suspicion of assault, theft, possession, "suspicion of suspicion" (an expression used by a respondent in describing his life). This was an ordinary experience for the street dude and often did lead to serious trouble. Over half of those interviewed claimed they had felony convictions.

The Structure of Street Time

Keeping cool and out of trouble, hustling bread, and looking for something interesting and exciting to do created the structure of time on the street. The rhythm of time is expressed in the high and low points in the day and week of an unemployed dude. I stress the pattern of the unemployed and full-time hustler because he is on the street all day and night and is the prototype in my interviews. The sometimes employed will also know the pattern, and he will be able to hit the street whenever released from the bondage of jail, work, and the clock. Here I describe a typical time schedule gleaned through interviews and field observation.

Characteristically the street person gets up late, hits the street in the late morning or early afternoon, and works his way to the set. This is a place for relaxed social activity. Hanging on the set with the boys is the major way of passing time and waiting until some necessary or desirable action occurs. Nevertheless, things do happen on the set. The dudes "rap" and "jive" (talk), gamble, and drink their "pluck" (usually a cheap, sweet wine). They find out what happened yesterday, what is happening today, and what will hopefully happen on the weekend—the perpetual search for the "gig," the party. Here peer socialization and reinforcement also take place. The younger dude feels a sense of pride when he can be on the set and throw a rap to an older dude. He is learning how to handle himself, show respect, take care of business, and establish his own "rep."

On the set, yesterday merges into today, and tomorrow is an emptiness to be filled in through the pursuit of bread and excitement. Bread makes possible the excitement—the high (getting loaded with wine, pills, or pot), the sharp clothes, the "broad," the fight, and all those good things which show that one knows what's happening and has "something going" for himself. The rhythm of time—of the day and of the week—is patterned by the flow of money and people.

Time is "dead" when money is tight, when people are occupied elsewhere—working or in school. Time is dead when one is in jail. One is "doing dead time" when nothing is happening and he's got nothing going for himself.

Time is alive when and where there is action. It picks up in the evening when everyone moves on the street. During the regular school year it may pick up for an hour in the afternoon when the "broads" leave school and meet with the set at a corner taco joint. Time may pick up when a familiar car cruises by and a few dudes drive down to Johnny's for a "process" (hair straightening and styling). Time is low on Monday (as described in the popular song, "Stormy Monday"), Tuesday, Wednesday, when money is tight. Time is high on Friday nights when the "eagle flies" and the "gig" begins. On the street, time has a personal meaning only when something is happening, and something is most likely to happen at night—especially on Friday and Saturday nights. Then people are together, and there may be bread—bread to take and bread to use.

Human behavior is rational if it helps the individual to get what he wants, whether it is success in school or happiness in the street. Street people sometimes get what they want. They act rationally in those situations where they are able to plan and choose because they have control, knowledge, and concern, irrationally where there are barriers to their wants and desires.

When the street dude lacks knowledge and power to manipulate time, he is indeed irrational. For the most part, he lacks the skills and power to plan a move up and out of the ghetto. He is "a lame" in the middle-class world of school and work; he is not ready to operate effectively in unfamiliar organizations where his street strengths are his visible weaknesses. Though irrational in moving up and out of the street, he can be rational in day to day survival in the street. No one survives there unless he knows what's happening (that is, unless he knows what is available, where to get what he can without being burned or busted). More euphemistically, this is "taking advantage of opportunities," exactly what the rational member of the middle class does in his own setting.

To know what's happening is to know the goods and the bads, the securities, the opportunities, and the dangers of the street. Survival requires that a hustling dude know who is cool and uncool (who can be trusted); who is in power (the people who control narcotics, fences, etc.); who is the "duker" or the fighter (someone to be avoided or someone who can provide protection). When one knows what's happening he can operate in many scenes, providing that he can "hold his mud," keep cool and out of trouble.

With his diploma in street knowledge, a dude can use time efficiently and with cunning in the pursuit of goods and services —in hustling to eat and yet have enough bread left over for the pleasures of pot, the chicks, and the gig. As one respondent put it, "The good hustler has the know-how, the ambition to better himself. He conditions his mind and must never put his guard too far down, to relax, or he'll be taken." This is street rationality. The problem is not a deficient sense of time but deficient knowledge and control to make a fantasy future and a really better life possible.

The petty hustler more fully realizes the middle-class ideal of individualistic rationality than does the middle class itself. When rationality operates in hustling, it is often on an individual basis. In a world of complex organization, the hustler defines himself as an entrepreneur; and indeed, he is the last of the competitive entrepreneurs.

The degree of organization in hustling depends frequently on the kind of hustling. Regular pimping and pushing require many trusted contacts and organization. Regular stealing requires regular fences for hot goods. But in Ghost-town when the hustler moved, he usually moved alone and on a small scale. His success was on him. He could not depend on the support of some benevolent organization. Alone, without a sure way of running the same game twice, he must continually recalculate conditions and people and find new ways of taking or be taken himself. The phrase "free enterprise for the poor and socialism for the rich" applies only too well in the streets. The political conservative should applaud all that individual initiative.

Clock Time vs. Personal Time

Negro street time is built around the irrelevance of clock time, white man's time, and the relevance of street values and activities. Like anyone else, a street dude is on time by the standard clock whenever he wants to be, not on time when he does not want to be and does not have to be.

When the women in school hit the street at the lunch hour and he wants to throw them a rap, he will be there then and not one hour after they have left. But he may be kicked out of high school for truancy or lose his job for being late and unreliable. He learned at an early age that school and job were neither interesting nor salient to his way of life. A regular on the set will readily admit being crippled by a lack of formal education. Yet school was a "bum kick." It was not his school. The teachers put him down for his dress, hair, and manners. As a human being he has feelings of pride and autonomy, the very things most threatened in those institutional situations where he was or is the underdeveloped, unrespected, illiterate, and underserving outsider. Thus whatever "respectable" society says will help him, he knows oppresses him, and he retreats to the streets for security and a larger degree of personal freedom. Here his control reaches a maximum, and he has the kind of autonomy which many middle-class males might envy.

In the street, watches have a special and specific meaning. Watches are for pawning and not for telling time. When they are worn, they are decorations and ornaments of status. The street clock is informal, personal, and relaxed. It is not standardized nor easily synchronized to other clocks. In fact, a street dude may have almost infinite toleration for individual time schedules. To be on time is often meaningless, to be late an unconsciously accepted way of life. "I'll catch you later," or simply "later," are the street phrases that mean business will be taken care of, but not necessarily now.

Large areas of street life run on late time. For example, parties are not cut off by some built-in alarm clock of appointments and schedules. At least for the unemployed, standard time neither precedes nor follows the gig. Consequently, the action can take its course. It can last as long as interest is sustained and die by exhaustion or by the intrusion of some more interesting event. A gig may endure all night and well into another day. One of the reasons for the party assuming such time dimensions is purely economic. There are not enough cars and enough money for individual dates, so everyone converges in one place and takes care of as much business as possible there, that is, doing whatever is important at the time—sex, presentation of self, hustling.

Colored People's Time

Events starting late and lasting indefinitely are clearly street and class phenomena, not some special trait of Afro-Americans. Middle-class Negroes who must deal with the organization and coordination of activities in church and elsewhere will jokingly and critically refer to a lack of standard time sense when they say that Mr. Jones arrived "CPT" (colored people's time). They have a word for it, because being late is a problem for people caught between two worlds and confronted with the task of meshing standard and street time. In contrast, the street dudes had no self-consciousness about being late; with few exceptions they had not heard the expression CPT. (When I questioned members of a middle-class Negro fraternity, a sample matched by age to the street set, only three of the twenty-five interviewed could not define CPT. Some argued vehemently that CPT was the problem to be overcome.)

Personal time as expressed in parties and other street activities is not simply deficient knowledge and use of standard time. It is a positive adaption to generations of living whenever and wherever possible outside of the sound and control of the white man's clock. The personal clock is an adaptation to the chance and accidental character of events on the street and to the very positive value placed on emotion and feeling. (For a discussion of CPT which is close to some of the ideas presented here, see Jules Henry, "White People's Time, Colored People's Time," *Trans-action*, March/April 1965.)

Chance reinforces personal time. A dude must be ready on short notice to move "where the action is." His internal clock may not be running at all when he is hanging on the corner and waiting for something to do. It may suddenly speed up by chance: someone cruises by in a car and brings a nice "stash" of "weed," a gig is organized and he looks forward to being well togged-out and throwing a rap to some "boss chick," or a lame appears and opens himself to a quick "con." Chance as a determinant of personal time can be called more accurately uncertain predictability. Street life is an aggregate of relatively independent events. A dude may not know exactly what or when something will happen, but from past experience he can predict a range of possibilities, and he will be ready, in position, and waiting.

In white middle-class stereotypes and fears—and in reality— street action is highly expressive. A forthright yet stylized expression of emotion is positively evaluated and most useful. Street control and communication are based on personal power and the direct impingement of one individual on another. Where there is little property, status in the set is determined by personal qualities of mind and brawn.

The importance of emotion and expression appears again and again in street tongue and ideology. When asked, "How does a dude make a rep on the set?" over half of the sample mentioned "style," and all could discuss the concept. Style is difficult to define as it has so many referents. It means to carry one's self well, dress well, to show class. In the ideology of the street, it may be a way of behaving. One has style if he is able to dig people as they are. He doesn't put them down for what they do. He shows toleration. But a person with style must also show respect. That means respect for a person as he is, and since there is power in the street, respect for another's superior power. Yet one must show respect in such a way that he is able to look tough and inviolate, fearless, secure, "cool."

Style may also refer to the use of gestures in conversation or in dance. It may be expressed in the loose walk, the jivey or dancing walk, the slow cool walk, the way one "chops" or "makes it" down the street. It may be the loose, relaxed hand rap or hand slap, the swinger's greeting which is used also in the hip middle-class teen sets. There are many refined variations of the hand rap. As a greeting, one may simply extend his hand, palm up. Another slaps it loosely with his finger. Or, one person may be standing with his hand behind and palm up. Another taps the hand in passing, and also pays his respect verbally with the conventional greeting "What's happening, Brother." Or in conversation, the hand may be slapped when an individual has "scored," has been "digging," has made a point, has got through to the person.

Style is a comparatively neutral value compared to "soul." Soul can be many things—a type of food (good food is "soul food," a "bowl of soul"), music, a quality of mind, a total way of acting (in eating, drinking, dancing, walking, talking, relating to others, etc.). The person who acts with soul acts directly and honestly from his heart. He feels it and tells it "like it is." One respondent identified soul with ambition and drive. He said the person with soul, once he makes up his mind, goes directly to the goal, doesn't change his mind, doesn't wait and worry about messing up a little. Another said soul was getting down to the nitty-gritty, that is, moving directly to what is basic without guise and disguise. Thus soul is the opposite of hypocrisy, deceit, and phoniness, the opposite of "affective neutrality" and "instrumentality." Soul is simply whatever is considered beautiful, honest, and virtuous in men.

Most definitions tied soul directly to Negro experience. As one hustler put it, "It is the ability to survive. We've made it with so much less. Soul is the Negro who has the spirit to sing in slavery to overcome the monotony." With very few exceptions, the men interviewed argued that soul was what Negroes had and whites did not. Negroes were "soul brothers," warm and emotional—whites cold as ice. Like other oppressed minorities these street Negroes believed they had nothing except their soul and their humanity, and that this made them better than their oppressors.

The Personal Dream

Soul is anchored in a past and present of exploitation and deprivation, but are there any street values and activities which

relate to the future? The regular in the street set has no provi-
dential mission; he lives personally and instrumentally in the
present, yet he dreams about the day when he will get himself
together and move ahead to the rewards of a good job, money,
and a family. Moreover, the personal dream coexists with a
nascent political nationalism, the belief that Negroes can and
will make it as Negroes. His present-future time is a combination of contradictions and developing possibilities. Here I will
be content to document without weighing two aspects of his
orientation: fantasy personal future and fantasy collective future. I use the word fantasy because street people have not yet
the knowledge and means and perhaps the will to fulfill their
dreams. It is hard enough to survive by the day.

When the members of the set were asked, "What do you really
want out of life?" their responses were conventional, concrete,
seemingly realistic, and—given their skills—rather hopeless.
Two-thirds of the sample mentioned material aspirations—the
finer things in life, a home, security, a family. For example, one
said, in honest street language, "I want to get things for my
kids and to make sure they have a father." Another said, jokingly, "a good future, a home, two or three girls living with me."
Only one person didn't know, and the others deviated a little
from the material response. They said such things as "for everyone to be on friendly terms—a better world . . . then I could
get all I wish," "to be free," "to help people."

But if most of the set wanted money and security, they wanted
it on their own terms. As one put it, "I don't want to be in a
middle-class bag, but I would like a nice car, home, and food
in the icebox." He wanted the things and the comforts of
middle-class life, but not the hypocrisy, the venality, the cold-
ness, the being forced to do what one does not want to do. All
that was in the middle-class bag. Thus the home and the money
may be ends in themselves, but also fronts, security for carrying
on the usual street values. Street people believed that they already had something that was valuable and looked down upon
the person who made it and moved away into the middle-class
world. For the observer, the myths are difficult to separate from
the truths—here where the truths are so bitter. One can only

say safely that street people dream of a high status, and they really do not know how to get it.

The Collective Future

The Negro dudes are political outsiders by the usual poll questions. They do not vote. They do not seek out civil rights demonstrations. They have very rudimentary knowledge of political organization. However, about the age of eighteen, when fighting and being tough are less important than before, street people begin to discuss their position in society. Verbally they care very much about the politics of race and the future of the Negro. The topic is always a ready catalyst for a soul session.

The political consciousness of the street can be summarized by noting those interview questions which attracted at least a 75 percent rate of agreement. The typical respondent was angry. He approves of the Watts incident, although from his isolated corner of the city he did not actively participate. He knows something about the history of discrimination and believes that if something isn't done soon America can expect violence: "What this country needs is a revolutionary change." He is more likely to praise the leadership of Malcolm X than Lyndon Johnson, and he is definitely opposed to the Vietnam War. The reason for his opposition is clear: Why fight for a country which is not mine, when the fight is here?

Thus his racial consciousness looks to the future and a world where he will not have to stand in the shadow of the white man. But his consciousness has neither clear plan nor political commitment. He has listened to the Muslims, and his is not a black nationalism. True, the Negro generally has more soul than the white. He thinks differently, his women may be different, yet integration is preferable to separatism. Or, more accurately, he doesn't quite understand what all these terms mean. His nationalism is real as a folk nationalism based on experience with other Negroes and isolation from whites.

The significance of a racial future in the day to day consciousness of street people cannot be assessed. It is a developing possibility dependent on unforeseen conditions beyond the scope of their skill and imagination. But bring up the topic of race and tomorrow, and the dreams come rushing in—dreams of superiority, dreams of destruction, dreams of human equality. These dreams of the future are salient. They are not the imagination of authoritarian personalities, except from the viewpoint of those who see spite lurking behind every demand for social change. They are certainly not the fantasies of the hipster living philosophically in the present without hope and ambition. One hustler summarized the Negro street concept of ambition and future time when he said:

The Negro has more ambition than the whites. He's got farther to go. "The man" is already there. But we're on your trail, daddy. You still have smoke in our eyes, but we're catching up.

6

Urban Samurai: *The "Karate Dojo"* *

Glenn Jacobs

The current interest in things Oriental embraces not only philosophy and religion, but also the Japanese martial arts such as judo, aikido, and karate. Schools have sprouted all over, and the arts are included in the athletic curricula of many high schools and colleges; most newsstands now carry a selection of magazines and paperbacks devoted to these subjects. Aside from their obvious exotic character, which seems to render them unique, the schools where these arts are taught exhibit traits which put them in the company of as diverse an assortment of groups as boys' gangs, men's fraternal organizations, religious cults, and high school athletic teams. Accordingly, this study examines a karate dojo (school) as a reality within a world of multiple realities. As the veils of mystery and secrecy are peeled away, the realities of group life are revealed.

Glenn Jacobs, instructor of sociology, University of Wisconsin, Rock County Campus, is a doctoral candidate at that university.

* This study was presented in an abbreviated form as a paper entitled "Communication and Mystification in the *Karate Dojo*" at the 1969 Annual Meeting of the American Sociological Association in San Francisco, September 3, 1969.

The Setting

During the day, lower Manhattan's drug and cosmetic district is filled with the hustle of people moving through the many wholesale and retail stores. It resounds with the cacophony of truck and automobile horns, reflecting the irritation of truck drivers, commuters, and businessmen anxious to perform their rounds and seek refuge in comfortable offices and homes. The shabby offices and lofts above the stores house the outlets of a staggering diversity of goods and services, only barely cataloged in the yellow pages of the telephone directory of a vast metropolis.

For the human traffic, the area is just another annoying bottleneck to be suffered while going somewhere else or while "picking up a few things"; not many are aware of the upstairs of these buildings. Sandwiched in among these upstairs nooks is a converted loft containing the *Goju Karate Dojo* (*Goju* meaning "hard-soft," a style of karate; *dojo,* a place where the Japanese martial arts are studied).

The *dojo* is open to its membership evenings from 6:30 to 8:30, and on Sundays from 12:00 to 4:00 in the afternoon— the hours when the neighborhood changes into a deserted array of shabby buildings.

The decor of the *dojo* is designed in such a way as to convince the spectator that he has at once entered a place pregnant with the mysteries of the East, the austerity of a professional's office, the savoir-faire of a ballet school, and the "men only" atmosphere of a boys' hangout. The rows of observation benches and the training equipment, rice paper lamps, documents written in calligraphy, and mazelike partitions dividing the place are all orchestrated to conjure up the exotic and the bizarre. Coupled with this, one is struck by the rather unorthodox movements, gestures, and vocalizations associated with the practice of the

art. The formalism of the various drilled techniques, the ho-
mogeneity of barefoot members in baggy white muslin uniforms
combined with the quasi-oriental atmosphere, are attractive to
tourists and prospective members.

Proficiency in karate calls for strength, stamina, and speed.
This makes the sport uncongenial to older men, women, and
young children. As a result, the membership consists largely of
males ranging between the ages of fourteen and forty. Their
occupational backgrounds are varied, with a skewness toward
older high school and college males and young middle- and
working-class men. In our *dojo* there was one minor celebrity, a
cartoonist for *Playboy* magazine. There were also several policemen studying karate. Reminiscent of cheap western movies,
they deposited their revolvers at the desk before exercises.

The Company Chart

The formal organization of the *dojo* consists of a scheme involving the student's progression through hierarchically ordered
statuses, the ranks being indicated by the color of the cotton
belts. Each status group also must learn the techniques appropriate to it. The specifications of skill and acquisition of particular
techniques are partially determined by the customary standards
of Japanese *dojos*, and partially idiosyncratic to a given school.
The succession of statuses are: (1) white belt—*shirobi* (*obi*
meaning "belt"); (2) green belt—*midori obi;* (3) brown belt—
chowbi; (4) black belt (first through third levels)—*kurobi;*
(5) black belt (fourth and fifth levels)—*renshi* (meaning "expert"); (6) black belt (sixth through eighth levels)—*kyoshi*
(meaning "wizard"); (7) black belt (ninth level)—*hanshi*
(meaning "chief"); and (8) black belt (tenth level)—*hanshi
seiko-sheehan* (meaning "chief master"). Honorary belt colors
for the fourth through fifth, sixth through eighth, and ninth and
tenth degrees are, respectively, black-red-white, black-red, and
solid red. (Both ninth and tenth levels of black belt are solid red.)
In the *dojo* of Mr. Urban, the master-proprietor, the highest

rank attained was the third level black belt; Urban himself was a seventh level black belt. The wearing of belts obviously makes it easy for members to identify one another as status equals, superiors, and inferiors, and the entire structure of the cliques are predicated upon formal group levels.

Hypothetically, mobility proceeds up or down, but in actuality the latter seldom occurs. Advance requires a formal examination of skill; demotion can result from unprincipled activity involving indiscriminate use of karate in or out of the *dojo*. In Japan the delinquent member is required to fight the master without pulled punches; but in the United States such authority cannot be exercised and the offender is simply dismissed. The prerequisites for advancement are satisfactory completion of and adeptness in the techniques of one's status. These include skill in various appropriate hand and foot techniques, free-style fighting or sparring (*kumite*) and, most important, excellence in the performance of forms resembling choreographic or shadow boxing routines (*katas*). *Katas* are symbolic representations in dance form of stereotyped fighting situations and appropriate techniques integrated into organized routines; each belt level has its own *katas*. Judgment of skill in *kata* is based upon criteria including rhythm and grace. It is considered the most important index of the acquisition of skill and proficiency in the art, and all the martial arts and the various styles of karate have their own series of *katas*.

As shall be stressed later, the status symbols of the upper belt ranks are communicated by loose clique formations, and the caricaturing of the most prominent *dojo* denizens. The more concrete signs of status typically include, for example, the amount of wear shown in a member's uniform, indicated by the degree of whiteness, limpness, and shrinkage produced by repeated washing and bleaching. The whiter, limper, and more form-fitting one's uniform is, the greater amount of seniority the member has attributed to him, even within a particular belt level, and hence, the greater amount of skill and proficiency that is imputed to him. As Gregory Stone has pointed out:

> ... the uniform is precisely any apparent representation of the self, at once reminding the wearer and others of an *appropriate* identity,

a *real* identity. The team-player is uniformed; the play actor is costumed. When we asked our informants their earliest recollections of wanting to wear any particular item of clothing, they responded almost unanimously by recalling their earliest self-conscious appropriations of the dress of their peer groups. In a sense, the earliest items of clothing they wanted comprised the *uniforms* of the peer circle.[1]

With the gaining of status also come greater privileges, such as the black belt prerogative of crossing the threshold into the sacrosanct confines of the master's "office," the greater accessibility of esoteric karate knowledge (such as *katsu*, a highly mystified art of resuscitation), and the acquisition of weaponry techniques other than the empty hands and extremities. With these privileges also comes the responsibility of teaching. This too is a privilege, since the best black belts are given the title "drill master." Like staff sergeants, and with the same demeanor, they drill the new recruits. The other black and brown belts do remedial work with deficient members, generally below their rank. The upper belts, then, through the teaching obligation, are given the authority to lord it over the lower ranking members and to ape the master's mannerisms.

Rites of Passage

Competition for all levels above white belt is keen. Tryouts are usually held on Friday evenings, and there is always a great deal of gossip and rumor circulated about who will compete and what his chances of success are. A member who has tried out for the same rank and failed, or one who has spent an excessive length of time at a lower level, will often become discouraged and quit. This is understandable, since the dropout's first group of peers has long since progressed to other levels. Quitting saves him humiliation at the hands of peers who are now his superiors.

At the tryouts a procedure is followed which resembles the initiation rites of so-called primitive societies, wherein the aspirants to a particular status in the *dojo* ritually go through symbolic separation from the old status, encounter the new status (transition), and experience incorporation into it.[2]

The aspirant, for example, must perform before the master and an audience, the class, seated on the floor on the periphery of the training area. First, he demonstrates his ability in *kata,* then he enters into *kumite* (sparring) with his "brothers" of the same level, and finally, with those of the aspired level. In this ritualistic sparring, the new member is bade welcome by his new group of "brothers." He has been admitted publicly into the establishment, so to speak. Achievement of the black belt marks one's real maturity within the *dojo.* In Japan, all levels under black belt are considered to be of minor importance. In short, "making black belt" means becoming one of the men. By sparring with his new peers, he has officially renounced his past. He is now ready to learn more esoteric techniques and skills, and has formally acquired the privilege to teach as well as learn.

When a member advances to any level he is given a diploma bearing his name, birth date, accreditation date, karate registration number, and certification of the fact that he has satisfactorily completed the requirements prerequisite to his new status. The new status incumbent is also given a letter of congratulation including an epigram or two, encouraging hard work and perseverance in what is assumed optimistically to be the student's upward mobile career.[3]

Years ago, among judo students in Japan, black belt initiation was marked by a "strangulation ceremony," where the master, usually in his own home, would literally strangle new black belt initiates into unconsciousness and then revive them by administering *katsu.* According to one writer, this was done "both to steel the victim's nerves and round off his experience."[4] It is conceivable that the American emphasis on status achievement on levels below black belt is a reflection of the differing focal concerns of American culture. The death and rebirth theme of such a psychological cataclysm understandably is prone to dilution in a competitive context, so it is no surprise that the achievement of statuses below black belt has everywhere become emphasized as the martial arts gain in popularity.

The Class Routine

The training of the karate student is conducted with strict discipline, and classes are run in militaristic fashion. Usually the beginning exercises apply to all belt levels, with one of the drill masters leading the class; in the *dojo,* the drill masters lead the routine class exercises. In addition, they transmit notices to the class and handle all remedial work for the lower belts. Thus, as in the manner of the military, the "orders of the day" are transmitted through the drill masters to the membership.

When the class is assembled, commands are given in Japanese: these act as cues to perform certain habitualized preliminary routines. Various stances are taken which correspond to the familiar "ten hut!" and "at ease!" No extraneous body movement is permitted, not even an adjustment of a uniform. No gestures other than those congruent with the spirit of the class are allowed. A prolonged smile or a whisper is met with a loud reprimand by the drill master. With regard to discipline, Urban says: "Decorum and procedure are necessary because they are better than we are." While such reverence for discipline is supposed to yield spiritual transcendence, it results in an idolatry of procedure here as well as in the Orient—*nirvana* never comes cheap! As Urban points out, he knows of no one who has achieved enlightenment in the *dojo.* According to him, the students get caught up in "the dance"; that is, they have yet to achieve the freedom that comes with the conquest of technique —or so the ideology goes.

Predictably, most of the techniques are performed in unison. Each belt level performs in its turn before a seated audience comprising the other levels. In this respect training and formal competition for belt statuses are the same. The audience plays a major role, even though it can never show approval by whistling, shouting, or applause of any sort. The final judgment of a performance rests with the master or an appointed referee. The karate *dojo* audience ostensibly differs from other conventional audiences; there is a mutual acquaintance between the players and the audience, and the first consideration of the player is for the approval or scrutiny of the referee. The main function of the audience then is to exercise the social pressure of simple spectatorship—the consciousness of many eyes on the player, the judgment of the spectators presumably reflecting that of the referee. Since the audience is never given the opportunity to disagree with the referee's decision during a performance, it can only disagree when it is disassembled, and hence, when it is not properly an audience.

A typical class begins when the drill master appears on the training floor of the main gym. The members immediately line up in formation, with arms apart, at attention, awaiting command. The teacher bows from the waist, making a salutatory utterance that sounds like "eesh." The class bows in return, and the "at ease" position is commanded. The order is then given to "loosen out." This is the warm-up period in which various calisthenics, similar to those used by ballet dancers, are executed. They are more strenuous, however, and include a succession of push-ups on the knuckles of the hands. Next, the whole class (all levels) goes through the *kihon*, referred to as the "bread and butter" techniques. *Kihon* is a standard drill series of techniques, constantly practiced and mastered in much the same fashion as a musician does his scales. Their mastery is considered necessary to the perfection of derivative techniques such as the *katas*. After the *kihon*, the teacher has each level go through specific procedures as dual preparation for *katas* and *kumite* (free-style sparring). Each level awaits its turn to perform and be instructed in the order of high levels to low. The same follows for the performance of *kata* and *kumite*, although in the latter, representatives from different levels may occasionally spar. Criticism by the teacher is frank but never abusive. Denigration is not necessary because of the tense atmosphere generated by the scrutiny of master and audience.

The main learning method is constant repetition of the teacher's example; the keyword is always *copy*. The teacher demonstrates before the class, sometimes with the assistance of another member, simultaneously explaining his actions throughout the performance. After the demonstration, the class is instructed to copy while the master and/or several drill masters inspect, observe, and criticize individual performances. If certain members have difficulty with something, groups may be formed of superior and inferior ability; after regular class the deficient members are sent to do remedial work with a drill master in the main or auxiliary gym, until they are able to keep up with the rest. To fall behind is considered an indication of laxity and neglectful home practice. The public division into two groups of different proficiencies acts as an impetus to catch up and maintain standards of acceptable performance. However, few are ever expelled as a result of deficient skills. As Urban puts it: "Those who can't make it fall by the wayside," not out of physical exhaustion, but out of embarrassment.

Thus far, the picture that has been formed of the *dojo* offers one the temptation to identify it as a microcosm of society. While the *dojo* does betray a sort of stratified organization, replete with statuses, roles, incentives, goals, rewards, and a quasi-judiciary authority, one must not draw hasty parallels. It is important to keep in mind the fact that the *dojo* exists in the midst of a large American metropolis. Its members bring into the *dojo* certain experiences from their lives in other groups and sub-cultures, with the various contradictions that go along with those experiences. Yet one must also keep in mind that the *dojo,* in a sense, has an existence apart from these inconsistencies; it is both apart from them and of them. Participation in the *dojo,* as in other recreational forms, offers a constancy which is sought by its members as an antidote, a replacement, a suspension of their everyday lives.

What follows will be devoted to the *dojo* peer group as a reality within a world of multiple realities.[5] It will touch on relevant aspects of peer group organization and values in society as they relate to the *dojo* and the cliques within it.

Cliques

The periods before and after class are about a half hour in length. On arriving at the *dojo* one immediately changes into uniform, in order to utilize every bit of free time for practice. "Locker-room" talk, although casual, mostly concerns karate.

Conversation tends to gravitate about the events of previous sessions, contests, meets with other schools, intra-*dojo* competition, also anecdotes about street fights, boasting, and gossip about other members, usually the upper belts. Preclass dressing-room talk is more abbreviated than after-class "bull sessions," since there is less time and everyone is anxious to get out onto the training floor to warm up.[6]

On the floor one exercises casually while chatting with someone nearby. Members may idle over toward acquaintances for small talk, which, again, revolves around karate, although with more specificity, since it usually focuses upon a particular technique or *kata* that is being practiced. A group of three or four might watch someone perform and comment on his ability and form. Sometimes this takes on a complimentary tone; at other times it may involve wisecracking, especially if the performer is too affected in his performance. Being too affected means that his facial gesticulations are exaggerated, that he pays inordinate attention to perfection, or that he uses ostentatious flourishes in executing a technique.

Individuals who are not working out will confine themselves to the periphery, some in casual aggregations, some solitary. Among those who stand by themselves are new members or, more distinctively, individuals of a type classed by the *dojo* membership as "*dojo* bums." The "*dojo* bum" is one who attends infrequently and goes from one karate *dojo* to another in the metropolitan area. Some may maintain multiple *dojo* memberships, or simply be visitors. They are often viewed with a folkloristic mistrust as "spies" who try to steal techniques or gather information useful to another *dojo* for a forthcoming competition. These "loners" will usually stay off by themselves; if by chance they begin to chat with a member, their manner is characteristically slick. One is tempted to liken them to the old displaced *samurai* or *ronin* of feudal Japan. Their social image corresponds to that of the strangers in other sports, such as skiing, tennis, and golf. Very often these "bums" have achieved a high rank in one *dojo* or another, and turn up on the Sunday when occasional exhibitions are held. They are often rough and are frequently disqualified during *kumite* (sparring).

Observation of the various aggregations on the gym floor

reveals that the various clumps of people conversing wear the
same colored belts or belts of adjacent levels (e.g., black belts
conversing with brown belts). Members with seniority will tend
to seek each other out to converse. The white belt groups are
larger and give the impression of huddling together for security
in the face of their inexperience in the *dojo*. In the course of
several weeks, the more experienced white belt members will
also break up into conversational groups among themselves, or
a few will talk with an upper belt. The various conversation
clusters, viewed together, begin gradually to give the appearance
of a "pool" of social interaction. As members climb in the
hierarchy, and as they become more experienced in learning
karate argot and *dojo* norms, shifts occur; some are left behind in
their original groups, and some make acquaintance with new
recruits, their peers having passed them by. Because of continuous promotions, the membership of a particular conversation
clique does not remain highly solidified. Often the fact of
seniority has a leveling effect, and people who have "hung
around" the *dojo* long enough will mingle with upper belt
groups.

Although members of like or contiguous belt levels usually
confine their attention to one another, one often finds single
black or brown belts conversing with a white belt or a group of
white belts. He is probably explaining something to the lower
belt members. He may be carrying out his teaching responsibility,
or, if the conversation is informal, is boasting about his experiences. The mien of an upper belt man is usually one of studied
aloofness. He will, for example, amiably show a lower belt
member a technique, but will rarely chat with him as an equal.
After class, in the dressing area, there may be some casual talk
between an upper belt member and several lower belts, but the
tone is that of a superior recounting his exploits to fledgling
admirers. He will usually take a know-it-all attitude and occasionally, if a personal question is asked, resume his formal,
instructor's composure. This happened once in the dressing room
when a white belt asked a black belt about the utility of karate
in a street fight. The black belt began to recount an experience
in which he took on three assailants. When the white belt asked
him if he ever lost a fight, the black belt replied: "Don't start

using karate unless you know what you are doing. Keep out of fights until you can handle yourself. When I was a white belt I was cocky and got into a lot of fights and lost some; but now I don't advertise that I know karate and only use it when I have to." That ended the conversation.

When black belts meet and converse among themselves, it is as if friends in a hobby club were getting together to tell each other about some new experience or project. This holds true among cliques of all levels, but is more apparent among black belts because they have acquired a great deal more karate lore and are more proficient in handling the jargon. The conversation will usually concern a meet, a newly acquired technique or *kata,* or will be devoted to the faults of a member known in common. New books on karate will be discussed, and their merits or demerits will be analyzed according to how much of the spirit of the art has been captured by the author. The more common "how-to" books are usually frowned upon because they are "wrong," the author did not study in Japan or under a Japanese, there is not enough "philosophy" in it, or because the style of karate advocated is too crude, too effeminate, not "traditional" (i.e., too eclectic), and so forth. Heroes of other *dojos* are maligned because they are "phonies," "just use a lot of fancy technique with no *kime*" ("heart" or strength), emphasize "too much speed and no strength," "would get whipped in a street fight," "would never have gotten those points in a meet if the ref was from our school." If white belts are standing nearby they will usually chime in and agree with all of these comments, so that they can get into the conversation and inject the small store of their own tidbits. However, they are usually ignored when they try to break into a conversation, or typically acknowledged with a halfhearted "yeah," or "uh, huh."

Making Faces

In general, the haughtiness of an upper level member is designed to maintain social distance through the mystifying aura of superior status. Another aspect of the composure of some upper level members is the highly dramatized caricaturing and aping of the master. From the time a member begins his stint in the *dojo,* he soon learns to adopt a frozen expression of mystical seriousness, aloofness, and reticence. This is designed to convey the belief and conviction that karate is serious business, that it is religious, intellectual, and "cultural." The "karate poker face" is adopted from Urban's own composure and may be defined as a symbolization of leadership, enlightenment, and skill. During drill, for instance, all smiling, giggling, and extraneous movement are forbidden. If this command is broken, the member is sternly reprimanded. The absence of visible emotion provides the "blank" upon which later embellishments are made.

As the member becomes socialized, the poker face acquires new meanings. He begins to notice that whole *dojo* personalities or trait constellations form about the seriousness of the facial expression, and that these are more pronounced among several upper level members. The more extreme caricatures serve to inculcate the meanings of these social masks into the membership body, despite the fact that they are cynically construed by some.[7]

Even black belt members criticize their peers who are prone to "put on the dog." An example of one such situation occurred when one member was running through some calisthenics on the training floor. He seemed to be devoting a lot of effort to perfecting a superfluous movement. Two black belts were watching, and one said: "He must think he's hot shit the way he carries on." His neighbor smiled in agreement and then went on to relate how so-and-so acted when he was called upon to perform, or how ridiculous so-and-so looked during *kumite* last week. The idea is that one can palm the act off on someone less sophisticated (e.g., white belts), but this sort of behavior "doesn't bounce" with peers, although one's public face belies this attitude.

Some of the more colorful *dojo* personalities reflect the diffusion of the master's image among the members. One black belt member affects an air of great pomposity. Since he is approaching middle age, it is generally acknowledged that he has passed his prime and is too old to compete any longer. He is a comical sight, strutting through eccentric ballet-styled calisthenics and explaining the more "philosophical" aspects of karate to younger members. One black belt peer of his exclaimed: "The way that guy acts, you would think he had a stick up his ass." Often, he performs with a lot of dainty flourishes. He is much like an old barnyard rooster relying on symbols of a bygone prowess and potency to gain respect. Should he make a mistake in executing some maneuver, he will grimace and shrug his shoulders in affected disappointment. If, during free-style sparring, one of the participants is injured, at a glance from the master, he runs to the aid of the vanquished to administer *katsu* (first aid). It is questionable that his ministrations bring relief to the injured, but since very few members have acquired the arcane methods of *katsu*, he is awarded the distinction of being the *dojo* healer. His behavior provokes a great deal of snickering and ridicule, but a perverse kind of respect is still held for him by master and membership alike, as for the punctilios of an ante-bellum southern aristocrat gone seedy. Much of the cynicism about him derives from resentment of his polished ways and the possibility of a superior station in life outside the *dojo*.

Another black belt member is also the butt of *dojo* humor and criticism. Despite his exceptional skill, he does not give the appearance of having much intelligence. Contrary to the previous member who presents himself as the quintessence of urbanity and sophistication, he acts like a tough, "dumb," army sergeant. His manner is gruff and crude, and he has been known to lose control and fail to pull his punches while sparring with lower belt members. He is disliked by the lower belts, and even a few of his peers have remarked on his lack of polish. He is never, however, criticized for his skill in karate, for his *katas* are perfectly executed and his fighting skill is exemplary. He is a drill master, and often conducts the lower belt classes. When the master is teaching, he assists in supervising and correcting students. While other upper level members will sometimes stop to explain a technique to a lower belt member, he always falls back on demonstration and imitation as his method of teaching. His response, when requested for some information or instruction, is always "Copy!" Unfortunately, he has a penchant for reciting some of the master's didactic metaphors and quaint,

stylized, Oriental anecdotes, and invariably twists the moral of
the tale until it loses its intended meaning completely; his unsophisticated speech makes a mockery out of anything more complicated than an order. Both men characterize the extreme ends
of a brains-brawn continuum of values, encapsulated in the *dojo*
peer group culture.

The Master as Peer Group Leader

As I have mentioned, the poker face and the caricatures have as
their source the image projected by the master. Urban exudes an
aura of invincibility. He is of medium height, but well-muscled,
and his hands, as a result of brutal conditioning, look like two
sledge hammers. His reticence is flawless. If in the elevator he is
encountered by a student, he will nod and without a smile utter
a perfunctory "hello." He will rarely engage anyone in casual conversation, and when interviewed behaves like a dignitary being
questioned by news reporters. He projects an image similar to
that of a general who must always be a source of strength and
morale for his men. The following dialogue elicited his views on
discipline:

Q: Is it considered admirable to maintain strict discipline?
A: The master must be one hundred percent autocratic.
Q: Do the people with higher belt positions have more privileges
   than those with lower belts?
A: The higher belts have *less* privileges! The whites [i.e., white
   belts] have more privilege to make mistakes.
Q: I've heard that only black belts may enter your office; is this
   true?
A: Yes, some black belts can enter; the admission is excellence.
Q: Do you have any personal contact with any of your students
   outside of the *dojo*?
A: No, this has to be—it is natural. I am not their friend, I am
   their teacher.

By maintaining social distance, and by the cultivation of an
air of enigmatic oriental wisdom along with brute strength and
skill, Urban never reveals anything to the membership other
than the symbolic features of a folk hero. As a result, the mem-

bership is provided with a somewhat apocryphal base from which to fill in any meanings or characteristics that they want to attribute to him.

Again, Urban portrayed himself as a father-figure:

> You're like a father. You represent the unattainable, and you're all alone. The students want to knock you down from where you are. They are always fighting the father, and when they get to the top they don't even thank you. Being a *sensei* [pronounced sen-say, meaning master] is a thankless job.

In short, he tends to characterize himself as a benevolent dictator "concerned for the welfare of his children," but often standing alone in the manner of the archetypal father.[8]

At this point one may be tempted to apply to Urban the Freudian interpretation of the father role, but given the facts of the "Americanization of the unconscious," to use John R. Seeley's expression, and Urban's own subscription to this rationale, a significant modification is in order. It is more appropriate, therefore, to visualize him as an adult peer group leader, a *mock* father; that is, a marginal composite, perhaps, of what the membership would like a father to be. In this respect, he resembles a coach or even the literary figures representing adult "friends" of children such as portrayed by Mark Twain, Dickens, and others. As Willard Waller put it:

> . . . the athletes stand in a very close and personal relationship to at least one faculty member, the coach, who has, if he is an intelligent man or a disciplinarian, an opportunity to exert a great deal of influence upon the members of the team. The coach has prestige, he has favors to give, and he is in intimate rapport with his players. Ordinarily he uses his opportunities well. As the system usually works out, the members of the major teams form a nucleus of natural leaders among the student body, and their influence is more or less conservative and more or less on the side of what the faculty would call decent school citizenship. The necessarily close correspondence between athletic prowess and so-called clean living is another factor which affects the influence of athletes upon nonathletes. . . . An antisocial coach, or a coach who allows his players to believe themselves to be indispensable, so that they wrest control of athletes from his hands, can vitiate the whole system. When the system does go wrong, athletes and athletics become an insufferable nuisance to teachers.[9]

Speak Softly But Carry a Big Fist

According to one scholar, the peer group offers a "defensive and offensive alliance in which they can experiment with ways to short-circuit the authority of parents, especially of mothers, and of parent substitutes." They test "social controls over the illicit,"[10] many times by behaving "aggressively."

Aggressiveness, while formally channeled in the *dojo,* is a prominent *dojo* value. During sparring, one's punches are supposed to stop short of contact; yet, the frequency of "accidents" and the absence of harsh reprimands for overaggressiveness testify to the fact that occasionally even violent behavior is considered a favorable attribute. Take, for example, Urban's own description of *kumite*:

> *Kumite* is ideally a realistic highly spirited practice of "*Shobu.*" *Shobu* is the term for actual combat. It is the responsibility of each individual to defend himself while practicing sparring in the *dojo* with others to keep from unnecessarily hurting them. Both the stronger and the weaker opponents should benefit from sparring practice. . . . Undue hostility and dangerous aggression are never tolerated during sparring in a well controlled dojo. . . . The orthodox *Jiu-Kumite* bout begins with an introductory phase whereby the fighters usually try their feinting techniques and various opening moves to check the reactions of their opponent. This is to see where the skills are the strongest. It then goes into the expository or infighting. It is here that the fighters' speed and close hand work come out. The conclusion then follows by the first fighter to take the initiative of a full focused attack resulting in a definite overpowering conclusion of the fight such as a knocking down of an opponent by a sweep or any series of body and head blows.[11]

It seems to be almost impossible to exhibit such ferocity and at the same time squelch the satisfaction of making contact. Once, while sparring in the *dojo,* an opponent did not pull a kick and an excruciating blow was delivered to the solar plexus. After the match the assailant, queried about his carelessness, replied, "I don't know what happened, I just couldn't control myself." The reprimand he received took the form of a brief lecture to the class, by Urban, on the danger of "losing your head" in a match. If one is injured during sparring, he is encouraged to continue fighting if he can, and to try to keep his adversary from recognizing the weakness. This is supposed to act as preparation for actual combat conditions. Several examples will make this more apparent.

During a sparring session, one of the antagonists had failed to pull a punch and had injured his opponent. The man would not continue fighting. He started to walk off the floor, but the drill master, who was acting as referee, called him back and ordered him to bow to his opponent. He did as he was told, showed no evidence of anger or resentment, and then left. There was wry joking about this among the spectators, but it was clear that any of them would have acquiesced in the same circumstances.

Another time a member broke a bone in his hand during a sparring competition for green belt rank. He was aware of the injury but kept on fighting and won. He fought again immediately and won the second time as well. This same person, a month earlier, was dealt an unpulled blow to the temple near the ear which, he subsequently learned, resulted in a minor concussion. His opponent, a black belt, either out of fear of being reprimanded or out of blind idolatry for procedure, hissed: "Keep fighting, keep fighting!" The injured man was unable to move, numbed by the blow.

This aggressiveness is not merely accidental, as is indicated by the number of dressing-room anecdotes boasting of street fights actually provoked by members under the guise of self-defense. The alleged brutality of the sport was rationalized by Urban during an interview:

Q: Some people consider karate brutal. What are your feelings about this?

A: Karate is not brutal; it's safe. Karate becomes brutal without ethics. One must have respect for the art, and respect is an art; and one must have self-respect to have the respect of others.

The enigmatic contradiction between violence and control is thus not a contradiction. Outright hostility is prohibited only in its most extreme forms, as when a particular member who continuously inflicts injury on his opponents is disqualified from a meet or dismissed from the *dojo*.

Aggression is a positive peer group value. While *dojo* aggressiveness is at times crude and relatively undisguised, its nature is intrinsic to childhood peer activities which, later on, in successor groups, becomes shunted off into more subtly disguised and socially approved forms, such as enterprising activity.[12]

As Bloch and Niederhoffer hypothesize, adolescent gang activity offers a substitute for the relatively ambiguous and undefined rites of passage in our society. In consequence, "equivalent forms of behavior arise spontaneously among adolescents themselves, reinforced by their own group structures which seemingly provide the same psychological content and function of the more formalized rituals found in other societies."[13] The *dojo,* stripped of all its accouterments, performs the same role. For the adolescent and young adult members, the karate *dojo* is either an adjunct to or a primary source of this satisfaction; for the older men in their late twenties and thirties, it is possibly a compensation for a childhood deficit or a continuation of peer activities, taking its place alongside such groups as fraternal organizations and athletic clubs. As A. M. Lee comments:

The strong appeal of men's social fraternities is to those who in childhood developed needs for the satisfactions possible in nonsibling peer groups. This appeal contrasts with the typical glorifications of sibling-type competitiveness by students who are "squares" (academic conformists) and by professors (frequently "squares" grown older).[14]

The hierarchy of belt status levels acts as a model for age-grading activity, which is so indistinct in our society. There one finds behavioral coordinates appropriate to his status. In this sense, the hierarchical grouping of statuses sustains social solidarity in the *dojo,* a solidarity inspirited with mystery. As Kenneth Burke has remarked, " 'order' is not just 'regularity.' It also involves a distribution of *authority.* And such mutuality . . . takes roughly a pyramidal or hierarchical form (or at least, it is like a ladder with 'up' and 'down')."[15] However, sometimes the reality of the world outside can intrude, as exemplified by the following exchange between two brown belt members after class:

Mr. "A": Jesus, all this training every night of the week knocks me out. I don't know how the hell I'm gonna get up tomorrow to go to work.

Mr. "B": Yeah, but it's great exercise—you can really sleep well
after training.
Mr. "A": Oh sure, what'll I do when I come in late tomorrow to
work—show my boss a *kata?*

Groups, no matter how impermeable their boundaries may
seem, no matter how solidary they are, exist within a larger social
context (something which the students of "small groups" and
"group dynamics" seem to have ignored), including other groups,
which, in turn, play a part in shaping the contours of the in-
group. In a society such as our own, with its industrial complexity, extensive geographical mobility, and ethnic, regional,
social class, religious, community, and associational diversity, an
individual's multiple group commitments sometimes make alter-
nation from one context to another a hazardous affair, as Mr.
"A" illustrates.[16] Groups cope with the threat of rivalry through
the cultivation of the various forms and manifestations of ethno-
centrism, to wit, the conglomeration of techniques, procedures,
esoterica, and decor which all enhance the elements of mystery
and secrecy in the *dojo*. In addition, the image of the master, and
the caricaturing of him, contribute to a growing store of karate
lore and myth. These aid in shielding the individual member
from other groups' claims. In effect, he is socialized into particular roles and assumes an identity which may "stick" across
group lines, an identity reinforced by the *dojo* hierarchy which
provides an alternate status universe to others in the world of
everyday life. The sociologist Frederick Thrasher in his classic
study, *The Gang,* saw similar factors operating in the cumula-
tive development of the culture of the adolescent gang.[17]

While children seldom have to pay for such peer group experience, the *dojo* member is charged a monthly fee for it, similar to
the prostitute's fee for sexual experience (it is always emphasized
how karate "will make a man out of you"), or even the fee paid
to a psychiatrist for social contact.[18] What at first glance appears
to be the natural course of a person's social development becomes an experiential commodity. But the *dojo* member gets a
good deal for his money. His *dojo* peers and their proprietor-
leader offer him the trappings of the secret society and the opportunities of group camaraderie. As the sociologist Simmel observed:

. . . The total action and interest sphere of the secret becomes a well-rounded unity only through inclusion, in the secret, of a whole complex of external forms. Under its characteristic categories, the secret society must seek to create a sort of life totality. For this reason, it builds round its sharply emphasized purposive content a system of formulas, like a body round a soul. . . . The particular emphasis with which the secrecy of the external element is thereby stressed . . . is necessitated by the fact that this secrecy is not required so obviously and much by sheer, immediate interest as is the secrecy of the objective group purpose. It must be added that, through such formalism, as well as through the hierarchical organization itself, the secret society makes itself into a sort of counter-image of the official world, to which it places itself in contrast.[19]

I would hasten to add that the *dojo* can be interpreted as playing a quasi-therapeutic role in mass society where denominational religion, along with conventional psychotherapy, is being phased out by emergent group forms of a therapeutic-religious character.[20]

Thus, I have traced the forms and processes of interaction in the karate *dojo*. What at first seemed to be a school is now understood as a successor or substitute for childhood peer group experience. Viewed from this perspective, it no longer remains an oddity or small point of interest. In terms of human needs and experience, it is comparable to other groups in the world of everyday life. It stands for its members as a place where some aspect of their many-sided selves can become rooted, a place where a uniform and a colored belt become the criteria of who they are and what they do, in this time, in that place.[21]

7

Poker and Pop:
Collegiate Gambling Groups

David McKenzie

There is a subversive element within the American tradition of individualism that is seldom noted: it is the role played by the childhood peer group and its successors in nurturing the values and attitudes of autonomy and enterprise. These groups, often pejoratively labeled "gangs," lie on the periphery of conventional views of morality and legitimacy. Yet, as we are prone to forget, they contribute to the molding of both heroes and villains in our folklore. David McKenzie probes one such crucible of identity—card-playing groups in a small midwestern university student union. In exploring the interwoven character of card-playing skills and sociability, he elucidates the manner in which these groups possibly socialize their members into lifeways often obscured by conventional education.

Mr. McKenzie, a senior at the University of Wisconsin, plans to continue his interest in sociology in graduate school.

The university educates people, and the student union "develops" them. It might indeed be claimed that education is not life, but something added to life. Childhood, adolescent, and adult peer groups are life to their members. Like other intimate groups, they are the measures through which we try to understand the larger world, including that of education. Students of large organizations have long been aware that the rational visible organizational layout often belies the influential presence of informal groups of personnel, which play a major role in the functioning of that organization as "enlightened management" has finally come to realize. Too often, we take the official definition of reality to be fact, and ignore the part played by these groups in shaping the development of institutions.

Among groups of this kind are the numerous student cliques inhabiting college campuses. Prominent among these are the Greek letter fraternities and sororities, but they are only a few of the varied and shifting groupings. Any visitor to the student unions, lounges, or any hangouts on campuses would soon discover that these places form natural environments for the proliferation of student cliques of various interests and orientations: some mirror student involvements with recognized campus organizations; others reflect the informal configurations of the various "crowds." The visitor to any midwestern university student union, for example, would see knots of "kibitzers" gathered aroung the makeshift gaming tables where the campus card players hold sway. These clusters are often foci of action even within a room filled with cigarette smoke, a booming jukebox, and animated conversations. But while there is action at the card table, it is not mayhem. The players are in various attitudes and poses: now one is pensive, tugging at his ear, tweaking his chin, wrinkling his nose, slyly smiling, and finally shrieking with joy or angered disappointment as the hand is called. Another seems businesslike, with no emotion crossing his face as he glances at his hand and scans the table, watching the cards fall. At one moment tension fills the air, and at the next it is gone as a hand ends and the group lapses into easy conversation, joking, and the relating of anecdotes while the next hand is dealt.

This type of setting is not necessarily typical of all university unions, but reflects particularly the character of a midwestern university branch campus as a two-year feeder extension to a large state university. The student population is small—the majority living in the surrounding community—and shows only slight participation in extracurricular events. In this respect, the formal organization has some apparent influence on the structure and operations of the card-playing groups, for the relative lack of involvement in extracurricular activities more or less leaves the students to their own devices. Radical political activity is almost absent due to the lack of upper classmen and other cultural influences. Hence, the environmental "press" lends to the card players the use of university facilities for unofficial activities. This expropriation of public space is quite visible and sets the card players off from the rest of the student population; they thus are defined by the latter and the institution's officials as mildly deviant.

At the midwestern university campus union under study, the geography of the setting reflects its ecology and the activities that take place in it. In various sections there are a pool table, a television viewing area, a canteen service and cafeteria, a jukebox and radio, and recreation tables. The card-playing area is unofficially marked off from the eating and recreation tables by a partition with pop coolers and vending machines; it forms a geographic barrier, although occasionally a player or two could be found on the other side of the "fence," as it is commonly called.[1]

As has been intimated, card-playing serves purposes other than simple recreation. The card-playing peer group becomes for many a universe where they can gain status and recognition, hung on the skeleton of gaming techniques and social skills.

The card games played the most often in the union are bridge and poker. Both games require counting and memory skills; that is, knowing what cards are out, to whom they have been dealt, what has been played, who melded what cards or who made which bid. Obviously, the person with a poor memory is handicapped. This can have disintegrative effects on any player's "face" in the group because stupidity (i.e., according to gaming criteria) "sticks out." Poker is a "showdown game." Fast judgment as well as a high level of skill are primary in terms of the ability to react immediately according to probabilities.[2] Bridge, on the other hand, is a performing game: that is, a player squeezes all the potentialities out of his hand through planned judgments. Playing a good hand is more important than being

dealt an unbeatable hand; that is to say, playing a hand better—
in terms of performance—than it would appear such a hand
could have been played. Victory is not prized per se. While bridge
is a partnership game with playing status most significant, both
status and money are important goals in poker.

Poker-playing is considered as an occupation by a few highly
skilled players in the union. One often hears the statement: "If
it weren't for cards, I wouldn't be able to pay my rent. . . ." Much
of this, however, is bragging. Penny-ante is usually played only
by "prize players" who have less skill and "play for money only
as a 'pocket book' edition of the true gambler";[3] prize players
play less often than regular gamblers, and hence have less skill:
they usually play for small amounts of money. On the whole, a
few players win a great deal and many lose a little. If the stakes
are small, players court luck and leave winning to the odds. It
is only the highly skilled players who can afford to gamble with
large sums of money. The degree to which playing becomes an
occupation depends on the combination of experience and financial need. The relationship of luck and skill is a subtle one
since "winning in poker is based on the careful development of
a pattern of unpredictable behavior."[4]

Some of the habitual players have visions of becoming professionals; at least one has played in Las Vegas or Reno. It is possible that some players in the union may already be classified as professionals. For example, while cash is paid on the
spot, credit is always given to a player who is running low: some
players actually carry account sheets which list their winnings
and amounts of indebtedness and which seem to caricature
double-entry books. An example follows:

"owsies"

J.B.	15.75
C.S.	140.36
K.M.	90.50
D.L.	4.76
J.C.	1.30
P.S.	120.50
G.H.	83.82

winnings 9/19/67–1/11/68 1,100.00 collected
uncollected 457.00
since 1/11/68 about 200.00 won

This particular player has won up to $440 in one sitting. An interesting perspective on expertise is the fact that some players are employed by other students to gamble and are paid according to their skill. I know of several players who were paid more than three dollars per hour. One player won $132 in twelve hours for a student and was paid a $36 commission for his services. This same player later won $108 and $107 for the same student and was paid accordingly. Ordinarily, such a practice would seem to be contradictory when the skilled player could, after all, profit more by playing for himself. However, two considerations render the practice understandable: (1) no matter how skilled the player, he still has to reckon with the vicissitudes of chance, and hiring himself out provides sure profit; and (2) being asked to play for someone is a testimony to the player's status and skill.

Hoyle Notwithstanding: the Role of Argot and Folklore

During the course of a game there is much conversation about group concerns other than cards: argot, folklore, jokes, conversation about "what's happening" regarding the dating scene, the local bands playing at the beer bars, exams, and so on. These conversations function to bring the group together as morale-building devices. The whole conglomeration of group-specific knowledge establishes in-group boundaries and conveys an air of group exclusiveness which puts off strangers and keeps newcomers hanging. If there is a new player in the group, he is almost always left out of the conversation and ongoing banter. The only conversational foothold he has is confined to the topic of cards; the argot includes terms which enable the players readily to distinguish insiders from outsiders. As one student of pool-playing groups put it: "The argot itself is not protected, but an open secret; that is, its meanings are easily learned by any outsider who wishes to learn them and is an alert listener and questioner. Argots develop partly to provide a shorthand way of referring to technicalities, but also as an elaborately inventive, ritualistic, often rather playful way of reinforcing group identity or 'we feeling.' "[5] Thus, the argot of the poker and bridge group sets it off not for the purposes of secrecy but rather to enhance the sense of colleagueship.

The following are examples of poker and bridge argot and the contexts in which they appear: "Christ, did I get zilched" (meaning "Did I ever get slammed!"); "I shot him the moon" (meaning to give someone a rotten card, which connotes a dirty trick. "Mooning" is an adolescent prank whereby the person pulls his pants down and contemptuously flaunts his buttocks); "How many did you eat?" (meaning "He took the queen of spades in the game of hearts"). Other less game-specific argot includes: "Ain't that a kick in the groin!" "You hairy whimp, butterball," and so on. Slang in everyday life has often originated from the argot of card-playing: expressions such as "passing the buck," "blue chips," "ace-in-the-hole," "trump his ace," "ante up," "four flusher," "poker faced," "stand pat," and "showdown" are typical examples.[6] There are also gestures, used illegally in bridge, such as hand signals between partners, and certain significant facial expressions—wincing, showing one's teeth, a nod of the head, and a deep smile.

The degree to which traditional folklore promotes stability in the card group depends on the degree to which these popular conceptions have been internalized. The myth that gamblers as a rule have no consciences—hence, no feelings—is certainly reflected in the "poker face" assumed by many in the peer group.

Informal conversation usually revolves around girls and dating and takes place while shuffling between games. Jokes and wisecracks also reflect these focal concerns and function to ease the complexion of the situation from seriousness to casual laughter. Representative of the typical repartee and banter encountered during a game are the following:

"The gas tank is falling off of my car."
"Well, I'll follow you out to the junkyard, Lois."

"Were you out to Mountview last night?"
"No, why?"
"You're lucky—about fifty boys to one girl, and they were all skags."

"Hey, see that girl over there? Well, if you want a nice piece of ass the first time, she's gotta be it. I guess she screws the first time."

"You mean the skinny blond over there?"
"Yeh, pretty nice, huh?"
"Yeh, where'd you ever find that out?"
"One of my friends took her out and . . ."
"Um, I'll have to take her out."

"Hey, you got a lighter I can use?"
"Yeh." (He pulls out a cigarette lighter)
"Christ, where'd you get that?"
"For Christmas."

"Hold out your finger and I'll snap it off!"
"No dice."
"That's no finger-snapper-offer—that's a killer!"

Conversation is rarely about school or grades. In addition, players often sing or hum along with songs on the radio or jukebox, a constant noisy accompaniment to all student-union activities.

The repetition of argot and topics of conversation borders on and serves the same purpose as a folklore—the development of interaction ritual, drawing of group boundaries, and strengthening of group solidarity. Repetition is the basis of habit and customs which resist modifying pressures from changes in the surrounding milieu, and hence limit the possibilities of variation of activity.[7] In this way, folklore and rituals in the card group are analogous to the myths of all societies. They reinforce group beliefs and practices and legitimatize the group's values. This explains the monotonous character of the endlessly repeated conversations about girls, the local bars, and weekend events.

A distinction should be made between group solidarity as a whole and team secrets within the structure of the game. The bridge team, for example, has additional practices and information which are privy to itself only, relevant to the context of a given match. In this respect, the card group teams perform in much the same way as the typical teammanship outlined by the sociologist Erving Goffman. Team activity transcends the formal requirements of the game as, for example, in the aforementioned use of gestures and hand signals.[8] Keeping team secrets is essential to the strategy of the game, and if the same teams play over and over again, these secrets grow into added psychological advantages. The same people usually play on the same team, unless, of course, one member is absent, in which case the other will search for a reputable alternative. Some teams definitely have higher status than others and therefore reinforce the status ordering of the group at large.

Intra-group hostilities usually result from disagreements concerning the playing of the game, but they are usually suppressed until the game has ended, at which time, in the case of individuals forming a bridge team, a person with a higher status will question the tactical motives of his partner and suggest different alternatives. When one member disagrees with another's playing tactics, the pressure about a blunder may build to the point of explosion. The casual resumption of activity after any interruption is typical, however. The players usually return to the game in short order, and give the impression that nothing has happened. If a member has shown himself to be a disagreeable player, or if his playing style is considered difficult to cope with, the other members may eventually avoid playing with him, especially in partnership games like bridge, since disagreements generally focus on the responsibility of one of the partners for the loss of a game. D.L. was rejected from the group because of his unpredictable and "crazy" bidding. As one player put it, "He would bid out of his mind!" Disagreements in poker are usually taken in stride, reflecting the attitude that the show must go on. This is not to say that poker is not played seriously, for play can be a very serious business when it involves maintaining status in the group.

The Communication of Status

The card group is, in fact, one of many in-groups determining these students' general social status.[9] Of course, this is not as simple as it seems to be. Status, or the sum total of an individual's statuses, may be consistent or inconsistent in rank; it is also relative to the degree and kind of commitments made by the individual to given institutional arrangements and group affiliations. These matters are pertinent to the understanding of the card player's status relative to the university as an institution.

Because the bridge and poker groups in the union for the most part consist of the same members day after day, they may be considered as cliques; that is, "as a small group of persons who customarily associate together in play or work and self promotion."[10]

The card-playing ability of the player is a major determinant of his status within the group. One could easily trace parallels here to the sociologist William Foote Whyte's citing of bowling scores in *Street Corner Society*. In Doc's group the status of each individual within the group structure was indicated by his bowling scores. But this only underlined his status in the group structure because bowling occupied only Saturday night and occasional week nights, whereas card-playing is a day-to-day occupation for many in the student union. Therefore, it not only indicates but also in part determines the status each person is to have within the group.

The criteria one can use to determine status within the group seem at first obvious, but as one becomes assimilated into the actual trade, he finds this can be very tricky. Likewise, upon first observation, a stranger can easily be deceived as to who really holds high status. One is often led to believe that the loud, boisterous players are the possessors of high status, but upon further observation, the calm players usually score highest and are the real leaders. Of course, leader in this context suggests more than the unidimensional leader-follower prototype. There are several dimensions of leadership, important among them being who has the greatest playing skill and, behaviorally, who is the object of address by most members. However, other members who are mediocre players are often well integrated into the group. Status, therefore, has its horizontal as well as its vertical dimensions, which is to say that playing skill as an index of status is crosscut by other qualities, such as sociability and adeptness at handling group-specific "knowledge"—argot, repartee, folklore, mythology, and so on. In some cases the two dimensions intersect, and in others they do not.

Skilled players often present an aura of invincibility through the demonstration of intricate and daring moves. In poker, for example, a leader remains aloof and rarely engages in conversation extraneous to cards; nevertheless he determines the tone of the betting. High status players give one the impression of an

"I-don't-give-a-damn" attitude. The players of less importance are usually the ones who get loud and slam their fists on the table, groan audibly from time to time, and show their displeasure through overt actions like kicking chairs. Rarely do the high status players lose their "cool." They appear less nervous and take advice willingly because they claim to want to learn new things about the game, and laugh their losses off as bad luck or something; this is their way of kicking chairs. Pretending to lack skill often hides the real leadership, especially when a conservative game is played to deceive a newcomer. Or it could be the case that "performers who have positions of visible leadership are often merely figureheads, selected as a compromise, as a way of neutralizing a potentially threatening position, or as a way of strategically concealing the power behind the front."[11]

It should be made clear, however, that the winners, the enterprising players, are not simply liked or trusted. While the steady winners always display good sportsmanship and pay their debts immediately, these can be considered mere tactics used to "cool the mark out," that is, to keep the interaction of the situation running smoothly and to prevent the hostility of losers from expressing itself in anything but obsequious admiration. The performances of all the individuals taken together help to maintain a definition of the game situation as an affable gathering of friends rather than a showdown game of cutthroat competition. A disgruntled loser is a threat to this ambiance. The appearance of the individual card player suggests one in which informal recreation and work are combined, and is directly reflected in the "poker face" of the most experienced card players. As an extreme example, the irate mother of a daughter made pregnant by one of the players burst into the student union and came after him with a butcher knife. She chased him around the room in silent-film-comedy fashion, and when she finally realized she was not going to catch him threatened him with strong language. When she left, he returned to the table, sat down, and without a word the group resumed the game as if nothing had happened.

"Dramatic realization" from time to time helps to intensify the image conveyed by a mask to "put on" (deceive) a kibitzer (one who gives unsolicited advice)[12] or an *arrivista* (newcomer):[13] this dramatic realization results supposedly from deeply stirred emotions.[14] The donning of such a mask may commence with the "short con," which may involve duping a person (the "mark") into underestimating the skills of the perpetrator so that he will be sucked in. When the mark realizes, too late, that he has been conned, he may be "cooled out"[15] by such remarks as "It happens to the best of us," or, "Don't worry about it, you'll probably win it back anyway." Again, these ploys are used as paraphernalia to sustain the smooth interaction and the dominant group definition of the situation. The attitude of good sportsmanship projected by these players acts as a bulwark against the creation of a scene by a dissatisfied loser.

High status players will often use dramatic realization in the form of extreme gestures to accompany excuses for consistent losing. They seem to lose their "poker faces" for the moment. The excuse may be bad luck, a test the hour before or after, a splitting headache, no sleep the night before, and so on. For example, after losing the sixth straight hand, a member of status was asked, "Christ, are you playing lousy! What the hell is the matter with you?" He exclaimed, "If you had the exam I just had, you wouldn't even be here, ring ding!" On the other hand, consistent winners try to display a modest attitude, as if it were only luck that enabled them to triumph. Should a member of low status win consistently, he will stress the element of luck, or explain his success by alluding to the fact that his skills are slowly being sharpened, in order to ingratiate himself with the upper status players. The modesty of the low status member reflects that of the sycophant, as opposed to the condescending modesty of a high status member. If he wins only one or two games, the player recognizes for the most part that the very nature of the game is luck—it is just that the players with more experience (and status) are more consistent winners.

Another skill already mentioned as part of the high status member's role involves "conning" a kibitzer or newcomer in order to entice him into a game. Here, "conning" refers to the deft manipulation of other people's impressions of reality, especially those involving the projection of contrived or false images.[16] The kind typically employed in this setting is the "short con" as distinguished from the "big con": the former merely concerns those practices designed to entice an opponent to the table and to keep him there, and to play with whatever money he has on hand; the "big con" is getting the "mark" to "go on the send" for money outside of the game situation (e.g., to call for more money, or go to the bank). However, even the short con is used with discretion because of the emphasis placed on good sportsmanship and sociability by the skilled players. In the union credit is usually granted. In this respect the leader resembles the poolroom hustler, who rarely puts the "short con" on unless he is hard up for money. They would just as soon play with the permanent members of the group, with the usual scapegoats typically providing the necessary money.

In terms of group processes, the scapegoats comprise lower status members who are used as targets for the wrath of higher status members in a losing streak, as well as convenient routine sources of easy winnings. A scapegoat is one who takes the blame for another, or for a group's or team's failure or embarrassment; a victim of jokes.[17] One player who functioned in this fashion knew he was not very good at the game but played regularly anyway, with the hope that one day he would strike it rich. His friends constantly criticized him for allowing himself to be taken advantage of, but he played and lost an estimated thousand dollars during the school year. I suspect that players such as these are aware that they are being used, but are willing to pay the cost for the limited comradeship that the group offers. Irving Crespi, a student of card groups, includes the scapegoat under the heading of "accidental players" that is, those who play only for the sociability offered in the group.[18]

Through the use of false modes of expression—such as exclamations like "Oh no!" and "Man, what a beautiful hand!" or an affected gasp as if he were dying, the master of the game can usually bluff the scapegoat, kibitzer, and newcomer into thinking he has something. Ordinarily, these would be obvious bluffs that even a naïve player could discern, but the skilled players use them so inconsistently that it is hard to second-guess them. Indeed, this is one of the basic stratagems of poker. As one student of the game has commented: "The poker hand must at all times be concealed behind the mask of inconsistent and irrational behavior."[19] The player who bluffs all the time will have his bluff called; similarly, the player who never bluffs is in trouble because he is too consistent. Often, several players will bluff cooperatively, and with gestures connoting disappointment play down their hands to keep the "suckers" in. To keep the disillusioned player in the game, he is "cooled out" by the winner and by the other players' exclamations regarding the role of Lady Luck with comments such as: "Today's my lucky day; tomorrow's yours." This tactic is not necessarily conscious but is patterned after group custom and habit.

Outsiders as Insiders

Despite their status as outsiders relative to the legitimate activities of the school, like many nonconformist groups they often turn the tables and merely ignore critical kibitzers and outsiders. Should outsiders try to make entry to the group and play, they generally foul up the argot, appear visibly uncomfortable, and feel nervous, as if one of the members would jump on them for a mistake. These signs of stress act as cues for the seasoned members, so that the nervousness of the newcomer is even more well founded in the facts of the situation. Even if a new player has high status in another clique, he has yet to prove himself to this one. The group is not going to recruit him. Hence: "The widespread attachment to membership in a status-giving in-group is perhaps the most invincible bulwark of tribalism in human thought. We attach values to ourselves and our status in-group in part by depersonalizing—even dehumanizing the members of outgroups."[20]

Women are commonly thought of as bad players because they "brood over their hands, take unwarranted gambles, but tell the truth."[21] That is, they do not bluff. In this connection, females are seen as insufferably practical, immune to the attraction of the amalgam of controlled unpredictability and chance. The proverbial inconsistency of the female does not seem to hold here. The male poker group feels less at ease when girls are spectators, and much less when girls are playing. They inhibit the flow of free and easy language among the men, and hence inhibit smooth group interaction, and thus are rarely found in the poker groups. Poker is more a game of chance than bridge which emphasizes sociability; it is considered more masculine, and this is enhanced by the possibility, albeit small, of big winnings, which also contributes to the masculine "breadwinner" aspect of the game.

If a girl wins, there is the possibility of degradation of a member's status. Then, too, she is inclined to consider card-playing merely a game, as opposed to the career orientation of the males.[22] But girls, for the most part, will not play, especially when money is involved, and will even discourage their boyfriends from playing, which makes them particularly repugnant to the group. In one instance, a girl threatened to break up with her boyfriend if he so much as put a penny into the pot. On the other hand, whether or not a player takes his girl out on the weekend will often depend on his winnings at the poker table. In general, poker is associated with the male world of club rooms and taverns, and women, if they do play, domesticate the game beyond the tolerance limits of the male ego. There are exceptions, of course. I knew two girls who would play poker any time and any place, but they were treated as "one of the boys" and were obviously willing to sacrifice, in this context, the considerations given to their sex in other situations. There were no poker groups consisting entirely of women.

The card player seldom runs into other students who openly "put him down." In terms of his status relative to the institution, the competitive, grade-seeking "good" students disapprove of him as do teachers and administrators. The rest of the student body tolerates him. He understands that his inveterate playing is mildly deviant, but takes criticism in his stride as a routine eventuality. Individual status in the card group and status outside of the card group seem, in fact, to have an inverse relationship; the higher one's in-group status, the lower his institutional status.

There are many reasons for this. Probably the most important is the fact that the card group is thought to subvert or weaken the general educational function within the institution. Those who devalue education, those for whom education is not of prime importance, tend to join the group. This is not to say that the

card players have entirely given up the idea of getting an education, but through frustration, unwilling or reluctant enrollment
in school, outside dependency factors, and the recognition of
cards as a source of income, "education" has become a secondary
goal. The social roles of such groups are offensive and defensive
alliances against parent substitutes who act as societal surrogates
of morality and presumed legitimacy. Hence, the card-players,
like fraternity men, become "anti-intellectuals."[23] Since the campus in question is a two-year school (students then feed into the
larger four-year schools), fraternities are absent, and athletic
competition is of minor importance. These groups and others
like them are therefore important sources of social support.

The "I-don't-care" attitude toward school gives the other students who stress the importance of their education the impression that the card players are "digging their own graves." Yet
their skill is admired, even by those who vow they would never
spend so much time playing cards. "How do they ever have time
for schoolwork?" is the usual comment. "I don't see how those
people can afford to spend the time playing as often as they do."
"Where do they get the money?—Why just the other day I heard
that Mike Tootsie lost sixty dollars in just a few hands—That's
something I'd never do is gamble, not even for a penny." "Those
guys must be stupid shits! Why did they come here in the first
place if all they're going to do is play all the time?" "I could not
see spending $120 a semester for tuition if all I was going to do
is play cards all of the time, could you?" "Why do they do it?"
"I think it's a lot of fun.—I wish I knew how to play better." "I
think it should be left up to the person how he spends his time,
and I think nobody should condemn him."

Although the card players may be "put down" or stigmatized
by professional educators and "mature students" within the institution, efforts at eradicating the practice have been futile, since
card-playing has widespread tolerance among the student body.
The card players, aware of the hostility of institutional officials
and the "goody-goodies" among the student body, seldom address
themselves to the issue and thus have not developed a counter-
ideology toward outsiders. But since the importance assigned to
card-playing seems to betray the fact that gambling is much more
of a career than schoolwork, leaders with the highest status view

members with good grades as failing to stress the same goals. Usually those with the better grades spend less time in the group, and hence may, from time to time, be left out of group secrets; they may eventually be considered a member of an out-group. For example, I heard one member say to another, "Gees, did you know I got a 'B' on that last exam?" The other member replied, "Well, you should, you dumb dinkle dorfus. That's all you've been doing lately is studying." He wasn't playing the role that the group felt he should be playing.

This can be related to the larger social question of the opposition of the peer group to conventional values, especially those values nurtured in sibling-successor group situations. Conventional values stress grades, whereas the card group sees the time spent on getting good grades as a threat to group cohesiveness. The grade point average of thirty highly representative players was found to be 1.5 (C−) (based on a 4-point scale) for an average of 2.3 semesters' work as compared to a grade point average of 2.6 (C+) for 2 semesters' work for the student body as a whole in the same time period. It was also found that out of these thirty students a total of eight had dropped out of school completely.

Yet, the social activity of the union may be at least as good a preparation for certain kinds of "life" as much that goes on in the formal routines of the college. Few "A" students make good salesmen; few "A" students are successful later as politicians; successful trial lawyers are rarely "A" students even in law school. In other words, the anti-intellectualism of the card player is aimed at one specialized type of intellectualism.

But before an outsider can understand why these groups are opposed to society's conventions, he must understand what influences them to behave the way they do. Siblings in the family, for example, compete for the recognition and rewards bestowed by an adult authority figure, the parent, and later, in successor group situations such as the classroom, by a parent substitute. Non-sibling peer groups, however, compete for recognition by the group at large, that is, by one's equals. We all establish peer and sibling-type relationships, but the ways we adjust to them differ. The card players represent a non-sibling peer group. Students join these groups because in the strictly academic environment they feel powerless and stifled. They are grasping for autonomy, for a way of reestablishing their sense of adequacy.[24] In this respect, the student power movement—which is, incidentally, making halting attempts to establish itself on this particular campus—deals with the matter in a consciously direct way by assaulting the bastions of institutional legitimacy and academic orthodoxy and demanding that education be "relevant" to life.

The card-playing student reacts to his powerlessness by looking to fellow students rather than the adult community for his social rewards. That is,

social power is defined primarily in terms of peer relations. Cut off from successful manipulative competition with adults, the adolescent may nevertheless exercise differential power in relationships with others of his own kind.[25]

Women can compete more successfully with females through the promise or use of sexual rewards, and hence appear less powerless in this setting, which may partly explain their relative absence from the card groups.

Many of the students at the two-year campus are still living at home; hence, they are caught in a sort of bind. They want independence, but this wish is frustrated by such needs as money, a place to eat, a place to sleep, and so on. This situation is the same for many college students who feel both dispossessed and subordinate in society's eyes. The peer group provides a universe where some independence is possible. In addition to power and independence, the card-playing peer group offers a protest against rationality—chance makes mockery of reason; a protest against stable middle-class values in that it defies the ethical imperatives regarding effort and reward; the pleasures of "thrill seeking"; and a chance to display their problem-solving talents. Moreover, card-playing quenches the thirst of a teleologically oriented mind. "All gambling puzzles possess a fascinating and challenging element of teleological mystery which functions to spur the curiosity to test the next event which can't be determined through the use of a scientific scheme."[26] In this counter-religion, the "goddess of luck" takes over.

In other words, the students join the card groups to create an *alternative status universe* in terms of what they can achieve.

But, also, "sociability" must not be overlooked: "The world of sociability—the only world in which a democracy of the equally privileged is possible without friction—is an *artificial world*," as Simmel pointed out.[27] Ironically, its artificiality is apparent only to the extent that it is counterpoised with the values it opposes.

The gaming world, in the double sense of its sociability and of its denotative characteristics, actually succeeds where the university fails. The school arrogates to itself the educative function, but these peer groups subvert its legitimacy through providing a milieu in which their members can work out their identities. As Frederick M. Thrasher says of adolescent groups, card players are an interstitial phenomenon, popping up like weeds at the interface formed by institutional legitimacy and the immoral mores of the real world of natural groups. To disintegrate and abolish the card groups in the union, therefore, would temporarily take away from many students a scholarship for study in the real world, for in a sense they do *live* poker.

8

The Home
Territory Bar[*]

Sherri Cavan

A good deal has been written in recent years on the phenomenon of territoriality in man, the lower primates, and the animal kingdom in general. Many of these writings extrapolate from lower phylogenetic forms and include territoriality as a component of basic human nature. However, most of this material has ignored the subject of human territoriality within its social context. The present essay exemplifies the social-symbolic meaning of space as exemplified by the home territory bar: the factors distinguishing it from other types of bar, and the routine patterns of interaction endemic to it.

Sherri Cavan is assistant professor of sociology at San Francisco State College.

Some public drinking places derive their special character from the fact that they are used as though they were not public places at all, but rather as though they were the private retreat

* Sherri Cavan, *Liquor License* (Chicago: Aldine Publishing Co., 1966).

for some special group. Those who use public drinking places in this way frequently designate them as "my" bar and often describe them as a "home," a "second home," or a "home away from home."

> An old woman came in and bought Ron a beer and then bought another beer for the fellow sitting next to him. Ron asked her if she were having one also but she replied that she was "on the wagon." She and Ron began talking about some of the people they knew in common; Ron then suggested that they go down to the R— (a bar down the street). "Why should I go to the R—," she said. "This is my home here."

> One of the patrons was explaining that he worked nearby and would drop in at this particular establishment occasionally after work. He went on to say, "N— is my favorite bar. It's the one I go to most frequently, I've been going there for eight years. It's like a second home."

Such establishments become in effect a kind of home territory, a setting where patrons may stake out proprietary claims and create an order of activity indigenous to the particular establishment, to be defended if necessary against the invasion of others.[1]

Those who make a public drinking place their home territory will be referred to as the "habitués" of the establishment. The term will be used to refer to the fact that the patrons of a particular bar share one or more features of their social identity, and this common bond forms the basis of defining those who are welcome in the establishment and those who are not. In many respects the English pub and what has been called the American "neighborhood tavern" stand as prototypes of the home territory use of the public drinking place, but the lines along which the patrons of the home territory are drawn are not necessarily limited to residential areas.

In Okinawa, for example, where some forty thousand American servicemen are stationed, in the course of time the bars and cabarets have become defined as home territories for groups differentiated along both racial and branch of service lines. According to one officer:

> It isn't only a racial problem. . . . Marines, paratroopers and sailors—they all have their favorite places. After a while these

places become, in effect, exclusive in their patronage. . . . It saves a lot of fights, I'll tell you.[2]

Racial and ethnic groups provide one type of collectivity that is likely to make some public drinking place their home territory: in San Francisco one can find bars that may be used almost exclusively by Negroes, by American Indians, by Mexican Americans, by Italians, by Irish, by Russians, by Chinese, by Filipinos, and by British subjects, to name just a few. One can also find bars that are used in the same way by the homeless, by the biographically blemished, by those whose organization of daily life is in part or wholly outside the typical range in terms of time and space, and by those who share a common fate that has little value in the everyday world. In San Francisco there are bars that are used as home territories by the unmarried who may have little else in common beyond their lack of a conjugal home; by newspapermen, actors, musicians, and seamen, whose daily round is somewhat apart from those with more conventionally timed or spaced occupations; and by the chronically unemployed and unemployable, the homosexual, the beatnik, and the petty criminal.[3] The collectivities from which the habitués of the home territory bar are drawn may also be compounded of a number of attributes: one can find bars that serve as home territories for elderly Italian men, middle-class homosexuals, or young, single Negroes of both sexes.

The attributes of some collectivities (e.g., class or marital status) are such that a sizable proportion of all bar patrons could utilize many bars as their home territory; in this case, whether or not one chooses to make a particular establishment his home territory is a matter of personal choice. This, of course, is true also even where the demarcation of the habitués is more limiting, so long as there is more than one establishment that could serve as a home territory for the more general group. For example, there are a number of establishments that are "open" to any Negro or any homosexual, regardless of any other attribute, but not all are patronized or used as home territories by all Negroes or all homosexuals in the community. The choice of one particular establishment over its possible alternatives by certified members of the collectivity may be a matter of such factors as residential propinquity, preexisting friendship networks, subtle differences in the standing behavior patterns of the various bars, or vagary, where one particular bar may become the place for a given collectivity to go for a while, to be superseded at a later date by another establishment. For example, homosexual home territory bars in San Francisco are often in and out of vogue, and one can find an establishment that was literally packed seven nights a week for some time to be virtually empty a month later, with many of its patrons at a new place that previously had little popularity. Of course, some homosexual bars maintain their popularity for long periods, and others, whether they are in or out of vogue among homosexuals in general, may still be patronized on a regular basis by some members of the homosexual population.

Among the habitués of any home territory bar one can differentiate between what Chandler has referred to as a "hard core of regulars," who may be found at the establishment on a frequent and recurring basis,[4] and those occasional patrons who may drop in once in a while but whose attendance is, in general, sporadic and unpredictable. But "hard core" regulars can be found in other types of bars as well, and their presence does not necessarily imply by itself that the establishment will be used as a home territory. Convenience bars often have patrons who use them on a frequent and recurring basis, some of whom prefer one bar to another that is equally convenient, although they still characteristically use the bar as a convenience.

Those who are not welcome in the home territory bar will be referred to as "outsiders," but not all who fall outside of the collectivities from which the habitués are drawn are outsiders. Some patrons who are not members of the habitués' collectivity may be present as invited guests of those who do hold membership, and in time they may achieve complimentary membership. In some home territory bars there may also be patrons who are not certified habitués, guest members, or outsiders, but rather are neutral persons whose presence may be tolerated: they may be in the bar but for the habitués they are non-persons. They may be permitted to join in the activities of the bar to a limited extent and for the time being, but not entitled to the privileges that are accorded the habitués, such as check-cashing, inclusion in raffles and pools, special parties and dinners, and dancing.

Neutral persons who are non-persons for the habitués are often found when a given establishment is characterized by more than one type of usage at one time. Thus, in one skid row bar that was used as both a home territory and a marketplace throughout the day, patrons who came to drink with the B-girls were for all practical purposes ignored by those patrons who used the bar as their home territory, the latter group customarily paying neither verbal nor visual attention to the former.

Some bars may be only occasionally used in more than one way, and the treatment that is there accorded to those who are not habitués varies. A number of bars in the vicinity of the football stadium that were used almost exclusively as home territory bars were occasionally patronized after the game by many who had gone to it. At these times, the habitués would characteristically extend a limited welcome to those who were using the establishment as a convenience bar. But in the home territory bars in the vicinity of the opera house, which experienced the same kind of occasional dual usage after a performance, the habitués would characteristically treat those who were using their establishment as a convenience bar as non-persons.[5]

Variation in the range of people who may be accorded a limited welcome in any given home territory bar is primarily a function of both the kind of collectivities that form the basis for the habitués and the indigenous culture that develops in the bar. Home territory bars that draw their habitués from relatively extensive collectivities or from collectivities that are compounded of more than one attribute are generally open, at least on a limited basis, to patrons who might be excluded if the habitués were drawn from less extensive collectivities or from collectivities with single attributes. For example, a number of bars that are used as home territories by young unmarried persons typically grant at least a limited welcome to those who are young and married and those who may be no longer young but who are still unmarried. In the same way, when the standing behavior patterns of a given home territory bar differ little if at all from those found in public drinking places in general (e.g., such as in the use of profanity), the range of people to whom a limited welcome may be extended is typically greater than it is when this difference in patterns is large.

Home Territory Behavior

Regardless of the categories from which the habitués may be drawn, the characteristic feature of the home territory use of the public drinking place is that the habitués treat the bar as though it "belonged" to them, as though it were no longer within the domain of public drinking places.

As a general rule, those who use the public drinking place in this way single out one establishment to treat as "their" bar. There are exceptions, of course. For example, a group of unemployed and unemployable men on skid row had two bars and a hot-dog stand that they used each day as home territories in a scheduled manner; they were at the first bar from about 10 A.M. to 2 P.M.; at the hot-dog stand from around 2 P.M. to 4 P.M.; at the second bar from around 6 P.M. until 9 or 10 P.M.; and back at the first bar again until 2 A.M. A similar phenomenon was found in a more respectable neighborhood: a number of patrons used one bar as their home territory on weekdays and another, which was a block away from the first, on weekends, although upon occasion they would patronize both places during the same evening. Again, two homosexual bars separated by two blocks were occasionally used by some of the same patrons, although by and large the patrons who went to both were very few compared with the number who used one or the other exclusively.

Once a collectivity has established itself in any particular bar, and assuming that the particular collectivity is one that the management of the establishment does not find repugnant,[6] proprietary acts on the part of the habitués become routine. Telephone calls and messages may be made and left at the bar, with the expectation that information will be forthcoming and delivery will be assured. The bar may be given as a mailing address, with the expectation that, like the general delivery department of the post office, items will be kept until called for. Money may be deposited, with the knowledge that the same sum will be available to the depositor when he returns at a later date. On occasion, items may be pawned, to be reclaimed at some future time, or money may be borrowed without a promissory note. The following examples come from a home territory bar located on skid row:

> Sammy came in and picked up his mail. The bartender said that he had letters for some of the other fellows, too (most of whom were seamen), but that he would send back all of the traffic tickets, writing on them, "Not at this address." A little while later, the bartender said that some fellow from one of the hotels down the street had pawned a watch with him for $10 and he wondered when he was going to reclaim it.

> Marv said that he left $1,800 at a bar in the tenderloin when he got out of the service, and for a while he charged drinks against it but finally took the balance out. The bartender then said that someone had left almost as much with him at one time.

The habitués of the home territory bar may also use the establishment for singing, dancing, and playing musical instruments, although the bar may have no entertainment license, and sometimes even for eating and sleeping, although for others the bar is neither a restaurant nor a hotel.

Over the course of time the routine patterns of behavior in the home territory bar may diverge in one way or another from the patterns that are more or less general for all public drinking places, crystallizing into a kind of indigenous culture within each. Perhaps one of the best examples of this divergence is found in the proprieties concerning the use of profanity and obscene language. As a general rule, public language is expected to be circumspect. Swearing and taboo sexual references are conventionally beyond the pale of acceptable words in polite society, and this is particularly true when women are, or possibly can be, present. In general, the rules governing such language in the public drinking place are analogous to the rules governing language in other public places. Even though the entertainers in night spots may be permitted a good deal of freedom in the use of double entendre and profanity, the license to use such language is typically not extended to the patrons, and its use by patrons in night spots, convenience bars, and many marketplace bars generally elicits sanctions from the management of the establishment.

On the other hand, there is much more variation in home territory bars with respect to the use of taboo language than there is in bars in general. There are some home territory bars in which swearing is characteristically absent altogether and others in which occasional swearing (but no more) is the rule. In others, both occasional swearing and taboo sexual references are acceptable, and in still others, bartender and patrons alike appear to engage habitually in the use of various taboo exclamations for their own sake. But whether such language is permissible or whether it is expected as a part of the ongoing activity is typically known in advance by those who use any particular bar as their home territory. At the same time, those who breach the expectations, either by using words that should not be used or by becoming offended by others using words that are locally acceptable, are typically a matter of concern for patrons as well as for management. Any sanctions that are meted out are just as likely to come from other patrons as they are to come from the management.

Mock sexual licentiousness provides another example of the lines along which the indigenous culture of the home territory bar may develop. In the marketplace bar, sexually oriented encounters that are to remain within the confines of the bar must be purchased by the drink; where such activity is without set price, it carries a possible implication that goes beyond the immediate setting. In home territory bars, however, where sexually oriented interaction becomes one of the characteristic patterns of behavior it is transformed into a game with special rules that are expected to be known and respected by the habitués.

Because the sexual activity of the home territory bar is defined as only a form of play, it is expected to be temporally delimited, to contain no meaning beyond the immediate moment. Thus, unlike sexually oriented encounters in the marketplace bar, there is never any question of eligibility. Passes, flirtation, embraces, and kisses are merely moves in a game for which typically neither long-term commitments (such as marriage or engagements) nor short-term commitments (such as dates) have any relevance with respect to determining who is eligible to play.

There were thirty to thirty-two people in the bar, and at least five couples were dancing at all times. A young man in a blue shirt, at the end of a number, kissed the woman with whom he had been dancing, returned her to the bar, and then went down to talk with his wife, who was sitting talking with two other men.

One of the Russians came over and asked me to dance, not saying anything to P.C., who was also sitting at the table. When we got back to the table, the fellow in the blue shirt came over, sat down on the bench, put his arm around me, and started talking to both of us. He eventually introduced himself, pointed out his wife, and then said that it was his anniversary.

During the course of the evening, dances, embraces, kisses, and lap-sitting were exchanged by almost everyone in the bar, but at a little after two, when the bar was being closed and good nights were said, the original couples, many of whom were married, paired up again.

While the previous example comes from a straight home territory bar in which the habitués are drawn along lines of class and ethnicity, a similar kind of sexual play can be found in homosexual bars that are used primarily as home territories:

Louie was insisting that everyone around him caress his Persian lamb vest, then winking at them and saying they could go farther if they wanted to. A number of times he grabbed at the genitals of men who went by him, and although upon occasion some of those who were so grabbed became embarrassed and hurried on, no one became indignant and no one appeared to expect anything more from him.

One fellow was goosed by another standing with a group near the bar. The former turned, smiled, and then went on.

Someone Morrie knew walked by him twice, goosing him both times in a very exaggerated manner. Everyone around laughed, including the one who had instigated the action.

Similarly, where sex is only play, it is not uncommon for straight females who are wise, and hence acceptable within the male homosexual home territory bar, to be singled out for mock flirtations.

There was a constant, although changing, group of men around an attractive blond in a black dress, admiring and flirting. The fellow sitting next to me nodded toward them and then said to the fellow on his right, "I hope that she doesn't take them seriously."

It was extremely crowded, with perhaps more than seventy persons clustered around the bar. I had just come in and was standing near the door when a patron motioned to me, smiled, raised his eyebrows, and in general indicated that I should come over to where he was seated, near the door end of the bar. I went over and he said, "Come on in." I said that I would but there didn't appear to be room. He said, "Of course there is plenty of room," and patted his lap, indicating that I should sit there.

Profanity and sexual play provide two examples of the lines along which special patterns of behavior within the home territory bar may develop, but they are not the only such cases. Joking relationships, topics of interest, noteworthy events of the past in the bar or in the life of the collectivity may all gradually come to be defined as part of the culture of each particular home territory bar, and for the habitués they may come to stand for the characteristic features of their bar.

Territorial Defense: the Habitués

The maintenance of the home territory use of a public drinking place is in good measure dependent upon the way in which the habitués are able to handle the problem of outsiders who may enter the bar because of its apparent public character. The particular behavior patterns associated with the bar and the degree of intimacy and control that the habitués have over their establishment may often be disrupted by outsiders who do not know what is going on or how the activity is to be carried out, or who may question the legitimacy of the activity. The most notable example of this is in the homosexual home territory bar, where both patrons and customary behavior patterns may be not only incomprehensible and repugnant to outsiders, but, once seen, may be made the object of police attention as well. Hence it is within the gay bar that the most elaborate forms of excluding outsiders are often practiced. In one such bar, the habitués routinely made outsiders appear out of place and feel uncomfortable about being where they were by breaching the outsiders' expectations that they would be inconspicuous within the establishment and by declining to accept any claims the outsider might make to being a respectable person.[7]

Like homosexuality, the play of licentious heterosexuality is also a vulnerable behavior pattern. In one straight bar, where temporary exchanges of partners and mock-sexual overtures were typical modes of behavior during the patrons' stay, the habitués would often distribute themselves around the bar in such a way that entering outsiders would be unable to get into the establishment easily or, once they were inside, would be unable to seat themselves at the bar. This barricade was no problem to entering habitués, who were either provided with a clear passage into the establishment or who merely barged through the mass of people at the door or around the bar, as they had a "right" to do.

But even where the divergence between the general features of bar behavior and the indigenous culture of the home territory bar is not so great, a bar can be considered as one's "own" bar only insofar as it cannot be considered as "everyone's" bar. Hence, the maintenance of proprietary interest in a bar is dependent upon the exclusion of others who, for some reason or other, appear to have no "right" to patronize the establishment.

Perhaps the most common form of tacit rebuff that an entering outsider is likely to receive upon entering a home territory bar is a conspicuous, questioning look, too long to be taken as a prelude to civil inattention, too intent to be taken as an invitation. As the patron of one home territory bar said of other establishments in the vicinity of "his" bar,

> You walk in these (other) bars and people look at you. You have to patronize them regularly if you want them not to look at you. You walk in them and you can see them thinking, "What's this guy want?"

Sometimes the look may be accompanied by an audible remark as well, as in the following example:

> When we entered the bar it was about three-fourths full. Two or three people at the bar gave us a long, somewhat questioning look, and then one woman said, quite loudly, "Oh, boy, make room for the paying customers." This was followed by much laughter.

Outsiders who enter home territory bars may also be pestered or treated in a purposefully annoying manner. The habitués may attempt to cadge drinks from them or to monopolize the dice boxes, pinball machines, or jukebox so that these facilities are not available to the outsider. The habitués may attempt to move past outsiders with a little more roughness than is routinely given to other habitués. They may attempt to bait the outsiders into entering arguments, make mock of their manner to the rest of the patrons in a way deliberately performed for the outsider as well, or request picayune information, as in the following example:

The fellow who had been at the door came over to me and said, "Do you have a skirt on?" It was quite obvious that I did, and he went on to say, "Well, I just wanted to make sure because you couldn't come in here if you didn't."

Further, the characteristic openness of bar patrons may be denied to outsiders in home territory bars.

As much as I tried to participate in the conversation, I could not do so . . . they were extremely loath to talk to strangers, especially one like myself who came unintroduced, alone, and then only irregularly about once a week.[8]

I had been sitting at the bar for about five minutes when a man came in, sat down one seat away from me and started telling the bartender about an accident down the street. I asked a question about it, but both the patron and the bartender ignored me. A second man came in and was included in the conversation from which I had been pointedly excluded.

Dean and Hal were discussing baseball when an older man, a little drunk and rather disheveled, came in and ordered a beer. He tried to enter their conversation a couple of times and finally Dean said to him, "You think you know all there is to know about baseball." The old man finished his drink and then left. Dean said loudly as he was leaving, "He thinks he's so smart."

A man from one of the bars on the street bordering the colored district came to Murphy's, began playing the jukebox, and tried to get friendly with the crowd. When he got no response, he called out, "How's that? You let me put my nickels in the jukebox and listen to my music, but you won't talk to me. What's the matter here? I'm as good as anyone of you guys." When he received no response, including no beer from the bartender, he remarked, "Well, at least I demand to be served like a human being. . . ." He carried on, with everyone in the tavern studiedly ignoring him. . . . The visitor left after a few more harangues against the treatment he was receiving.[9]

And, of course, the habitués may deliberately engage in routines of behavior that they know will be offensive to the outsider.

When we came in, there were about five patrons seated at the door end of the bar, and two lesbians seated three or four stools over from them. The conversation between the bartender and the patrons at the end of the bar seemed to be exceedingly loud, even by bar standards, and included a number of references to "diesel dykes" and "girls who look like Muni bus drivers." This went on for about five minutes, and the two women eventually left without finishing their drinks.

Once they were gone, the conversation continued as loudly, but with the topic changed to what might generally be considered "offensive" sexual references and overly descriptive homosexual matters, and we left soon afterward.[10]

For some home territory bars, the problem of outsiders never arises. In some cases, the existence of the premises may be unknown to those who might be potential outsiders, because the establishment is located in an area that outsiders do not frequent, because it is unmarked on the street, or because it requires a devious route to gain entrance. In San Francisco, one homosexual home territory bar is located at the top of a long flight of stairs and another presents a blank and dark façade to the street.[11] Similarly, a home territory bar for British subjects was unmarked on the street, requiring potential patrons to pass first through a small gift shop to get to the door. When asked about why the last bar was so concealed, one patron in the establishment stated,

They are particular about who comes in here. You have to find out about the place the hard way. Some friends told me about it, and now I come here regularly. This is a real British place—I have dual citizenship—this is just the way they behave in pubs in the British Isles. All the British subjects around here come here. Everybody behaves himself.

In other bars, the collectivity that congregates may be a matter of public knowledge, and those who are not eligible do not enter either because they know in advance that it is not the kind of place they would care to frequent or because they know in advance that, even if they would like to enter, they would not be welcome.[12]

There were five persons in the bar, a group of four men at the far end playing poker dice and another man sitting next to me. The patron next to me was explaining that he was on a dinner break and went on to say, "I actually like crowded bars best. This place would take about fifty people to make it look like it was full." I asked if there were any other bars he could go to in the area and he said, "No, this is the first one from where I work. You could go north to the J— Club. It's a little shorter I guess, but it's a dingy place, mainly for the characters in the tenderloin."

The bartender said, of a small bar a few blocks down the street, "Yeah, that's the place where all the kooks hang out. Prostitutes, pimps, gamblers, dope peddlers—you can find them all down there."

For some bars, such information may not be a general matter of public knowledge, but once the entering outsider has opened the door the character of the establishment may be immediately apparent to him and he may withdraw. The following statements came from a number of men in response to the question of whether homosexual bars should be marked:

"They don't need a sign. There's no mistaking what's going on. You wouldn't believe what's happening! A regular, or a straight guy, wouldn't want to walk into one of these places. Not if he's in his right mind."

"Yes. Those people should all go to their spots. Shouldn't associate with people that just want to have a drink. You can spot the action right away. A straight guy's not going to want to walk into something like this."

"They have to have some place to go. Let them have their own bars. I've gone into them. Accidentally. Just takes a couple of minutes to tell. Some of these places in Sausalito! Wow! Four of us guys went in, ordered a beer and sat down. The scene was too much!"

"Yes. That way it would protect tourists and people from being humiliated. Get those guys all together. Let them have their own entertainment, if that's what you call it. But keep it private. Let the rest of the decent people enjoy themselves in a normal fashion."

There are, of course, always some who may be unable to read the cues for what they are, as a final respondent indicates.

"Yes. Otherwise you don't know what's happening. They ought to have a sign outside or something. Let you know what's going on. They should put up a sign so everybody'd be aware of the situation. Gay bars might be all right but they're sure not for me."[13]

The following field examples both come from homosexual

home territory bars, the first patronized primarily by men, the second by women.

A very nicely dressed couple came in, stood for a few minutes at the door looking around and then left, apparently deciding that this was not the place for them.

Two young couples started to enter and then stopped at the door, looking around and apparently a little uncomfortable. One of the couples started to leave, paused, and then finally left. The other couple stood inside, right by the door, in a tentative manner, nervously peering at the ceiling and the signs and posters around the room, occasionally casting surreptitious glances at the patrons.

The knowledge that a particular public drinking place serves as a home territory for some particular collectivity can, of course, raise problems of its own for the habitués. In most home territory bars, the presence of outsiders is usually inadvertent; they patronize the establishment because of its "public" definition. However, bars that are known to be home territories for a variety of "exotic" or otherwise socially curious groups may find that outsiders have deliberately entered to observe the habitués and their activity, or, in some cases, to make trouble for those who are there. This is a rather persistent problem for some homosexual bars in San Francisco, and an occasional problem for others, as in the example below:

There were about seventy patrons in the bar; almost 80 percent of them were female and almost all of these were in pants, either tailored capris or levis or what appeared to be men's slacks. Two men in their late twenties came in and stood next to where I was seated. We started talking, and eventually they told me that they were both straight and that they had come into the bar because, as they put it, "this is a place where you can observe real life." One of them went on to say that he had been in all the bars along the street but that this was the most "alive" one he had found. (Of the eighteen bars along the street, two others were also home territory bars for homosexuals, but both of them had a predominantly male clientele.) When I asked him what he meant by "alive," he replied, "Well, it's the kind of place that things happen in. It's exciting."

We talked for a while longer, and it was apparent that they assumed by my presence in the bar that I was also a lesbian, an assumption I did not try to alter. Eventually they started telling me that I should find out what men were like and that once I had sexual intercourse with a man I would no longer be interested in women.

One of them suggested that we drive to a nearby park and he would show me what he meant.

When it was evident that I had no intention of leaving the bar with them, they began asking about what lesbian sexual relations were like, prefacing each query with statements to the effect that they were only academically interested in the subject, although their insistent questioning gave me the distinct impression that they were either baiting or mocking the kind of person they thought I was.

A while later they began talking to two girls standing nearby. From what I could overhear, the general drift was quite similar to the conversation that they had with me.

Homosexual bars are not the only establishments which outsiders may enter to observe. One bartender said that he would sometimes go to one or two of the Filipino bars not far from his establishment just "to see what they're up to," and occasionally would enter one of the bars on skid row for the same purpose. Similarly, bars that are used as a home territory for prostitutes and their pimps may also be treated by outsiders as scenes to be viewed:

There are (also) the tourists, the out-of-towners, who have heard of this strange club in the bad West End where practically everything is said to happen. They come, dressed either carefully in slacks and duffel collars, or unsuitably in off-the-shoulder dresses and stiff collars, not because they really appreciate good music or enjoy dancing in whatever space they can find in the ill-decorated club, but for the shiver in the spine at the vice bubbling beneath the surface, about which their friends have whispered or boasted of having seen break out, at the prospect of a fight or a girl being beaten up by her ponce, at the thought of spotting illicit love in a dark corner.[14]

Characteristically, the activity known as "slumming," in which respectable people intentionally visit settings of little respectability out of curiosity or for excitement, is usually carried out in public drinking places; one rarely if ever finds people slumming in other possible settings, such as cafeterias, parks, hotels, or movie houses.[15]

It might also be noted in passing that home territory bars are not the only type of public drinking place in which some patrons may be present primarily to observe other patrons. Some marketplace bars are treated in the same way, and one such place in San Francisco became so well known as a place where prostitutes made contact with their customers that the rites of the prostitutes and their clients became objects of interest, men bringing their dates to witness them. Similarly, in asking patrons about various public drinking places, they will often say of pickup bars that the activity that goes on is worthy of being viewed in and for itself.

Territorial Defense: the Management

The collectivity that utilizes a bar as a home territory typically expects that the management will actively support whatever claims it makes upon the bar and whatever indigenous culture develops there.[16] If the management does not cooperate, the collectivity may move in mass to some other establishment. The patron of one home territory bar said, "We all used to go to the K— bar, but Steve, the bartender, acted like he didn't want us there." In the same way, the movement of homosexuals from one establishment to another is sometimes explained by statements attesting to the owner's or bartender's lack of support. As one patron said of such a change, "Oh it was a nice place, but Del, the owner, wouldn't stick up for the gay kids."

Thus, the management will often take an active part in controlling the entrance of outsiders into home territory bars, if for no other reason than to assure the habitués that they are welcome, although the probability of real trouble—physical assaults or melees—may be a factor as well. One example comes from an establishment that was used as a home territory by middle-age, middle-class unmarried people. Since most of the habitués worked during the day, the owner kept the bar closed until late in the afternoon, when what he called "his" patrons would end work. His explanation was that if he opened earlier, "all the winos and drunks, with their filthy language" would come into the bar. He would also ask potential patrons who did not appear as though they might fit in to leave, because as one patron said, "This is a place for gentlemen only."

The treatment bartenders may give to winos who attempt to enter skid row home territory bars, even upon those occasions

when they can pay for their drinks, is even more severe. They
may be bodily thrown out if they make any claims on the establishment, such as sitting down at the bar, for the social distance
on skid row between those who have a proper establishment they
can call their own and those who typically drink on the streets
is often very slender, and the former can little afford to be reminded that they recently were, or soon may be, in the latter
category.

One of the winos came in, holding a fifty-cent piece out before him.
Mario (the bartender) told him to go away; when he didn't leave
immediately, Mario started to come out from behind the bar. About
half an hour later he came back in and acted as though he were
going to sit down at the bar. Mario took him by the jacket and
pushed him out. Fifteen minutes later he came in again and got as
far as sitting down at the middle of the bar, with his elbows
stretched far out on either side of him. Mario took hold of him very
roughly, shook him, and then literally threw him out the door. He
muttered as he was on his way out, "Oh, that's okay—forget it."
One of the patrons at the bar told me that they do that just to annoy
the bartenders, that they know they will not be allowed in but they
enjoy baiting the bartenders and disrupting the bar.

Outsiders who do not appear to the bartender to be capable
of assimilation into the bar may be more indirectly rebuked by
slow or unpleasant service.

If I don't know a patron, I give him a warm glass routine. Part of
the bar equipment is a large draft beer box and in this is a compart-
ment for chilling glasses. Behind me is a bamboo curtain covering a
portion of the back bar shelves. On these shelves is the extra supply
of glasses, which are warm, of course. When I serve a stranger, I
reach behind me and get him a warm glass. . . . The act of giving
the warm glass says, "I don't know this person. No one is to talk
to him until I have a chance to find who sent him."[17]

The bartender, recounting an incident which occurred earlier in
the evening, said, "This guy butted right into our conversation and
wanted to argue. That's all he was looking for, a fight. If he had been
nice, well, that's a different story. I told him to leave and instead he
orders another beer so I gave him a flat one that I opened last
night and I guess he finally got the hint because he left without
finishing it."

There were only about sixteen people present when we entered, although they took up all of the seats at the bar. I sat down at one of
the small tables along the wall opposite from the bar, and P.C. went

to the bar to get our orders. The bartender was standing almost in front of him, more or less listening to the conversation between two patrons. It took the bartender almost five minutes to make the drinks for him which were very, very light.[18]

Two couples, who were younger than the indigenous population of the bar and rather "tough" looking, were seated at one of the small tables, sporadically playing the bowling machine. One of the young men came up to the bar and asked for a beer. The bartender was standing less than a foot away but ignored him. The patron asked three times, each time with a little more insistence in his voice. The bartender finally, in a very slow and deliberate manner, took the bottle from the beer box, uncapped it, and put it down on the bar in front of the patron. Along with this rebuff went a long and unpleasant look at both the patron and his companions behind him. A little later, one of the four said, "Let's go down to the queers' place," and they left, their drinks unfinished.

Outsiders may also find that, in contrast to the liberal pouring of other patrons' drinks, their own are being measured with too much precision, or that they are being charged somewhat more than other patrons for similar orders.

Checking identification cards for age when it is apparent that they do not need to be checked to establish one's majority is yet another way in which the management can attempt to control the entrance of outsiders. Frequently, in gay bars, an employee will be stationed at the door for just this purpose. While the use of an ID check for controlling entrance is not exclusive to gay bars, it appears that only in gay bars and nightspots will there be an employee whose primary function is that of gatekeeper. But in nightspots, the only concern of the management is typically that the patrons be of legal drinking age.

A routine, legitimate ID check is usually undertaken with dispatch, so that the potential patron's status can be determined without undue embarrassment to him. In contrast, the exclusion-oriented ID check is usually a prolonged and elaborate procedure, during which the employee looks at the documents, looks at the patron, looks again at the documents, and then coolly returns them.[19]

Two young men in suits came in, sat down at the bar, and called out their order to the bartender, who was about three or four feet away. The bartender walked over to the two of them and said, "Lemme see your ID's." The patrons, who both appeared to be about twenty-five or twenty-six, looked somewhat annoyed, but took out their billfolds and handed some papers over to the bartender. The bartender looked at each identification paper very intently, then at each person. He handed them back with a small shrug and said to the patrons, "Now, what was it you wanted to drink?" in a slightly solicitous manner. One of the men said, "Oh, forget it," and the two of them got up and left.

I asked the bartender, after they left, why he had asked for their ID's since they both appeared to be obviously over twenty-one. The bartender said, "Aw, they looked like troublemakers."

The function of checking ID's in such situations becomes quite apparent when it is noted that the process may be terminated even before the documents are initially handed over by the patron if someone inside the bar greets the potential patron, or if it becomes apparent that he is with others who unquestionably have entrance rights.

The doorman asked for my ID just as we got in, but midway during the process of getting it out of my purse, Alan, the bartender, called out to him, "Hey, it's okay. I know them." The doorman then waved his hand to me in a way that signified I could enter without producing any papers and offered a small, apologetic smile as well.

In return for the assistance which the management provides the habitués in maintaining a bar as home territory, those who utilize a bar in this way will often take it upon themselves to attend to a variety of matters routine to its operation while they are present. They may act as waiters, taking drinks to patrons seated away from the bar and removing their empty glasses and ashtrays when they leave. They may, if the bartender is busy, reach over the bar and phone for a cab for a departing patron. At the end of the evening, they will often shut off the outside lights, unplug the jukebox, lock the door (or unlock and relock it as patrons leave after 2 A.M.), move the glasses on the bar down to the sink area, put empty beer bottles in cases, straighten out the bar stools, tables, and chairs, and, upon occasion, sweep the floor.

In addition to routine operating matters, habitués of a home territory bar will often take it upon themselves to assist with or handle a variety of problems that may arise. They may go on errands for necessary supplies such as ice, change, or fuses, make emergency repairs when equipment breaks down, or volunteer their services when the bartender must be temporarily absent from the premises or, as in the example below, when he is unable to function.

> The bartender (who was also the owner) had been drinking quite heavily and finally left from behind the bar to sit on the other side. One of the patrons went behind the bar and began mixing drinks, making change, cleaning up, and in general taking over the bartender's duties. Occasionally he would grumble, "I don't know where the glasses . . . where the ice is . . ." but his actions were apparently quite voluntary.

> Eventually the auxiliary bartender arrived, but before going behind the bar he sat down, ordered a drink, and chatted for a while with some of the other patrons. When he finally did go behind the bar, the patron-bartender left to take the owner home.

In the same way, social difficulties that are the responsibility of the management in other types of establishments may be handled by patrons in the home territory bar. The problems of ejecting persons too inebriated to be served or to manage physiological control of themselves, pacifying those who are disruptively obstreperous, and cooling-out those who have been socially violated may all be taken over by the habitués as a matter of course.

In short, the habitués of the home territory bar typically behave as though the premises were their own home, for which they themselves are responsible. Thus, they actively engage in the work of making sure that the guests are properly cared for while they are there, that unforeseen events do not disrupt their visit, and that the room is put in order when they leave.

In summary, once a bar has been staked out as a home territory by some collectivity, the maintenance of the definition in effect requires the habitués to treat certain courses of action as consequential. If territorial defense has the character of a seriously pursued activity, presumably it is because the viability of the home territory use of the bar is in large measure dependent upon it. Were no patron to be defined as an outsider, the obverse definition of an habitué—with the implication of activity that definition carries—would be difficult to maintain. Thus, just as variations in use may modify to some extent the standing patterns of behavior typically associated with the public drinking place (as in the night spot), so, too, may variations in use modify to some extent the inconsequentiality typically associated with the setting.

iii

CAREERS STRAIGHT
AND OTHERWISE

9

Summertime Servants: The "Shlockhaus" Waiter

Mark Hutter

The lower middle-class Jewish resort hotel is a phenomenon on the wane as the first generation of immigrants dies off and succeeding generations become assimilated and more affluent. Nevertheless, the shlockhaus *has made its contribution to the American scene. Viewers of late night television, for example, are used to seeing entertainers reminisce about their early careers in the "Jewish Alps" or the "borscht circuit." And there are the countless Marjorie Morgensterns and Noel Ehrmens who nostalgically look back on their summers in "the mountains" toiling away as waiters, busboys, counselors, musicians, and so on, for seven days a week, and yet remembering it all as fun. The nostalgia perhaps owes its pleasantness to the fact that the Catskills represent the essence of the human comedy, for which the* shlockhaus *dining room and kitchen provides the stage.*
Mark Hutter is assistant professor of sociology at Temple University.

"Fool! Why do you wash that plate? Wipe it on your trousers. Who cares about the customers? *They* don't know what's going on. What

is restaurant work? You are carving a chicken and it falls on the
floor. You apologise, you bow, you go out; and in five minutes you
come back by another door—with the same chicken. That is restaurant work. . . ."—GEORGE ORWELL, *Down and Out in Paris and
London*

Located sixty miles north of New York City in Sullivan County,
New York State, is the Catskill Mountains resort area. This summer resort region caters almost exclusively to lower-middle-class
Jewish residents of New York City. There are three major types
of accommodations for the summer vacationers: bungalow colonies which cater primarily to young couples who have small or
teen-age children and who want to spend the entire summer
away from the city; the large resort hotels which offer their
guests all the conveniences (indoor swimming pool, golf course,
fancy nightclub, etc.); and the small resort hotel.[1]

The small resort hotel is called by its Jewish staff members
a *"shlockhaus,"* a Yiddish derogatory term referring to the
slovenly preparation and service of food, the poor sleeping accommodations for the guests as well as the staff, the lack of
recreational facilities except for a small swimming pool, and
the general disregard and dislike for the guests by the staff and
the owners.

The dramaturgical perspective of symbolic interaction will be
utilized in the analysis. More specifically, our concern will
center around the viewing of the *shlockhaus* as a "social establishment." A "social establishment is any place surrounded by
fixed barriers to perception in which a particular kind of activity
regularly takes place."[2]

Setting: the Staff and Guests

The small resort hotel can accommodate up to 250 people,
but usually averages 150 during most of the summer. Its business peaks during July, tapers off in August, and has a brief re-
surgence on Labor Day weekend. The specific type of hotel being
observed is a one-family operation, with its head an elderly
Jewish man who has been in the business all his life. Because
the hotel is small, he has direct control over every aspect of its

administration, and he runs it in much the way a dictator governs his country. He is usually active from six in the morning, supervising the kitchen and planning the day's menu, until one the following morning, personally seeing that all unnecessary lights are out. The hotel is his only business, and because the season is so short he must extract the maximum profit the limited time can yield. He therefore skimps wherever possible on expenses. Because any adverse conditions can ruin him financially, he and his family are usually nervous wrecks by the end of the summer.

The guests can be divided into two groups. The majority, comprising 80 percent of the clientele, are elderly East European Jews. Usually foreign-born, they are living or have lived on the Lower East Side of Manhattan. They speak little English and converse mainly in Yiddish. The remaining 20 percent are young American-born Jewish couples and their children.

The hotel obviously fulfills different needs for the two groups. The older people are mostly retired and are on Social Security. The low rates permit them to get away from the hot city without appreciably denting their budget. At the hotel, they can relax with people of the same cultural heritage. The food is strictly "kosher," and all Jewish dietary laws are observed. It is prepared and served in familiar ways, compatible with their tastes. The entertainment is also geared to their cultural heritage: Yiddish comedians and singers deal either with life in the East European "*shtetl*" or on New York's Lower East Side. The same routines appear week after week and season after season. But the guests seem never to tire of them, even though they may have seen the same act or slight variations of it countless times.

For the smaller group of young couples in the lower-middle-income bracket, the *shlockhaus* has important advantages which the bungalow colony or the larger more expensive hotels cannot match. Expenses are low, and there is the convenience of a camp which keeps the children busy all day. The hotel also provides for counselors to look in at the small children until midnight when the parents are out. Except at mealtimes, these guests are seldom seen on the hotel's grounds. They visit friends at the better hotels, where the nightclubs are open to outsiders for a small cover charge and other facilities are available for a minimal fee. At the *shlockhaus* the young crowd can then play the role of the "big shot" or "big spender."

Because most of the clientele are elderly it is a welcome relief for the staff to serve these younger people, who have no special diet problems and are usually bigger tippers. They are also preferred in the casino or playhouse, where the band likes to play popular songs for a lively audience as a change from the Yiddish music which they usually have to play. The frontstage staff bolsters these people's ego by kibitzing with them, and are frequently rewarded for their subservience by the guests' buying them a drink.

The staff of the small hotel is divided into three groups: (1) the "housemen" supervisors—chef, salad man, baker, maître d'hôtel, and bookkeeper; (2) the "non-housemen prestigious" personnel—waiters, busboys, counselors, bookkeeper's assistant, lifeguard, band, and children's waiter; and (3) the "non-housemen nonprestigious" personnel—dishwashers, kitchen men, chambermaids, and maintenance men.

The housemen are usually middle-aged, of East European Jewish origin. Their cohesive strength lies in their loyalty to the owner rather than to the other staff members who are under their supervision. The amount of administrative strength each member of this group has over his subordinates is determined by the owner. Strong feelings of dislike are frequent among members of this group as each one tries to run the other's department.

The non-housemen prestigious staff are second in the pecking order because of their occupational position and their religious and class background. This group is usually composed of American-born Jews between the ages of eighteen and twenty-four, all of whom are college students from the lower middle class. The group derives its cohesiveness from its common cultural background, its dislike for the owner and housemen, and its disrespect for the clientele, with which it has frontstage or face-to-face relations.

The non-housemen nonprestigious staff is composed of socio-economically deprived Negroes and Puerto Ricans and a smaller number of whites who are recruited from New York's Bowery by employment agencies. With the exception of the chambermaids, these form a transient group, who often stay at a hotel just long enough to pick up one or two paychecks and then move on.

There is very little interaction among these groups outside the formal organization; their members tend to segregate themselves, and the owners tend to support this segregation. The groups are separated in their living quarters; the housemen are given inexpensive rooms, the non-housemen prestigious staff is given barrack-type accommodations that are barely habitable, and the non-housemen nonprestigious staff is provided with what is euphemistically called "Hawaiian shacks," small wooden buildings large enough for a bed. The groups are segregated also in respect to their dining areas: the first eats with the owners at a special table in the kitchen; the second in the dining room or in the children's dining room; the third in the kitchen.

The quality of the food for the "help" also varies with the occupational group. The food provided for housemen is the same as the guests eat; the food served the other two staff groups consists of leftovers, recooked and tasteless. For the prestigious staff, there is hardly enough to fill one's stomach. The nonprestigious staff, dishwashers, kitchen men, etc., receive a larger quantity than the waiters or busboys, because they do not have the opportunity to "scoff" (pilfer) food from the kitchen. (Thus, the owner reinforces an "unlawful" behavior pattern.)

The food usually provided the non-housemen staff consists of a passable breakfast: a small glass of juice, cereal, scrambled eggs, reheated coffee and/or a glass of milk. Dinner is usually a bowl of soup (yesterday's, of course), and the scraps left from the meat which could not have been served the guests, made into hamburger. The bread at breakfast and lunch is stale, and the "butter" is margarine. Dinner, being a "meat" meal, prohibits the use of "butter."

It is important to note that the ethno-racial factor is an important determinant of formal and informal group membership. A possible explanation is that the social status the worker brings with him from the outside community plays a large role in determining his attitudes toward his fellow workers and their attitudes toward him. For example, the management feel that they can demand more from the black than the white employee.

The assistant cook, if he is Jewish, is usually a houseman; if he is black, he is not. If he is Jewish, he frequently has an assistant—a kitchen man; if he is black, he does not. Furthermore, the black assistant cook would have nowhere near the administrative power that the Jewish employee would have. He would get paid less, and he would eat with the non-housemen nonprestigious staff, by choice if they were black, and also as a result of subtle hints by the owner. Finally, he would be almost completely cut off from informal contact with the housemen; his accommodations would usually be better than those of the non-housemen nonprestigious staff, but would not be as choice as the housemen's.

Waiter-guest relations are similarly influenced. One incident in particular stands out; it occurred during Rosh Hashanah, the Jewish New Year holiday, which that year was a week after Labor Day. Most of the frontstage staff had had their fill of the mountains for the year and had gone home after Labor Day, so the owner was shorthanded in the dining room for the holiday. He hired a Black, who was an experienced waiter, to be a busboy for one of the white waiters, a Jewish college student. He was treated the same as the other busboys by the staff. In fact, he was given better service in the kitchen by the housemen, to show that they were not prejudiced. However, the guests took advantage of him, as they would not have dared had he been a "nice Jewish boy." They treated him as a servant, which is not really surprising, considering the importance of the personalization of the guest-waiter relationship when the waiter or busboy is a college student. They also tipped him accordingly. The other busboys who had the same size station earned more than twice what the black busboy earned. The guests simply took advantage of the color of his skin and saved a "buck."

Workplace: Frontstage and Backstage

The *shlockhaus* dining room, like the restaurant, is a combination product and service unit: it differs from a factory, which is solely a production unit, and a retail store, which is solely a service unit.[3] Utilizing Erving Goffman's terminology, I will refer to the production area as "backstage" or "back region" and the service area as "frontstage" or "front region."[4]

The frontstage, the dining area, is where the performance takes place; that is, where the waiter and busboy serve the guest. Here the activities which most clearly embody and maintain the image of the hotel take place. Frontstage staff, maître d', waiters, and busboys, are all expected to comport themselves in a manner fitting the impression which the hotel wishes to project.

The backstage, the kitchen, is where the product is made and distributed to the frontstage staff. Impressions fostered by the performance on the frontstage are knowingly contradicted backstage, as a matter of course.

The *shlockhaus* dining room is open for three meals a day, seven days a week. All members of the dining room staff come to the dining room to eat and prepare the service an hour before the guests arrive; after the meal they clean up the dining room and set the tables for the next meal. The average workday begins at 7:30 A.M. and ends at 9:30 P.M. with approximately a one-hour break in the morning and a three-hour break in the afternoon. Each member of the staff works every meal throughout every week of the season—approximately ten consecutive weeks, 70 consecutive days, and 210 consecutive meals.

The maître d' is paid $85 to $100 a week plus food and lodgings; the captain of the waiters, the waiters, and the busboys all receive $15 a week plus food and lodgings. The captain, the waiters, and the busboys derive their income primarily from guests who tip at the end of the week or the end of their stay, the tips averaging $140 a week for the captain, $120 for the waiters and the captain's busboy, and $90 for the busboys.

Free meals and lodgings are, of course, included in calculating an employee's salary. The *shlockhaus* owner prefers to deduct the cost of the employee's meals and lodgings—the cost according to his calculations—rather than pay the employee's actual value. If the employee requests cash instead of meals or the lodgings, his request is denied; the owner would sooner have him quit than increase his pay envelope. In one hotel, where the accommodations for the waiters and busboys were particularly bad, I inquired how much the owner would charge for the least expensive guest room available. He wanted $10 a week, the equivalent of two-thirds my weekly salary ($15). When I told him that I did not want lodging included in my contract, he refused to consider such an arrangement.

As mentioned, the particular image that a restaurant wishes to project will determine the behavior expected of the frontstage staff. In the *shlockhaus* dining room a certain degree of informality is encouraged. The owner knows most of his guests by name and frequently interacts with them informally outside the hotel's dining room. However, he is no longer able to supervise both backstage and frontstage areas directly because of the large number of employees and because of the physical separation of the frontstage from the backstage. Rather than relinquish supervisory control in the kitchen, which is of crucial economic importance to him, he delegates control of the frontstage staff (waiters and busboys) to a maître d'.

The maître d', usually middle-aged and of East European Jewish origin, takes a personal interest in seeing that the guests are seated with people they will find compatible, and in general tries to make each guest feel that he is his personal friend. One ploy which he likes to use is to let the guest overhear instructions given to the waiter to give him or her particular attention.

Controlling the selection of the guests that comprise a station (all the guests served by one waiter-busboy team), he can subtly or not so subtly control the amount of money each team will make in tips during a particular week by giving a station old guests or young ones. He can determine how good a tipper a new arrival is by experience, or by knowing whether the guest has registered for the cheaper or better accommodations. In many *shlockhauses* he demands monetary compensation from members of the frontstage staff if they want good tippers on their stations.

As long as the dining room is running smoothly, the maître d' permits his staff certain privileges prohibited by the manager. The most important of these privileges is allowing the staff to "scoff," or pilfer, food from the kitchen and eat it after he finishes serving the guests. If the maître d' is permissive—and most of the time he is not—the frontstage staff may scoff everything from a quart of milk to a steak.

He may also reward the staff for performing adequately by overlooking minor infractions of the rules. On the other hand, he may zealously enforce them, and penalize the guilty station by cutting its size or by loading it with bad tippers.

The maître d' in a sense is caught in the middle. The guests can complain to him about the waiter, and can then complain about him to the owner. He can also receive criticism from the frontstage staff concerning alleged favoritism and/or poor timing in handling the seating. He must thus present two faces on the job. To the staff, he must play the role of the stern boss; to the guests, the humble servant anxious to please. Behind the scenes in the kitchen, he may be cursing out a waiter or busboy or ridiculing a guest's mannerisms. Ten seconds later in the dining room he is again the well-mannered "host."

In the larger *shlockhaus*, assisting the maître d' to keep the waiters and busboys in line is the "captain of the waiters." Usually the most experienced waiter in the hotel or a relative of the owner, he has the station with the best tippers and is first on the serving line. It is his job to see that there is no "goofing off" in the dining room before, during, and after the meal, nor any confusion in the kitchen. He tries to minimize friction among the waiters and busboys; it is also his job to see that no one sneaks ahead on the kitchen serving line where the food is distributed to each waiter. He assigns to each waiter and busboy a "side job" before and after a meal, varying from distributing bread to each station to collecting the dirty linen after a meal. To enforce his authority he can assign a desirable side job or create an undesirable one for members of the staff who displease him.

His position is a difficult one; he is both a member of the working staff and a member of the ruling faction. Since he is the peer of the other staff members and is in direct contact with them in the formal setting (and in the informal one as well), he is subject to a great deal of pressure from them. At the same time he must share the responsibility of the maître d' and the owner, although he rarely shares in the making of it. The effectiveness of group pressure will determine how effective he is.

The functioning unit in the dining room is the waiter and his busboy. They serve approximately thirty guests a meal (four tables), and on weekends they may serve forty or more. Guests are served by the same waiter and busboy team throughout their stay at the hotel. Only on rare occasions do guests complain about the service or their dinner partners, and ask to have their tables changed. As mentioned, the waiter and busboy and the tables they serve are called a station; in the small hotel, there are usually three to six stations. The number of stations varies, of course, with the number of guests in the hotel.

The waiter's role is to take the orders and serve all the main courses, i.e., appetizer, soup, entree, etc. It is the busboy's role to clear the table of "dirty" dishes (finished courses), and to get side orders that guests may want. He must help the waiter set up before the meals and after them. In general, he is the waiter's assistant. However, what makes him unique as compared to other busboys in the restaurant industry is that he is tipped separately by the guest. The guests usually tip the waiter $5 a week per person and busboys $3, although smaller tips frequently occur. Occasionally a station may be "stiffed," that is, not tipped at all, but this happens rarely. In addition, the waiter tips the busboy $5 a week or a percentage of his tips for services rendered. In the next section of this paper, we will discuss in detail the waiter-busboy-customer relationship. Here we will focus our attention on the waiter-busboy relationship and their relationship with the rest of the staff.

The waiter and busboy are not passive recipients of the housemen's authority. They have two ways, among others, of fighting it. The first is to "bitch" to the guests about the quality of food which the employee has to eat. This device is used frequently in the *shlockhaus* for it satisfies the guests' needs to mother the waiter or busboy, besides allowing him to "get back" at the owner. It may also involve telling the guest not to order a particular dish because it is yesterday's leftovers, or simply because it is "lousy," which hardly helps the image the owner wishes to project. The second device is "killing all livestock": that is, wantonly destroying food which can be served again. Such items range from pats of butter to full containers of milk and occasional main dishes which have not been touched. This hits the owner hard—in his pocketbook—and when costs rise, he is smart enough to know the cause. He may fire some members of the frontstage staff whom he considers prime offenders, but more frequently he tells the frontstage supervisor to "get off the waiters' backs."

The waiter-busboy relationship is important, for the two must act as a unit in taking care of their station. The mutual dependence of each man cuts across the occupational structure. If the waiter gets "bombed," that is, falls behind in his orders, the busboy comes to the rescue. On occasion the waiter may be clearing a table while a busboy brings out "mains."

Although informally they may be close friends, in the formal setting the subservient role of the busboy must be observed. However, it should be noted that outside status and social relations have important influence on the formal work relationships. The following incident will serve to illustrate how these informal relations influence work relations in the dining room. One of my busboys was a particularly close friend; in fact, our parents are our mutual "godparents." During one meal, bombed with additional orders, I was frantically running around in the kitchen trying to get them filled, when I noticed my busboy "chewing the fat" with one of the dishwashers. I lost my temper and attempted to "pull rank" on him. Immediately after I finished my tirade, I felt like a jackass. My busboy simply looked at me and said, "Don't pull that waiter crap on me," and walked away. After the meal, I felt I had to apologize for my breach of conduct.

We have considered the frontstage staff's interrelationships; equally important is their relationship with the backstage staff. In the *shlockhaus* the waiter and busboy are in direct contact with cooks, salad men, and bakers—the housemen prestigious staff. In giving and picking up orders, should the waiter or busboy tell them to hurry up, the result may well be a slowing of the service. On the other hand, the waiter knows a few routines to get his orders filled promptly, ranging from simple flattery and the use of psychology to bribery. In one *shlockhaus* where I worked I found it useful to give the salad man a six-pack of beer every week. My orders were usually filled ahead of those of my competitors, resulting in their envy and better service for my station. When they asked me to account for my success, I attributed it to my dazzling personality and good looks. When in time they learned the ropes, they did the same, and I lost the advantage.

Another routine is for the waiter to order more than he needs. Then, if a guest asks for that item, he has it right at hand. If the waiter overestimates the demand, rather than return the extra orders to the kitchen and be censured he simply "kills" the extras, or eats them.

The waiter knows how to get even, as well as how to get around, with members of the backstage staff. Consider what happened to the salad man in one *shlockhaus* who impressed us with the fact that he was boss in his domain. He was a particularly nasty individual, and we decided to give him the works. We told the guests that the best thing on the menu was the "Hawaiian salad," a particularly time-consuming one to make; usually there were only four or five orders for it. One day, because we pushed this salad, there were approximately thirty-five orders. The salad man was "really bombed." We estimated that he lost ten pounds during the meal. The next day, he made about twenty such salads beforehand, anticipating the same demand. Accordingly, we changed our tactics; we did not push the salad, and he was caught with fifteen extras at the end of the meal, which he had to "break-down."

Workface: The Waiter-Guest Relationship

In high status restaurants the waiter-customer relationship is on a very formal basis; the lower the status of a restaurant, the more informal will be the relations between waiter and customer. In the low status restaurant deference from employees is neither expected nor rewarded. Whyte notes that waitresses in such restaurants had certain standards of behavior that they expected the customer to live up to, and they took action to "put him in his place" if he "got out of line."[5] He also notes that customers did not resent such treatment; in fact, they rewarded it by leaving better tips than they did for waitresses who treated customers according to middle-class standards of respect and deference.

The waiter-guest relationship in the *shlockhaus* is also characterized by informality, but with this important difference: the waiter and busboy have each personalized his relationship to the guest. The only outlet for the frontstage staff to relieve dining room pressure is by kibitzing with the guests and hoping that the sanctions imposed by the more sympathetic will curb the "bitchy" behavior of others. He cannot talk back to the guest, for by doing so he will destroy his image.

The guest has two sources of control over the waiter or busboy. He can complain about the service, usually to the maître d', but sometimes to the owner. Complaints to the superiors are signs of unsatisfactory service, as well as unsatisfactory relationships between waiter and guest. In the *shlockhaus,* individual complaints are a serious matter, because the guest is usually a repeater who spends one or two weeks every summer with his friends and relatives at the hotel, and the owner is afraid of losing his patronage.

The second and more important source of power is the tip. The guest usually gives his tip at the end of the week or at the end of his stay at the hotel, and since the *shlockhaus* is a family hotel, the guest represents more than himself. Alienating him may mean alienating his family and friends. In fact, on some occasions, a station may be composed entirely of one family or one group of friends.

A word here about the tipping system may be in order. The tip has traditionally been a reward for good service. However, the restaurant and hotel owner have exploited this generous custom to get the public to pay the wages of their staff. As indicated previously, in the *shlockhaus* the tip accounts for 90 percent of the waiter's earnings and approximately 80 to 85 percent of the busboy's. The economic importance of the tip cannot be underestimated.

Besides the payroll savings for the owner, the tipping system also serves to assure him that the customers receive good service. Problems, however, arise when the waiter or busboy knows from previous experience whether a particular customer is a good or bad tipper. They will naturally make special efforts to please the customers who reward them well at the expense of those who tip poorly. Thus one guest who made a pest of herself for two weeks "stiffed" (left no tip at all) her waiter and busboy. The next year when she returned to the hotel and while she was registering, we told the hotel owner in her presence that we would refuse to serve her unless she tipped us in advance. In fact we threatened to quit en masse unless she did. When the guest refused, the owner was forced to guarantee us that she would tip when she left. At the end of her stay, rather than face any additional humiliation, she tipped us the customary amount and left the hotel quietly.

But tipping should not be thought of solely in economic terms. The tip is also viewed by the waiter or waitress as an expression of feeling; it represents what the customer thinks of him. The stiff is even more disturbing to the ego than to the pocketbook. Of course, the tip also symbolizes the customer's superior position. The waiter is dependent upon his whim and is thus placed in an inferior position.

Many of the frontstage staff in the *shlockhaus* indicated they would prefer a service charge system—but only if the service charge were comparable to their average tip. They preferred this system rather than working on a straight salary, feeling that the owner would rather sacrifice service to the customers than hire enough stations if he had to pay a fixed salary. Perhaps if tipping were abolished the quality of the service in the *shlockhaus* would suffer. Certainly, there would be less kibitzing with the guests; the personal relations which arise between the staff and the guests would largely disappear. There would still exist some informality in the dining room, but the staff would not interact with the guests outside of it. The owners of the hotels I worked in always asked the staff to participate as much as possible in the guest's social activities. He knew the guests liked to have younger people around. When the staff did not participate, they would complain that the hotel was like an old-age home. And, of course, without the staff, the younger guests could not play the role of big shots.

In addition to the absence of informality which is characteristic of customer-waiter-busboy relations, the generally good service would deteriorate. Since tipping is the primary incentive for drawing conscientious work, the frontstage staff in the *shlockhaus* would probably grow careless in its work and indifferent to its customers; the "bad" customer especially would suffer even worse service if he did not have the economic power of the tip.

The tipping system, then, is tied up with the status issue. At the same time the frontstage staff in the *shlockhaus* does not have the servant attitude which is characteristic of the traditional waiter. Middle-class college students who take seasonal jobs to help finance their education know their social standing does not depend on the job. As I overheard a guest remark to her husband, "Don't be so demanding, he's working hard so that he can get through college."

The inconsiderate guest is inclined not to permit the staff member to forget his "place." Should he fail in this, there are other ways for the guest to show his lack of consideration. The guest who demands immediate service is a problem, but the one who demands more service than the waiter is able to provide is a "lulu." Should he order the "blue-plate special" with no substitutions allowed, he proceeds to substitute for every item. Or if he asks for a side order—for example, more bread—he expects the waiter or busboy to fill other requests "while he is in the kitchen."

Still another type of nuisance is the man or woman who usurps the waiter's time by telling him his troubles. This type appears to be quite prevalent in the *shlockhaus* because of the informality encouraged by the management in the staff-guest relationship. Then there is the type who does not know what he wants to order, yet refuses to accept the waiter's suggestions. Only when the waiter is preoccupied with other duties does he finally decide to give his order. As often as not he changes his mind, and the waiter has to return the order to the kitchen. Or he doesn't want a beverage with the meal, but when he receives his order he decides he does want it, thus forcing the waiter to make an additional trip to the kitchen.

Whyte says the first question to ask when considering the customer relationship is: "Does the waitress get the jump on the customer, or does the customer get the jump on the waitress?"[6] The waiters and busboys in the *shlockhaus* are no exception.

They aim to have guests favorably impressed with them from the beginning to ensure a good tip. If they personalize their relationships with the customers, their tips will improve. To this end they concern themselves with the personal problems of the guests; perhaps commenting favorably on how good looking their grandchildren are, as seen in their photographs, or trying to impress the guests with the fact that they are poor boys just like their grandsons, working their way through college under slave-like conditions. This personalized relationship prevents the guest from treating the waiter and busboy solely in terms of their occupational roles, but rather as individuals.

It is interesting to note that the "economically deprived worker" routine becomes institutionalized over the years in all the small hotels. The guests, especially the old-timers, become skeptical when they hear it again. Ironically, because the routine has become institutionalized, the failure to utilize it may actually hurt the size of one's tips.

The waiter and busboy also employ other routines to help assure their tip. They talk vividly about how hard it is to get a special order, how they argue vehemently with the cook or salad man for it. If they do not want to get the order because they know it takes a long time to prepare or they are afraid of a "run" (everyone will order it), they tell the guests that the kitchen will not prepare it or that the kitchen has run out of the particular order. An excellent device utilized occasionally is the failure to wipe their perspiration from their faces—a powerful sign to indicate how hard they work.

The waiter's behavior, then, is determined by the image the *shlockhaus* wishes to project. However, no matter what the framework of appearances maintained by the hotel, there is usually little feeling behind the appearances. Group attitudes and behavior are almost completely reversed when frontstage employees leave the dining room. Waiters and busboys derogate the guests in a way greatly unlike the face-to-face treatment prevalent in the front region. Guests treated with respect in the dining room are often ridiculed, cursed, and criticized. In the kitchen, the waiters refer to them by belittling code names; their speech and mannerisms are imitated and ridiculed. This derogation serves to maintain the solidarity of the particular station and of the frontstage staff against the common enemy; it probably also compensates for the loss of self-respect that may occur from the constant flattery of the customers.

Backstage derogation takes other forms, usually revolving around the preparation and social treatment given to the guests' food. The contempt and dislike for particular customers is shown in the way the food is handled. A guest who did not want any bones in his "flanken" (boiled beef) ate the flanken after the waiter, unknown to him, removed the bones from the meat with his hands. Another incident which comes to mind is the many times a staff member spat in the guests' soup bowls to get even for the hard time the guests were giving him.

There are other forms of derision, such as casting knowing looks to fellow employees when in the presence of a bad customer; or what Goffman calls "communication out of character,"[7] when one member of a team performs his role for the secret and special amusement of his audience. For example, the waiter may take his guest's order with an affected enthusiasm that the guest does not realize to be mockery. Thus, waiters usually ask a particularly obnoxious guest for his exact wishes on how he wants his steak prepared. He then randomly selects any steak from his tray and gives it to the customer, who is usually quite pleased with this special service.

A similar form of team collusion occurs when one team member attempts to tease another while both are engaged in a performance. The object is to make one's teammate burst out laughing or somehow lose his poise. For example, in the *shlockhaus* one of the waiters "scoffed" a blueberry cupcake and was about to eat it after the meal when the maître d' entered the dining room to ask the waiter about some seating arrangements for the next meal. The waiter had no time to hide the cupcake in his service stand, so he cupped it in his hand and put his hand behind his back. I witnessed this little drama, and walked over to the waiter while he was talking to the maître d' and squashed the cupcake in his hand. The waiter just managed to control his laughter. The performer, by mocking the audience and teasing a teammate, is not bound by the official interaction. It also shows that the performers feel they have this interaction so much under control they can toy with it at will.

All of the above forms are ways in which the employees can free themselves from the restrictive requirements of the formal pattern of interaction. In all of them the audience is unaware that the performers are deviating from the regularized patterns. Goffman states that the performers often attempt to speak out of character in a way that will be heard by the audience but will not openly threaten the balance of the situation.[8] Thus, in the official working consensus which guarantees the waiter-customer relation, there is usually an unofficial line of communication which each group directs at the other: mimicked accents, well-placed jokes, veiled hints, significant pauses, etc. The communicator is able to deny that he meant anything by his action if questioned by the recipient. For instance, the owner of one of the small resort hotels could not pronounce the letter "v." Thus, one of the waiters, Victor, was called "Wictor" by the owner. When he would ask where Victor was, we would reply that "Wictor" was in the dining room. The owner, however, never accused us of having said something unacceptable to him.

Goffman notes that by "putting out feelers," one team can extend a definite but non-compromising invitation to the other. This takes the form of requesting that social distances and formality be increased or decreased, or that both teams shift the interaction to one with a new set of roles.[9] For instance, it was mentioned earlier that college students try to let their customers know who they are because they have discovered that the customers warm up to them in conversation and leave better tips.

Often, team solidarity and the self-enhancement of the waiters are further maintained through establishing sexual superiority over women guests who are higher in social status. Quite frequently a younger female guest and her children stay at the hotel during the week, while her husband returns to New York City to work until the weekend. While husband's away, the wife is free to play. Although it is true the waiter is in a subordinate position in the dining room, his sense of identity is not defined by him or by the guest by his occupational role, but by his being an upwardly mobile college student, and of potential sexual interest.

The redefinition of the service relation into a sexual one has great prestige value with one's teammates. This higher status external to his work can significantly influence social relations within the work structure. Thus, service employees always have anecdotes to tell about their alleged conquests.[10]

The frontstage staff sees the customer as the common enemy; hence, incidents occur in which the staff member must disguise his informal relations with the guest outside the dining room to be acceptable to his teammates. For example, I enjoyed playing chess with some of the older guests in the afternoon; I preferred this activity to playing basketball under the hot sun. However, I had to explain my actions by telling my teammates that I was after a larger tip. In fact, I had frequently to employ many forms of communication out of character with my new teammates, the older guests, in the presence of my fellow staff members, to make my true intentions known to the guests.

In this discussion of communication out of character we have seen that the performance given by a team is not a spontaneous, immediate response to the situation. Nor does the team's performance absorb all its energies and constitute their sole social reality. The following will emphasize the social sources of embarrassment which often result from unintended actions.[11]

A prime source of embarrassment is the unmeant gesture. This is defined as inadvertent acts which convey inappropriate impressions, as when a waiter who has just finished serving a party leans back, relaxes, and suddenly is shocked to attention by an unexpected shout from a guest. Another is the intrusion of a guest into the backstage. Imagine the reaction of the customer when he witnesses activity such as takes place in the backstage of the restaurant—the kitchen.

There are various techniques employed to handle the intrusion, but none of them are really effective. For instance, the performers may try to switch rapidly from their backstage performance to one that the intruder will feel is proper. Thus, the waiter will remove his fingers from the pudding he is sampling, the bread which has fallen on the floor will be placed in the garbage (only to be removed and used when the intruder leaves), the dirty dishes which have been only wiped clean and used are sent to the dishwasher to rewash, etc.

A technique infrequently used is to continue one's performance as if the intruder belonged, or to incorporate the intruder into some aspect of the performance which his definition of the situation would accept. This is never successful. A third technique is the one most frequently employed. This is simply to usher out the intruder as quickly as possible; he is told, quite unceremoniously, to stay out. His status on frontstage carries no weight in the kitchen.

A further source of embarrassment is the *faux pas*, the verbal statement or non-verbal act whose full significance is not appreciated by the individual who contributes it to the interaction. The *faux pas* jeopardizes the image self-projected by the team and the image which the restaurant wishes to project. An incident which occurred in one *shlockhaus* will serve to illustrate this. A busboy began setting up his station for the next meal before he finished serving all his guests. It had a rush effect on his guests. The management did not see him do it but his fellow staff members did. They told him that his actions were against the rules, that the policy of the hotel was that employees were part of a great organization and not part of a *shlockhaus*. His action, then, as observed by the guests was not compatible with the image which the hotel wished to project. Further, he hindered his own image by this careless act.

The final major form of performance disruption is called the scene. By creating a scene, an individual acts to threaten or destroy the polite appearance of consensus. While he may not act simply to create such dissonance, he usually does so with the knowledge that it will most likely result. A frequent type of scene which occurs is when one of the teammates can no longer take the other's inept performance and bursts into criticism in front of the audience. This misconduct is often devastating to the performance which the teammates wished to project. Thus, in the small resort hotel, no public disagreement between the team of waiter and busboy occurs in the dining room. If a busboy forgets an order, for example, the waiter suppresses his displeasure until after the meal or in the kitchen. Immediate public display would only disrupt the situation further and make the guests witnesses to a scene that should be reserved for the two of them only. Quarreling in front of the guests destroys not only their capacity to function efficiently, but also shatters the reality-order they present to the guests as close friends who work as an efficient team.

To prevent these major forms of performance disruption— unmeant gestures, inopportune intrusions, *faux pas,* scenes— and their consequences, the performers in the interaction must sustain certain attributes for saving the performance: loyalty, discipline, and circumspection.[12]

Loyalty is the defensive measure used by performers to save their own show. If the restaurant is to sustain its image its employees must act as if they have accepted certain moral obligations. The frontstage staff is usually disloyal to the management of the restaurant in order to further its own aims—better tips, for instance. They describe their working conditions and their treatment by the management in terms that make Simon Legree look a saint. It is hoped that the guests will be so moved by sympathy that they will increase the size of their tip. (Their pity frequently takes the form of smuggling out food from the dining room for the staff.) Regrettably, the management, to defend itself against such disloyalty, does not improve the existing working conditions. Instead, it tries to develop high in-group solidarity within the establishment, and to create an image of the customer sufficiently inhuman to allow the employees to cozen them with emotional and moral immunity.

The second attribute, discipline, means that the actor is able to show intellectual and emotional involvement in his performance, but must not allow himself to get carried away. Being carried away by his own performance may destroy his ability to sustain it. That is, the disciplined performer does not commit "unmeant gestures" or *faux pas.* He must also be able to suppress his emotional response to his private problems, to his teammate's mistakes, and to the audience when they arouse his hostility. The waiter who maintains his self-control in the above-mentioned situations does not jeopardize the image which he is trying to project, and thus does not jeopardize his tips.

We have seen that loyalty and discipline are attributes required of the actors if the performance they are putting on is to be sustained successfully. Circumspection is useful when the members of the team exercise foresight and design in determining how best to stage the performance. Obviously, if the management of the restaurant wishes to project a certain image, it must choose employees who are loyal and disciplined. In addition, the degree to which these attributes are possessed will markedly affect the likelihood of carrying off the performance. For these reasons, the owner of the *shlockhaus* hires for his frontstage staff "nice Jewish boys," just as the owner of the hash house hires waitresses from the same social background as the customers, and the owner of the high status restaurant hires waiters who show the proper respect for the clientele.

In addition to the three attributes of impression management, there is a counterpart in the tactful tendency of the audience and outsiders to act in such a way that they maintain the performers' projected image. For example, access to the back and front region is controlled not only by the performers, but by the audience as well. Thus, in one of the hotels I worked there were only two entrances to the dining room from the main lobby. One was through the kitchen, and the other was by going outside the building and crossing the lawn. On a rainy day, the majority of the guests preferred to "brave the elements" rather than walk through the back region. Those guests who did use the kitchen walked with their eyes straight ahead and thus saw as little of the back region as they could.

Another way in which the customer may show his tact is by "not seeing" a discrepancy between the fostered impression and a disclosed reality. Also, at moments of crisis for the waiter, the guests may come into tacit collusion with him in order to help him out. Thus, on a busy weekend the guests who are staying at the hotel for two or more weeks may tell the waiter to serve the weekenders first, so that he may get a better tip by giving them good service. A further display of tact occurs when the customer realizes that the waiter is a beginner and frequently shows extra consideration in refraining from the difficulties he might otherwise create.

In most cases the customers are tactful because they identify with the performers, or because they wish to avoid a scene. However, in some instances their motivation to act tactfully is to ingratiate themselves with the performers for purposes of exploitation. Thus, the guest who is staying at the hotel for a considerable time permits the waiter to serve the weekenders first because this will enable him to demand special service during the week. His second motive may be to rationalize the poor tip which he will give at the end of his stay by being so considerate of the waiter and busboy.

In conclusion, we may say that viewing the small resort hotel's dining room as a social establishment brings coherence out of what at first seems perceptual chaos. While it is true that man is a toolmaker, an organizer, a political creature, a rational-economic being, it is also true that he is primarily a meaning-creating, imaginative, and dramatic animal, and this is really what makes him worth studying. Even the *shlockhaus* can become a thespian's delight!

10

The Hustler*

Ned Polsky

In his book, Hustlers, Beats and Others, *in an essay entitled "Research Method, Morality and Criminology," Ned Polsky admonishes sociologists for having "copped out" of their responsibility to gain reliable data on the criminal world in the overuse of in-prison interviews of convicted criminals and in the heavy reliance on statistics, rather than direct observation of the criminal milieu. Poolroom hustling is a morally deviant occupation, and Polsky's portrait of it from the inside out therefore enables us to view hustlers on their own terms. It thus reflects a new emphasis on social problems, initially prompted by reflections on the moral transparency of the Prohibition era, which suddenly made deviants of many of us; that is, sociologists began to see the role that law and society itself played in creating deviance. Polsky's approach to the poolroom hustler treats his occupation like any other "normal" occupation in terms of the structure of work, required skills, on-the-job relationships, and the hurdles that must be overcome in the pursuit of a career.*

Ned Polsky is associate professor of sociology at the State University of New York at Stony Brook.

* Ned Polsky, "The Poolroom Hustler," *Social Problems*, Vol. 12 (Summer, 1964).

"Such and such a man spends all his life playing every day for a small stake. Give him every morning the money that he may gain during the day, on condition that he does not play—you will make him unhappy. It will perhaps be said that what he seeks is the amusement of play, not gain. Let him play then for nothing; he will lose interest and be wearied."—BLAISE PASCAL

"They talk about me not being on the legitimate. Why, lady, nobody's on the legit when it comes down to cases; you know that."—AL CAPONE[1]

The poolroom hustler makes his living, or tries to do so, by betting his opponents in various types of pool or billiard games; and as part of the playing and betting process he engages in various deceitful practices. The terms "hustler" for such a person and "hustling" for his occupation have been in poolroom argot for decades, antedating their application to prostitutes. Usually the hustler plays with his own money, but often he makes use of a "backer." In the latter event the standard arrangement is that the backer, in return for assuming all risk of loss, receives half of the hustler's winnings.

As a necessary and regular part of their work, hustlers break certain of America's generally agreed-upon moral rules, and because of this they are stigmatized by respectable outsiders. More knowledgeable outsiders see the hustler as one who violates an ethic of fair dealing, as a quasi-criminal who systematically "victimizes" people. Less knowledgeable outsiders (the large majority) regard hustlers as persons who, whatever they may actually do, certainly do not hold down respectable jobs; therefore this group also stigmatizes hustlers—"poolroom bums" is the classic phrase—and believes that society would be better off without them. Hustling, to the degree that it is known to the larger society at all, is classed with that large group of social problems composed of morally deviant occupations.

However, in what follows I try to present hustlers and hustling on their own terms. Insofar as I treat of problems, they are not the problems posed by the hustler but for him; not the difficulties he creates for others, but the difficulties that others create for him.

My approach is basically that of Everett Hughes to occupational sociology. In this paper I deal chiefly with questions about the work situation: How is the hustler's work structured? What skills are required of him? Whom does he interact with on the job? What does he want from them, and how does he try to get it? How do they make it easy or hard for him?

Previous Research

A bibliographic check reveals no decent research on poolroom hustling, sociological or otherwise. Apart from an occasional work of fiction in which hustling figures, there are merely a few impressionistic accounts in newspapers and popular magazines. With a couple of exceptions, each article is based on interviews with only one or two hustlers. No article analyzes hustling on any but the most superficial level, or even provides a well-rounded description. The fullest survey of the subject not only omits much that is vital, but contains numerous errors of fact and of interpretation.[2]

The desirability of a study of hustling first struck me upon hearing comments of people who saw the movie *The Hustler* (1961, rereleased spring, 1964). Audience members who are not poolroom habitués regard the movie as an accurate portrait of the contemporary hustling "scene." Now, the movie does indeed truly depict some social characteristics of pool and billiard hustlers and some of their basic techniques. But it neglects others of crucial importance. Moreover, the movie scarcely begins to take proper account of the social structure within which hustling techniques are used and which radically affects their use. *The Hustler* is a reasonably good but highly selective index of the poolroom hustling scene—as it existed not later than thirty years ago. And as a guide to today's scene—the terms on which it presents itself and on which the audience takes it—the movie is quite misleading.

Method and Sample

My study of poolroom hustling extended over eight months. It proceeded by a combination of: (a) direct observation of hustlers in action; (b) informal talks, sometimes hours long, with hustlers; (c) participant observation—as hustler, as his opponent, and as his backer. Since methods (b) and (c) drew heavily on my personal involvement with the poolroom world, indeed they are inseparable from it, I summarize aspects of that involvement below.

Billiard playing is my chief recreation. I have frequented poolrooms for over twenty years, and at one poolroom game, three-cushion billiards, am considered a far better than average player. In recent years I have played an average of more than six hours a week in various New York poolrooms, and played as much in the poolrooms of Chicago for most of the eight years I lived there. In the course of traveling I have played occasionally in the major rooms of other cities, on Market Street in San Francisco, on West 25th Street in Cleveland, and the room on 4th and Main in Los Angeles.

My social background is different from that of the overwhelming majority of adult poolroom players. The latter are of lower-class origin. As with many American sports (e.g., baseball), pool and billiards are played by teen-agers from all classes but only the players of lower-class background tend to continue far into adulthood. (Even at the teen-age level the lower class contributes a disproportionately large share of players.) But such differences—the fact that I went to college, do highbrow work, etc.—create no problems of acceptance. In most good-sized poolrooms the adult regulars usually include a few people like myself who are in the poolroom world but not of it. They are there because they like to play, and are readily accepted because of this.

The poolroom I play in most regularly is the principal "action room" in New York and probably in the country, where heavy betting on games occurs most often; sometimes, particularly after 1:00 A.M., the hustlers in the room well outnumber the non-hustlers. Frequently I play hustlers for money (nearly always on a handicap basis), and occasionally I hustle some non-hustlers, undertaking the latter activity primarily to recoup losses on the former. I have been a backer for two hustlers.

I know six hustlers well and during the eight months of the study I talked or played with over fifty more. All are now usually based in New York, except for two in Chicago, two in Cleveland, one in Philadelphia, and one itinerant hustler whose home base is in North Carolina. However, those based in New York are of diverse regional origins; almost a third grew up in other states, where their careers started.

It is not possible to demonstrate the representativeness of this sample because the universe (all United States pool and billiard hustlers) is not known exactly. But those I asked about the number of real hustlers in America, i.e., the number of people whose exclusive or primary occupation is hustling, generally agree that today the number is quite small. In response to my queries about the total number, one hustler said "thousands" and another said "there must be a thousand," but the next highest estimate was "maybe four hundred" and somewhat lesser estimates were made by nineteen others. Moreover, the three hustlers making the highest estimates have rarely been out of New York, whereas over half the others either come from different parts of the country or have made several road trips. It seems safe to assume that the sample is at least representative of big-city hustlers. Also, it is highly probable that it includes the majority of part-time hustlers in New York, and certain that it includes a good majority of the full-time hustlers in New York.

Poolroom Betting: The Structure of "Action"

Hustling involves betting one's opponent, by definition. But the converse is not true. The majority of poolroom games on which opponents bet do not involve any element of hustling. In order to understand how hustling enters the picture, one must first establish a perspective that encompasses all betting on poolroom games, hustled or not.

In pool or billiard games, the betting relationship has three possible modes: (1) player bets against player; (2) player(s) against spectator(s); (3) spectator(s) against spectator(s). In most games only the first mode occurs, but combinations of the first and second are frequent, and slightly less so are combinations of the first and third. Combinations of all three are uncommon, but do occur when there is more "ready action" offered to the player(s) than the player(s) can, or wish(es) to, absorb.

I have never seen the second mode occur alone, nor a combination of second and third. I have seen the third mode occur alone only twice—at professional tournaments. The betting relationship then involves the mode player-vs.-player, whatever additional modes there may be.

If two mediocre players are betting, say, upwards of $15 per game, and at another table two excellent players are playing for only a token amount, the first table will invariably draw many more people around it. The great majority of spectators, whether or not they bet much and whatever their own degree of playing skill, are attracted more by the size of the action than the quality of the performance. (A visiting Danish billiardist tells me this is not so in Europe, and also that betting on poolroom games is far less frequent than in America.)

There is an old American poolroom tradition that players should make some kind of bet with each other, if only a small one. This tradition remains strong in every public poolroom I know. (It is weak in the pool or billiard rooms of private men's clubs.) When one player says to another, "Let's just play sociable," as often as not he means that they should play "for the time" (the loser paying the check). It is only some of the newer and least skilled players who refuse to bet at all (want to "split the time"), and nearly always they rapidly become socialized to the betting tradition by a carrot-and-stick process—the stick being that it is often hard to get a game otherwise, the carrot that better players are always willing to give poorer ones a handicap (a "spot"). Most of the regular players will not even play for the check only, but insist on a little money changing hands "just to make the game interesting." The player who claims that just playing the game is interesting enough in itself is regarded as something of a freak.

Although few serious bettors (hustlers excepted) care for big action, nearly all (including hustlers) want fast action. They may not want to bet much per game, but they want the cash to change hands fairly quickly. Consequently, in an action room the standard games are redesigned for this purpose. Some are simply shortened: players gambling at snooker will remove all the red balls but one; or three-cushion billiard players will play games of 15, 20, or 25 points instead of the usual 30, 40, or

50. In straight pool (pocket billiards), where the standard game is 125 or 150 points, good players are usually reluctant to play a much shorter game because scoring is so easy—any good player can occasionally run more than 50 points—that shortening the game makes it too much a matter of chance. Therefore, in an action room one finds most of the pool players playing some variant of the game that requires high skill and minimizes luck, and that therefore can be short (takes only 5 to 20 minutes per game). Today the chief of these variants are "nine ball" and "one pocket" (also called "pocket apiece").

Every poolroom has at least one "No Gambling" sign on display, but no poolroom enforces it. The sign is merely a formal gesture for the eyes of the law (and in some cities required by law). It is enforced only in that the proprietor sometimes may ask players to keep payoffs out of sight—not to toss the money on the table after the game—if the room is currently heaty, e.g., if an arrest has recently been made there. Police are never really concerned to stop the gambling on poolroom games, and everyone knows it. (But police sometimes check to see that the minimum age law is observed, so proprietors will often ask youths for identification.) Betting is so taken for granted that in most poolrooms the proprietor—the very man who displays a "No Gambling" sign over his desk—will on request hold the players' stake money.

However, in no poolroom does the house take a cut of the action; i.e., the proprietor gets no fee for permitting gambling or holding stake money, and wouldn't dream of asking for one. His payment from bettors is simply that they comprise most of his custom (in equipment rental).[3] And hustlers, as he and they well know, count in this regard far beyond their numbers, for they play much oftener and longer than other customers; indeed, they virtually live in the poolroom.

Non-hustled Poolroom Gambling

Hustling is not involved when the games played for money are any of the following:

(a) Non-hustler vs. non-hustler. A "sociable" game in which

the bet is a token one. The only betting is player vs. player.

(b) Non-hustler vs. non-hustler. A game for significantly more than a token amount. The players play even-up if they are fairly equal. If they are aware of a significant difference in skill levels, the weaker player is given an appropriate handicap. Usually the betting is just between players; rarely, one or both players will bet spectators; spectators do not bet each other.

(c) Hustler vs. non-hustler. The players are aware of the difference in skills, and this is properly taken into account via an appropriate spot. Usually the betting is only player vs. player, though sometimes spectators bet players or each other. The hustler tries to avoid this type of game, and agrees to it only when he has nothing better to do.

(d) Hustler vs. hustler. Each player knows the other's mettle, if only by reputation ("Minnesota Fats" vs. "Fast Eddy" in *The Hustler,* for example). The hustler, contrary to the impression given by the movie, does not prefer this type of game (though he does prefer it to the foregoing type) and does not regard it as hustling. But he plays it frequently because he often can't get the kind of game he wants (a true "hustle"), and this alternative does offer him excitement—not only the greatest challenge to his playing skill, but the most actions. The average bet between two hustlers is much higher than in any other type of poolroom contest.[4] And the betting modes 2 and 3 (player vs. spectator, spectator vs. spectator) occur much more often.

Be that as it may, the hustler much prefers to hustle, which means to be in a game set up so as to be pretty much a sure thing for him, a game that "you're not allowed to lose" as the hustler puts it. In order to achieve this, to truly hustle, he engages in deception. The centrality of deception in pool or billiard hustling is perhaps best indicated by the fact that the poolroom hustler's argot originated that widespread American slang dictum, "Never give a sucker an even break."[5]

The Hustler's Methods of Deception

The structure of a gambling game determines what methods of deception, if any, may be used in it. In many games (dice, cards, etc.), one can deceive one's opponent by various techniques of cheating. Pool and billiard games are so structured that this method is virtually impossible. (Once in a great while, against a particularly unalert opponent, one can surreptitiously add a point or two to one's score—but such opportunity is rare, and usually involves risk of discovery that is judged to be too great; it seldom means the difference between winning and losing anyway, so no player counts on it.) One's every move and play is completely visible, easily watched by one's opponent and by spectators; nor is it possible to achieve anything via previous tampering with the equipment.

However, one structural feature of pool or billiards readily lends itself to deceit: on each shot, the difference between success and failure is a matter of a fraction of an inch. In pool or billiards it is peculiarly easy, even for the average player, to miss one's shot deliberately and still look good (unlike, say, nearly all card games, where if one does not play one's cards correctly this is soon apparent). On all shots except the very easiest ones, it is impossible to tell if a player is deliberately not trying his best.

The hustler exploits this fact, so as to deceive his opponent as to his (the hustler's) true level of skill (true "speed"). It is so easily exploited that, when playing good opponents, usually the better hustlers even disdain it, pocket nearly every shot they have (intentionally miss only some very difficult shots), and rely chiefly on related but subtler techniques of failure beyond the remotest suspicion of most players. For example, such a hustler may strike his cue ball hard and with too much spin ("english"), so that the spin is transferred to the object ball and the object ball goes into the pocket but jumps out again; or he may scratch (losing a point and his turn), either by "accidentally" caroming his cue ball into a pocket or by hitting his cue ball hard and with too much top spin so that it jumps off the table; or, most commonly, he pockets his shot but, by striking his cue ball just a wee bit too hard or too softly or with too much spin, he leaves himself "safe" (ends up with his cue ball out of position, so that he hasn't another shot). In such ways the hustler feigns less competence than he has.

Hustling, then, involves not merely the ability to play well, but also the use of a kind of "short con." Sometimes the hustler doesn't need to employ any con to get his opponent to the table, sometimes he does; but he always employs it in attempting to keep his opponent there.

The best hustler is not necessarily the best player among the hustlers. He has to be a very good player, true, but beyond a certain point his playing ability is not nearly so important as his skill at various kinds of conning. Also, he has to possess personality traits that make him "rocklike," able to exploit fully his various skills—playing, conning—in the face of assorted pressures and temptations not to exploit them fully.

The Hustler's Cardinal Rule

As the foregoing indicates, the hustler's cardinal rule is: don't show your real speed. Of course, an exception is permitted if by some miracle the hustler finds himself hustled, finds himself in a game with someone he thought would be easy but who turns out to be tough. But this is not supposed to happen, and it rarely does. For one thing, hustlers generally know each other, or of each other, and their respective skill levels. Second, any type of pool or billiard game is overwhelmingly a game of skill rather than luck—even in the chanciest type of poolroom game the element of skill counts for much more than in any card game whatsoever—and this means it is possible to rate the skill levels of various players (to "handicap" them) along small gradations with a high degree of accuracy. For example, if one has seen the three-cushion billiard players X and Y play various people over a period of time, it is possible to arrive at the judgment "On a 30-point game, X is 2 or 3 points better than Y" and to be dead right about it in at least eight out of ten contests between them.

The corollaries of the hustler's chief rule are: (a) He must restrain himself from making many of the extremely difficult shots. Such restraint is not easy, because the thrill of making a fancy shot that brings applause from the audience is hard to resist. But he must resist, or else it would make less believable his misses on more ordinary shots. (b) He must play so that the games he wins are won by only a small margin. (c) He must let his opponent win an occasional game.

It may be thought that once a hustler has engaged an opponent, a bet has been agreed upon and the stake money put up, and the game has started, the hustler might safely let out all the stops. This would be very shortsighted.

In the first place, as noted earlier, the typical non-hustler bets only a small amount on the game. The hustler's only hope of making real money, therefore, is to extend the first game into a series of games, entice his opponent into doubling up when he is behind, and so on. If he does this well, the opponent will hang on for a long time, may even come back after the first session to play him on another day, turn into a real "fish" (the poolroom term for an inferior opponent who doesn't catch on that he's outclassed and keeps coming back for more). And when the opponent starts demanding a spot, as sooner or later he will, the hustler can offer him his (the hustler's) average winning margin, or even a little better, and still have a safe game.

Secondly, there are spectators to take into account. Some of them will bet the hustler if he offers the non-hustler a seemingly fair spot. More importantly, some of them are potential opponents. Nearly all poolroom spectators are also players (except for the inevitable contingent of poor and lonely old men, who use the poolroom as a poor man's club). The hustler doesn't want to look too good to spectators either.

He knows that as he beats various opponents his reputation will rise, and that increasingly he'll have to offer spots to people, but he wants to keep his reputation as low as possible as long as possible with as many people as possible. He also knows that he has to play superbly on occasion—that he will play fellow hustlers when there's no other action around, and that then he must show more skill—but he wants to keep these occasions few. (It helps considerably, by the way, that because hustler-vs.-hustler games occur when hustlers give up hope of finding other action, these games usually take place after midnight when there aren't so many potential victims around to watch.)

The sooner everyone in the poolroom knows the hustler's true speed, the sooner he exhausts the real hustling possibilities among the room's regular players. Then, he either must move on to a room where he's less known or, if he stays in the room, has to take games he shouldn't take or else restrict his pickings to strangers who wander in.

Job-related Skills and Traits

Although the hallmarks of the good hustler are playing skill and the temperamental ability to consistently look poorer than he is, there are other skills and traits that aid him in hustling. Some are related to deceiving his opponent, some not.

Chief of these is argumentative skill in arranging the terms of the match, the ability to "make a game." The prospective opponent, if he has seen the hustler play, may when approached claim that the hustler is too good for him, or ask for too high a spot, i.e., one that is fair or even better than that. The hustler, just like the salesman, is supposed to be familiar with standard objections and with ways of overcoming them.

Another side of the ability to make a game reveals itself when the prospective opponent simply can't be argued out of demanding a spot that is unfair to the hustler, or can be convinced to play only if the hustler offers such a spot. At that point the hustler should of course refuse to play. There is often a temptation to do otherwise, not only because he is proud of his skill but because action is his lifeblood (which is why he plays other hustlers when he can't find a hustle), and there may be no other action around. He must resist the temptation. In the good hustler's view, no matter how badly you want action, it is better not to play at all than to play when you are disadvantaged; otherwise you are just hustling yourself. (But he often will, albeit with the greatest reluctance, agree to give a fair spot if that's the only way he can get action.)

The hustler, when faced, as he very often is, with an opponent who knows him as such, of course finds that his ability to make a game assumes greater importance than his ability to feign lack of skill. In such situations, indeed, his game-making ability is just as important as his actual playing ability.

On the other hand, he must have "heart" (courage). The *sine qua non* is that he is a good "money player," and can play his best when heavy action is riding on the game (as many non-hustlers can't). Also, he is not supposed to let a bad break or distractions in the audience upset him. (He may pretend to get rattled on such occasions, but that's just part of his con.) Nor should the quality of his game deteriorate when, whether by miscalculation on his part or otherwise, he finds himself much further behind than he would like to be. Finally, if it is necessary to get action, he should not be afraid to tackle an opponent whom he knows to be just about as good as he is.

A trait often working for the hustler is stamina. As a result of thousands of hours of play, all the right muscles are toughened up. He is used to playing many hours at a time, certainly much more used to it than the non-hustler is. This is valuable because sometimes, if the hustler works it right, he can make his opponent forget about quitting for such a "silly" reason as being tired, can extend their session through the night and into the next day. In such sessions it is most often in the last couple of hours, when the betting per game is usually highest, that the hustler makes his biggest killing.

Additional short-con techniques are sometimes used. One hustler, for example, entices opponents by the ancient device of pretending to be sloppy-drunk. Other techniques show more imagination. For example, a hustler preparing for a road trip mentioned to me that before leaving town he was going to buy a soldier's uniform: "I walk into a strange room in uniform and I've got it made. Everybody likes to grab a soldier."

Finally, the hustler—the superior one at any rate—has enough flexibility and good sense to break the "rules" when the occasion demands it; he will modify standard techniques when he encounters nonstandard situations. An example: Once I entered a poolroom just as a hustler I know, X, was finishing a game with non-hustler Y. X beat Y soundly, by a higher margin than a hustler should beat anyone, and at that for only $3. Y went to the bathroom, whereupon I admonished X, "What's the matter with you? You know you're not allowed to win that big." X replied: "Yeah, sure, but you see that motherfucking S . . . over there? [nodding discreetly in the direction of one of the spectators]. Well, about an hour ago when I came in he and Y were talking, and when S . . . saw me he whispered something to Y. So I had a hunch he was giving him the wire [tipping him off] that I was pretty good. And then in his middle game it looked like Y was stalling a little [missing deliberately] to see what I would do, so then I was sure he got the wire on me. I had to beat him big so he'll think he knows my top speed. But naturally I didn't beat him as big as I could beat him. Now he'll come back cryin' for a spot and bigger action, and I'll nail him." And he did nail him.[6]

The Art of Dumping

As we saw, the structure of a pool or billiard game makes it virtually impossible for the hustler to cheat his opponent. By "stalling" (deliberately missing some shots, leaving himself out of position, etc.) and by "lemoning" or "lemonading" an occasional game in the session (winning in a deliberately sloppy and seemingly lucky manner, or deliberately losing the game), the hustler keeps his opponent on the hook and entices him into heavier action, but such deception falls short of outright cheating. However, in examining betting we saw that there is considerable variation in the interpersonal superstructure of the game, i.e., that there are several possible types of betting relationships between and among players and spectators. One of these varieties does lead to outright cheating by the hustler—not cheating of his opponent, but cheating some spectators.

When two hustlers play each other, not only is the betting between players relatively heavy, but the betting of spectators against players is also, typically, at its height. Therefore, two hustlers sometimes will agree before their session that if, on any game, there is a good disparity between the amounts of action that each gets from spectators, the player with the most to gain from side bets with spectators will win the game and the players will later share the profits. The amount that spectators bet each other is of course irrelevant to such calculations; and in such circumstances the amount that the players bet each other auto-

matically becomes a phony bet, strictly for deluding the spectators.

For example, one such game I know of went as follows:
Hustler A played hustler B for $70. A's side bets with spectators
totaled $100, and B's side bets with spectators totaled $380.
Therefore A deliberately lost to B, paying him $70 and paying
$100 to spectators, with B collecting $70 from A and $380
from spectators. Later, in private, B gave A $310 (the $70 that
A had "lost" to B, the $100 that A had paid to the audience, plus
$140 or one-half the overall amount won from the audience).
Each player thus made $140 on the deal.

Sometimes the hustlers will set up the audience for such disparity in side betting, via previous games in the session. An
example: Hustler X played hustler Y for $20 per game. By pre-
arrangement, both players refused to make side bets with
spectators on the first three games, and player Y deliberately
lost the first three games. At the end of the third game Y became
enraged, claiming that bad breaks had beat him, that X was
just lucky, etc.; he raised his bet with X to $50 and also offered
to bet spectators. Naturally, he got lots of action from spectators
—and just as naturally he won the fourth game.

More commonly, however, such setting up does not occur.
Rather, the hustlers will agree before their session that they will
play each other in earnest and the bets between them will be real,
but that if there is a disparity in side betting with spectators on
a given game and one player gives the other a prearranged
signal (gives him "the office" as the hustler's argot has it), the
player with the most side action will win.

In the hustler's argot, the above type of deliberate losing is
called "dumping." It is always distinguished from "lemoning"
(where deliberate losing is strictly a means of conning one's
non-hustler opposing player). Though all hustlers use the verb
"to dump" in referring to a game that the hustler deliberately
loses for the purpose of cheating spectators, they vary in the object they attach to the verb. Some would say that the hustler who
lost "dumped the game," others that he "dumped to" his opponent, and others that he (or both players in collaboration)
"dumped the bettors." Some hustlers on occasion prefer a nomi-
nal use: "the game was a dump."

Because dumping involves outright cheating and could lead to serious, indeed violent, reprisals if discovered, it is the aspect of hustling that hustlers are most evasive about. A profession not merely has "open secrets" which only novices and outsiders don't know about, but, as Erving Goffman noted, also has "strategic secrets" which professionals often talk about among themselves but try to keep from outsiders, and "dark secrets" which professionals not only try to keep from outsiders but seldom talk about even with each other. Dumping falls in the "dark secret" category. No hustler likes to own up to dumping, even in talk with other hustlers. One learns about dumping indirectly, via hustlers' comments on other hustlers, hardly ever through a hustler's direct admission that he has engaged in it. It is my impression that such reticence is always pragmatic rather than moral, i.e., that no hustler has strong compunctions about dumping and that every long-time hustler has dumped at least on occasion.

Although dumping is a possibility whenever two hustlers playing each other make unequal amounts of side bets with spectators,[7] it actually occurs in only a minority of such situations, perhaps a sixth of them. For dumping is risky even when it is not literally discovered, i.e., sometimes the spectators' suspicions are aroused even though nothing can be proven; and hustlers can't afford to have this happen often, because it would kill their chances of side betting.

In this regard there are two kinds of spectator-bettors that the hustler distinguishes and takes into account. First, there are the ignorant majority who don't know about dumping; the hustler doesn't want talk, much less actual knowledge, of dumping to reach their ears. Second—and equally important to the hustler because, though they are in the minority, they bet more—there are some knowledgeable spectators (including other hustlers) who know about dumping but also know that it occurs in only a minority of hustler-vs.-hustler contests and therefore will often risk a bet. That is to say, just as some horse players assume that at certain tracks there probably will be one race per day that is fixed (one race "for the boys") and are willing to discount this because it's only one race out of eight or nine, similarly there are poolroom spectators who will bet on one hustler against another because they know that dumping occurs but seldom.

(Among the knowledgeable spectators there are also, of course, some cautious types who refuse to make such bets because of a possible dump, even though they know the odds are against it.)

In sum, the fact that spectators will be players in hustler-vs.-hustler games not only permits dumping but at the same time restrains the extent of it. Hustlers must severely limit their dumping, both to prevent it becoming known to the ignorant and, just as importantly, to prevent knowledgeable spectators from feeling that hustlers generally dump when they play each other. No one wants to get a reputation as a dumper; therefore he cautiously picks his spots. As a result, dumping provides only a small portion of his true hustling income, i.e., his "sure-thing" income. The great bulk of it derives from his games with non-hustler opponents.

The Hustler and His Backer

The hustler frequently uses a backer, who plays the losses if he loses and receives 50 percent of any winnings. Contrary to the movie, a backer hardly ever assumes any managerial function. All he does is put up the hustler's stake money in return for a half share in the profits.

Once in a very great while, a hustler will work out a standing agreement for backing, i.e., have someone agree to back him regularly. There is no time limit specified for such an arrangement; the deal lasts only as long as both parties consent to it.

But almost always—again contrary to the movie—the hustler has no standing agreement with a backer. Rather, he looks for backing on an *ad hoc* basis as the occasion for backing arises. The "occasion" is not that the hustler decides, in the abstract, to play on someone else's risk capital; it is a specific match with a particular opponent, whose handicap terms (if any) the hustler has already arranged or knows he can get. Indeed, even a top-notch hustler rarely can get backing without being able to tell the backer who the prospective opponent is and what the terms of the game are; he has to convince the backer that the particular deal is a good one.

After tentatively arranging a game with his opponent, he asks one of his acquaintances in the room to back him, and if he can't find backing in the room he phones a potential backer to hurry on down with some cash. Sometimes the hustler enters the poolroom with his backer in tow.

The backer specifies the maximum amount per game that he is willing to invest, but makes no guarantee about a total investment. That is, if the hustler starts to lose, the backer can pull out after any game. And if the hustler starts winning, he cannot then bet only his "own" money and dispense with the backer; the backer is in for 50 percent of the profit made on the entire session.

Under what conditions does the hustler seek a backer? The obvious answer is that when he is broke or nearly broke (as he very often is), he looks for backing, and when he has his own money to invest he plays with that. This is indeed how the average hustler operates. The superior hustler, however, figures more angles than that. As one of the most intelligent hustlers explained to me: "If you've got lockup action [a game impossible to lose] and you're broke or maybe you need a bigger stake, you should first try like hell to borrow the dough. It's crazy to cut somebody in on action like that unless you have to. The other big thing—what some of these jerks don't understand—is that when you have a real tough game you should always look for a backer, even if you've got the dough. You should take out insurance."

The backer, then, should not assume he is being approached for backing because the hustler can raise stake money no other way (though this is usually the case), but has to consider the possibility that it's because he has a very difficult game he wants to "insure."

Also, the backer must consider the possibility that he may be dumped: if the hustler is playing a colleague, they may have agreed that one of them will win the good majority of games and that they will later split the profits. (When both hustlers making such an agreement are using backers, the decision as to which hustler will lose is more or less arbitrary. If one is using a backer and the other is not, it is, of course, the former who agrees to lose.) Or, if he is playing a non-hustler with whom no such collusion is possible, he may deliberately lose on the backer's money until the backer quits, and then, after the backer has left the room or on some other occasion, the hustler playing with his own money will slaughter the opponent he has set up on the backer's money.

All in all, it takes as much sophistication to be a good backer as to be a good hustler.

The Hustler as Con Man

As several parts of this study illustrate in detail, hustling demands a continuous and complicated concern with how one is seen by others. Attention to this matter is an ineluctably pervasive requirement of the trade, and is beset with risks and contradictions. The hustler has not only the concerns that one ordinarily has about being esteemed for one's skills, but develops, in addition to and partly in conflict with such concerns, a complex set of special needs or desires about how others should evaluate him, reactions to their evaluations, and behavior designed to manipulate such evaluating.

The hustler is a certain kind of con man. And conning, by definition, involves extraordinary manipulation of other people's impressions of reality and especially of one's self, creating "false impressions."[8] Now, if one compares the hustler with the more usual sorts of con men described by David Maurer in *The Big Con,* part of his specialness is seen to lie in this: the structural contexts within which he operates—the game, the setting of the game within the poolroom, the setting of the poolroom within the larger social structure—are not only more predetermined but more constraining. Structures do not "work for" the poolroom hustler to anywhere near the extent that they often do for other con men, and hence he must involve himself in more personal ways with active, continuous conning.

The point is not simply that the hustler can't find an ideal structural context, but that much less than the ordinary con man is he able to bend a structure toward the ideal or create one *ab ovo* (come up with an analogue of the con man's "store").

That is, he is far less able to be a "producer" or "director" of ideal social "scenes." To a much greater degree he must work in poor settings, and to a correspondingly greater degree he must depend on being a continuously self-aware "actor."[9] (In this connection, note the ease with which many passages of this essay could be restated in dramaturgical or Goffmanical terms.)

The nature and degree of the hustler's concern about the evaluation of him by another person vary, of course, with the specific kind of "other" that the person represents. For the hustler the three main types of significant others are: outsiders, intended or actual victims, and colleagues. His shifting concerns about each group relate not only to particular work situations but to his general life style and career line.[10]

11

Life in the Colonies:
Welfare Workers and Clients[*]

Glenn Jacobs

In recent years the notion "subculture of poverty" has achieved wide currency. In fact, where once the invisibility of our poor was considered problematical, the opposite may now be true. The danger of concepts such as subculture lies in the fact that they overgeneralize about the realities they attempt to describe. As they become incorporated into the policies and procedures of decision-making men and organizations, they finally lose whatever descriptive value they had and instead take on the coloring of their new environment. The career of the concept of subculture, then, has traveled the route from troubleshooting to "reification"; that is, with respect to the issue of poverty, the notion has outlived its utility as an identifier and instead has objectified the phenomenon beyond the bounds of reality. This paper describes some aspects of the day-to-day operation

[*] Glenn Jacobs, "The Reification of the Notion of Subculture in Public Welfare," *Social Casework*, vol. 49 (November, 1968), pp. 527–34.

*of an urban welfare center. It focuses on the roles and con-
flicting social personalities shown by the caseworker as he
tries to manage the different forces impinging on him in
his work. In addition, the worker is seen as a mediator of
the leveling effects of the gigantic welfare apparatus on the
poor, an apparatus which actually creates a poverty subculture that it was designed to eradicate.*

Nowadays the social scientist is likely to include in his con-
ceptual toolbox the notion of subculture. Although the term subculture is used to denote a sociologically acceptable concept,
it has been assimilated into the *lumpensociologese*—to coin an
expression—of popular literature. Traditionally, social scientists
agree that a subculture is "a sub-division of a national culture,
composed of a combination of factorable social situations, such
as class status, ethnic background, regional and rural or urban
residence, and religious affiliation, but forming in their combination a functioning unity which has an integrated impact on the
participating individual."[1]

By examining the social-psychological dynamics of the interplay between the poor people in our society and the representatives of a middle-class social order—the public agency
bureaucracy—I shall attempt[2] to demonstrate that a pseudo-
subculture, which fosters dependency and functions as a self-
fulfilling prophecy, has been created. The data, although
impressionistic, were culled from my own experience as a caseworker in the New York City Department of Welfare (now the
Department of Social Services) from March, 1965, to July, 1966.

The Uses of the Subculture Concept

Because the connotations of the term subculture vary to a
great extent, a review of some of the uses of the concept seems
to be an essential preliminary step in establishing the thesis of
this article.

In recent decades, the term subculture has achieved wide

currency in the study of deviant behavior, especially juvenile delinquency. Albert K. Cohen defines it as a shared means of adjustment within "a community of individuals."[3] Cohen's interpretation of the concept is not novel, however, either in sociology or in the study of juvenile delinquency. It is implicit in Frederick M. Thrasher's work on the emergence of gang action as a response to the opposition of the conventional social order.[4] The adjustive aspect of subculture is also apparent in the phenomenological perspectives on deviance advanced by Howard S. Becker and others.[5]

Educated laymen and "applied sociologists" interpret the concept in an unscientific manner, that is, as a tool of identification used by social practitioners in what Richard Korn designates the "human service bureaucracies."[6] It has become, in fact, an integral part of the process of labeling social problems and, as such, tends to simplify the problems myopically. The simplification is part of the groundwork for facilitating the flow of funds through public agencies. In the final analysis, however, it provides a functional *raison d'être* for the bureaucracies. As used, the concept enables the bureaucrats to define policy for the staff and the administrative personnel of public welfare agencies, and to focus on the bureaucracy's objectives in regard to segments of an individual client's situation or local "community" problems. C. Wright Mills suggests that the inability of "social pathologists" to escape conservative particularism represents a "cultural lag" that may actually create problems. "The aim to preserve rurally oriented values and stabilities," he states, "is indicated by the implicit model which operates to detect urban disorganization; it is also shown by the stress upon community welfare. The community is taken as a major unit, and often it sets the scope of concern and problematization."[7] This condition, especially within the public welfare agency, is derived partly from a confused democratic-liberal idealism and partly from the intrinsic mechanics of the large-scale bureaucratic setup. The idealism stems from a common-sense notion of the "medical model of the social expert."[8] The medical analogy was drawn from the apparent efficiency with which medical institutions tackle public health problems and has led to proposed "injunctions against self-prescription by the patient and unauthorized treatment by the unqualified."[9]

Inherent in such an ethos of expertise is the anticipation of the time when the social work practitioner, like his medical and public health counterparts, will confidently "deal with . . . (the citizen's) personal and social problems."[10] As Korn suggests, the resultant structure would be based on control rather than the humanistic "enlargement of men's powers of self-realization."[11] Obviously, the direction of such an approach, especially in regard to poor people, is toward the development of a "colonialist" social attitude focusing on the relationships between caretakers and natives. In the colonial nations, now called the Third World, this attitude fostered a reaction that may be called a mass dependency syndrome. In our society, particularly in large urban areas in which racially and ethnically distinct ghettos exist, a similar phenomenon is emerging.

Clearly, an orientation to social problems based on a medical analogy carries the implication that poor people, because of their poverty subculture, are the locus of infection—poverty. Moreover, the orientation often results in the facile juggling of labels.

Lewis A. Coser and Bernard Beck and other writers who follow Georg Simmel's masterful analysis of poverty as a social or moral category that emerges through societal definition include the poor person as an object of sociological inquiry among other phenomena called deviant behavior.[12] Apart from the economic indices of poverty, the most significant sociological index, in Coser's view, is the assignment of a person, through the granting of public assistance, to the category of the poor. Such classification, he declares, is accomplished by means of a degrading initial and continuing investigation carried out by caseworkers to determine the person's eligibility for assistance. Limitations are thus imposed on the rights and prerogatives of poor people in maintaining the distinctions between private and public life. In addition, Coser sees the professionalization of welfare work as a neutralizing factor that removes the element of mutual personal responsibility from the worker-client relationship.[13] As a result, the client's position becomes one of unilateral dependence.

For describing the worker-client relationship, A. M. Lee's concept of group culture is more useful than the subculture concept, since it retains the critical notion of adjustment while dispensing with the encumbrance of a notion that has become part of organizational ideology. The group culture concept is more relativistic and therefore more scientifically effective. In addition, retention of the subculture idea (ideology) necessarily leads to confusion between a concept of subculture, so-called, and a theory describing a pseudo-phenomenon, which is what the oversimplified idea of poverty is.

The Bureaucratic Group Culture

The welfare agency's dealings with a client reveal consistent indications of a prototypical parent-child relationship. The roots of the interaction are to be found in the goals, policies, and procedures of the agency bureaucracy; the ambiguous and conflicting aspects of the worker's role; and the isolated and dependent social position of the client.

In the main, the public welfare agency's contact with the client is sustained through the worker-client interactions. Virtually all major policy decisions concerning clients are therefore mediated, if not determined, by the worker. Except for the reports of the agency, and the city hospitals, the information that is compiled about a client is almost entirely the product of the worker's communications. The bulk of the case record is composed of the worker's reports of visits and other communications with the client, and the decisions that are based on his and his superiors' evaluations of data on the client's social, medical, occupational, and legal history. The record, therefore, may be seen to reflect the individual worker's orientation toward the client and, indirectly, the agency's. In a sense, the worker functions as the conveyor of images. He is a selective reporter whose biases and judgments determine the extent and kind of information the agency receives concerning the client. Similarly, the client's view of the agency is largely derived from his perceptions of the worker as its official representative.

The Socialization Process

Because the worker acts as the contact between the two social spheres, his role in the agency and his role with the client are often in conflict and are reflected in a confusion of social personalities that the worker must assume in making his occupational life comfortable. As the worker sees it, in order to keep his relationships on an even keel in either realm, he must potentially jeopardize good diplomacy in the other.

In the face of often contradictory demands, he must do some fancy ground-shifting to preserve the tricky balance he strikes between the bureaucratic and the client-centered realms. In doing so, the worker, especially the novice caseworker, "learns the ropes." He acquires a variety of techniques for short-cutting procedure and for holding the client at bay so that the complications of his role within a gigantic organization may be minimized.

At first sight, the job appears to involve simply the acquisition of necessary information and skills in order to perform formally outlined duties. In reality, the completion of an assigned task (not to mention a service that is unaccounted for or disapproved by procedure) entails circumvention of the bureaucratic system. The caseworker is placed in the paradoxical position of having to abide by rules and at the same time bypass them. He resolves the dilemma by appearing to follow the rules while actually violating them, either with the knowledge and consent of the "rulers" or without their knowledge. As a caseworker, I observed administrators in relatively high positions violate important rules concerning emergency funds without apparent uneasiness, despite the fact that I, a caseworker who was bound by the rules, was present. Because the majority of the procedures are related to the daily functions of the caseworker, rule-breaking is naturally more overt among the caseworkers but is, nevertheless, prevalent at all levels. Whether the worker's "wheeling and dealing" is fully known to his superiors is a moot point. It seems likely, in view of the fact that most administrators were once workers.

Rule-breaking is an important part of the socialization process for the worker. An experienced worker is often evaluated by his colleagues and superiors on the basis of his speed in accomplishing procedural shortcuts. Such work-saving efforts often involve delicate maneuvering to obtain supervisory approval of grants and client services without the requisite clerical work. The workers pridefully refer to such maneuvering as "sneaking it under the supervisor's nose." A newly appointed supervisor may be expected to return the request marked "incomplete." Although aware that the worker has tried to put something over on him, he is usually not angered; rather he takes a sort of comical pride in his own slyness. Such interaction frequently involves good-natured banter, with the supervisor playing the sly old fox and the worker, the precocious young pup. The experienced supervisor, on the other hand, may be expected to look the other way in the face of the worker's antics. His long experience has immunized him against all hope of keeping the cards honest (or bureaucratically regular), and too often he resorts to similar trickery in coping with his superior, the case supervisor.

Despite the fact that such informal flouting of procedure is widespread, officials are keenly sensitive to the public and the press. A supervisor frequently cautions a worker to give in to a client's demands after the client has gone over the worker's head and issued a complaint to the central office, even though the demand may be unreasonable or contrary to policy. The advice is based on a bureaucratic administrator's fear of public exposure of the agency's backstage behavior. Edgar May, a critic of current public welfare programs, recounts an incident in which the details of a case were kept secret under the cloak of professional confidentiality:

In New Jersey, while I was discussing a welfare problem case with the local commissioner, he cautioned me not to use the details even though the family could not be identified. "You know, good casework is not to talk about a family's problems unless you can help them," he said. . . .

Occasionally, confidentiality is used not to hide the failure of the relief recipient from public view but rather to hide the failure of the welfare department. All-purpose confidentiality of this sort is simple censorship and is contrary to the public interest.[14]

Korn defines this issue more abstractly:

When and if the young professional persists in questioning why his colleagues do not more vehemently and urgently communicate their problems to the public, he very quickly is confronted with his second major disillusionment. He learns that his colleagues, though quite aware of their own ineffectuality, are quite opposed to sharing this awareness with the public. . . . If public confidence is undermined, the security and prestige of the profession will be endangered.[15]

It is interesting to note the response to a situation in which a novice embarrasses the organization. For example, a welfare union magazine published an article I had written describing much of the informal functioning of the welfare department.[16] One might expect that such exposure would arouse the ire of workers and administrators. In fact, the only response was silence. The bureaucracy thus covers up its embarrassment by means of the subtle social-control mechanism of disregarding dissent.

The newly recruited welfare caseworker often has high ideals, but he lacks training in social science or social work, since the only educational prerequisite for the position is a college degree. Once the facts of agency life are revealed, he either stubbornly fights for his principles or succumbs to established practice and relinquishes hope of maintaining the awareness that comes with dissent. If he chooses the latter course, he follows the "line" of the department and the unions. Although opposed to much of the welfare department's policy and procedure, the union representatives almost invariably confine their complaints to wage disagreements and focus their attention on the building of professionalism.

The experience of a trainee with whom I had contact illustrates one way in which the worker is taught the rules. The trainee's shortcomings had been discussed at a meeting, and he had accepted the criticism. He subsequently learned that a colleague was asked by the senior case supervisor for an evaluation of him. The colleague had replied, "He's young and idealistic and wants to help people." The supervisor's response was, "Well, please tell him what the story is!" Knowing the "story" means keeping one's ideals to oneself and includes the so-called uplifting of the client as this is defined on paper. The ideals are permitted to exist only as polite fiction, providing grist for the public relations mill. The "story" means one must perform the everyday functions, whether legitimate or otherwise, in a manner that is no secret to anyone who keeps his eyes open. Witness the myth of services —the matching of ambiguously defined case problems with equally ambiguous services supposedly performed by the worker. Although a large part of his function is supposed to embrace this area, the worker is never given an adequate schedule of agency procedures. Instead, he receives an elaborate code of instructions for recording services he never really performs. The deception has grown out of the need to fulfill the terms of the reimbursement procedure of the federal and state agencies. In order to receive reimbursement for funds paid out, the city has to prove that the specified services were performed. Korn describes the effect of the deceit on the "human service functionary":

> It is in the course of grasping these relationships that the human service functionary must cope with the severest disillusionment of all: The knowledge that the organization can survive only at the expense of systematically betraying the responsibilities it was designed to fulfill. If he is a policeman, the functionary must live with the knowledge that the largest single category of persons systematically and daily violating the law are his fellow policemen. If he is a mental-health worker, he must accept the fact that the largest single aggregate of persons engaged in the daily mistreatment of the mentally ill are his fellow employees at the mental hospital. If he is a correctional specialist, he must work with the awareness that prisons, reformatories, and training schools constitute society's most comprehensively organized and effective means for preventing rehabilitation. If he is a welfare worker, he must work with the realization that neither the landlord nor the loan-shark can compete with the relief agency in its readiness to crush the souls of the poor.[17]

Although the worker receives ample instruction in the intricacies of bureaucratic procedure, he is given little preparation in working with the persons who should be of primary importance —the welfare recipients. He is taught little more than an interviewing technique or two and a mulch of common-sense approaches to the determination of financial eligibility that are more suitable to police and detective work. Consequently, he must rely on his own inappropriate knowledge, compiled from his own experience and from witnessing the actions of subordinates and superiors, the helpers and the helped, and the exploiters and the vanquished, to enable him to cope with clients. Since his experiences are probably limited to his interpersonal relationships in childhood, adolescence, and college, it is no wonder that the peculiar game he plays with his clients takes on characteristics that are very different from those normally expected in a therapeutic relationship.

The bureaucratic structure further complicates the welfare worker's role by placing him in a position of continually compromising himself before the client. The other reality, the field, is the world in which the worker must make excuses for the effects of bureaucracy on the client. Much of the worker's time, therefore, is spent in justifying his actions, for his commitments to the agency and client are often at odds.

The welfare worker has the added disadvantage of occupying the lowest rank among popular conceptions of the professions. Moreover, large discrepancies exist between the unions' conception of his occupation and what he actually believes it to be. The unions have been preoccupied with the obsession of "professionalizing" his role. In New York City, the change in Civil Service title from social investigator to caseworker was met with wry comments. Such title-granting is reminiscent of the proliferation of vice-presidents in large corporations. Titles, in this context, are merely overstated status symbols that are bereft of power and prestige.

Signs of Change

Not long ago several strikes were conducted by schoolteachers and social welfare caseworkers—the caretakers of the ghetto. The strikes were particularly meaningful because they involved more than mere wage demands; they were aimed at achieving improved conditions of work and role clarification. The strikes embarrassed the officialdom because they had the flavor of exposés. They bring to mind Lee Rainwater's clarification of E. C. Hughes's conceptualization of "good people and dirty work,"[18] for, as Hughes would contend and Rainwater does, strikers are perceived as threatening the solidarity of the group. The striking teachers and caseworkers, most of whom are middle-class white persons, had been mandated by society, perhaps unknown to themselves, to deal with categories of people socially insulated from the rest of society by barriers of social distance. It is reasonable to speculate that the time must come when the professional in such a situation is faced with an occupational identity crisis—when he realizes, for example, that as a teacher in a ghetto school he is functioning only as a disciplinarian and that no learning is going on in his classroom, or that as a caseworker he is functioning in the capacity more of a manipulator or fixer than of a social worker. It is at this point that, collectively, he strikes or, distributively, he quits, rebels, or accepts his identification and becomes co-opted into the system.

The Worker-Client Group Culture

The earlier analogy to the colonialist approach is useful in understanding the social-psychological dynamics of the worker-client relationship in the public welfare agency. O. Mannoni's analysis of social conditions in Madagascar provides valuable insights into the psychological aspects of colonialism.[19] In a similar vein, Frantz Fanon depicts the creation of the native character type out of the Third World substratum, a type similar to our own Uncle Tom.[20] Mannoni notes that the native, in typical fashion, seldom expresses thanks for gifts and handouts from the colonialist. "The gifts which the . . . (native) first accepts, then asks for, and finally, in certain rare cases, even demands, are simply the outward and visible signs of . . . (the) reassuring relationship of dependence," which has become the native's mode of adjustment. "They are essential to what might be called the life of the relationship."[21] The natives' dependency needs are complemented by the European colonialist's culturally induced will for power, stemming from a culturally conditioned inferiority complex.[22]

In more formally sociological terms, Barry Schwartz notes in his analysis of the exchange of gifts that the process acts as a means of development and maintenance of identity and as a mode of social control.[23] In regard to the debate about whether public assistance grants should be made in the form of cash or goods, he observes:

Social workers are more prone to argue in favor of the former alternative, often on the basis of its implications for the psychological autonomy of the recipient. Opponents of this policy argue that the presentation of money severely limits the welfare department's band of control, for cash may be spent on disapproved commodities. Its abstractness dissolves the authority of the giver, which is inherent in concrete terms.[24]

The dependency relationship of the worker and the client takes the form of a game. Each seeks to manipulate the other in the hope of gaining either personal or material rewards. The worker's rewards are largely personal and the client's, material. For the client, personal rewards are of secondary importance. The worker, on the other hand, gains most of his satisfaction by maneuvering himself into a position in which he, like his colonialist counterpart, sees his role as that of a philanthropist or, more overtly, as a symbol of authority. Since the only area in which the worker can exercise a recognizably controlling influence is in his contact with clients, he must make the most of it, especially in demonstrating his power before his peers. Inevitably, therefore, the sound of a worker shouting down a client during a telephone conversation is heard in a welfare center. One welfare worker was faced with an embarrassing situation during a home visit when the client's child asked him why he sounded so different on the telephone. She referred, of course, to the contrast between the authoritative "telephone voice" and the subdued and personal face-to-face manner.

The tactics used by the clients and the workers in pursuit of their objectives are quite apparent. A client's letter appearing in a New York City Department of Welfare magazine contains a list of methods used by workers "to accomplish the deprivation of our families." The methods are "indirect answers, intended to confuse; negative answers and demeaning attitudes, in order to discourage; eventual allowing of a 'skinned down to the bone' version of the original request, if one is persistent enough; . . . intimidation, if one is not appropriately grateful."[25]

Although the client is obviously partial, and it is impossible to agree that the "methods" are used as simply as she imputes, the list itself may be construed as the automatic responses of the worker in his self-defense game with the client. It also represents the stratagems used by the worker in coping with obligations that, in many cases, are impossible to fulfill. In general, the strategies and ready responses of the client are not unlike those used by children to wangle something out of a parent: persistent requests, angry threats and demands, temper tantrums, and cajolery.

Such techniques are not used at the outset of the relationship, but their use follows a predictable pattern. The new client may begin by stating his request in a reasonable and adult manner, and the worker may record it without suspicion or tongue-in-cheek agreement. Eventually, however, the huge amount of prescribed clerical work and the multiplicity of client requests prevent the worker from attending to the requests, and he is compelled to make excuses to the client. In time, the client's next move is to ask for more than he hopes to receive eventually. At this stage of the relationship, all the maneuvers and responses have come into play, but no resolution of the problems is brought about; the worker never catches up, and the client has additional needs. Moreover, the worker sees the client as a swindler, and the client sees the worker as a begrudging, authoritarian miser. By the time the worker is assigned a new case, or the client a new worker, the previous experience of each has already led to a stereotype of the other. The final effect is a self-reinforcing sedimentation of attitudes and practices that is transmitted from generation to generation of workers and clients.

Although this kind of relationship emerges as an effort on the part of both clients and workers to make their association more understandable and predictable, it evolves into a relationship based on deception and the dehumanization of the other person.

By refusing to become part of the efforts of society to keep the poor people invisible, the "dirty workers" have brought all the elements of the poverty "problem" to the fore. If their strikes are interpreted as danger signals or warnings, as they should be, social reconstruction seems possible. Such reconstruction is hampered, however, by the adherence to a subculture concept that views poverty as an intrinsic, centripetal phenomenon. And if, as Robert A. Scott points out with respect to welfare policies in dealing with the blind, "programs of services . . . are often more responsive to the organizational needs of agencies . . . than they are to . . . (client) needs,"[26] then we must, indeed, view the so-called subculture of the poor as a pseudo-conception.

If the subculture concept is to be used appropriately, it must be based on the understanding that poverty in society is a social status that emerges from the processes of labeling and the leveling effects of large bureaucratic organizations. The result is a phenomenon strikingly similar to the "third culture" anthropologists speak of in referring to much of the underdeveloped world, or more critically, a variant of "neocolonialism," a term used by the militant denizens of the Third World. Not intending to smack of political agitation, I would insist that such an analogy transcends the limits of mere metaphor. The existence and ministrations of the welfare bureaucracy reinforce dependency and make "it possible for people to enter welfare careers without feeling a moral burden in doing so."[27] The urban ghetto, then, is a "primary mechanism by which persons . . . could find themselves mutually reinforcing one another and mutually legitimating the pursuit of such a career."[28] Indeed, the conditions for an internal colonialism are thereby set, for as Rosenberg maintains in the case of Mexican migrants:

The Mexican sites are deliberately placed outside city limits in inconspicuous places, on unbeaten paths where they are not likely to be seen. This practice does not materially differ from that of the Nazis who threw a sop to the public conscience by hiding concentration camps. People are encouraged to wear blinders and thus to develop a kind of tunnel vision. Whether one chooses to see it or not, this nasty business is . . . internal colonialism. . . . But, "The difference between the traditional and the new colonialism is that our colonial natives are kept with us within distance when we want them. . . ."[29]

12

A Field Experience in Retrospect[*]

Elliot Liebow

An account of the participant observer's subjective involvement in his fieldwork is as valuable as the rest of his observations. Several books have already appeared which deal with the methodology of participant observation. It is to be hoped that this livening of interest will not be reduced to formulas, for the methodology of participant observation realizes itself in the career of the fieldworker, blends in with his experience, and thus shares in the individuality of the study itself. Elliot Liebow's reminiscences about his work, which culminated in the modern sociological classic, Tally's Corner, *yields a fruitful record of one man's drift into his fieldwork career.*

Elliot Liebow is chief of the special projects section, Mental Health Center, National Institute of Mental Health.

* "A Field Experience in Retrospect," in Elliot Liebow, Tally's Corner (Boston: Little, Brown and Co., 1967). See also footnote 1.

Robert read the book slowly and with feeling, pausing only occasionally to take a swig of gin and chase it quickly with some beer. Lonny listened quietly and watched with blinking eyes as Robert changed his voice for each of the characters, assuming a falsetto for Snow White. But my own interest started to wander, probably because I had already read the book and seen the movie.

Suddenly Robert raised his voice and startled me back into attention. I looked at Lonny—placid, eye-blinking Lonny—and at Ronald—a handkerchief around his head and a gold earring stuck in his left ear making him look like a storybook pirate—and wondered what the hell I was doing there with these two guys, drinking gin and beer and listening to *Snow White and the Seven Dwarfs*.

I thought back to the events leading up to this situation. From this perspective, everything looked normal and reasonable. I retrieved my can of beer, sat back and listened to the rest of the story. Robert gave it a damn fine reading.

(Field Note, April, 1962)

Background

When I came to the Child Rearing Study Project on January 1, 1962, this NIMH-supported study of "Child Rearing Practices Among Low Income Families in the District of Columbia" was well into its third year. My job was to collect field material on low-income adult males to complement the data already secured through family interviews.

From the very beginning I felt comfortable with the prospect of working with lower-class Negroes. I was born and raised in Washington, D.C. My father and mother were both Jewish immigrants from Eastern Europe—my mother from Latvia, my father from Russia. My father was a grocer, and we lived in rooms above or behind the various stores which he operated. All were in predominantly Negro neighborhoods.

School and playground were white, but all of our customers and most of the neighbors were Negroes. Among them and their children I had many acquaintances, several playmates, and a few friends. The color line, retraced daily at school and playground and home, was always there; but so were my day-by-day contacts with Negro men, women, and children in the store, on the street, and occasionally in their houses; watching a crap game in Sam's place; witnessing the Devil being exorcised from a woman writhing on the floor of a storefront church from my seat in the back row; shooting crap for pennies in a dark hallway; sitting with Benton on the curb, poking aimlessly at debris, waiting for something interesting to happen. It was not until I was seventeen and enlisted in the Marine Corps that I began to move in an almost exclusively white world.

Preparing for the Field

I spent the first week familiarizing myself with the project and with the work that had already been done. I had several informal discussions with Dr. Hylan Lewis, the director of the project, and gradually gained a feeling for the kind of material that was wanted. It was significant that he laid down no hard-and-fast ground rules on the assumption that the job could best be done if I were free to feel my way around for a few weeks and discover for myself the techniques that were most congenial to me. His one prescription was that the work be securely anchored in the purposes of the project, remembering, too, that "everything is grist for our mill." As I think back on this now, I see a clear connection between his instructions and his fondness for the quotation, "The scientific method is doing one's darndest with his brains, no holds barred."

Having partially digested the project literature, I told the director that I was ready to get started. He suggested a neighborhood that might be "a good place to get your feet wet." His instructions were: "Go out there and make like an anthropologist."

"Out there" was not at all like the Indian village of Winisk on Hudson Bay in which I had done field work. I was not at all sure how one "makes like an anthropologist" in this kind of "out there." Somewhat wistfully, perhaps, I thought how much neater things would be if anthropologists, as they had done in the early thirties, limited themselves to the study of "wholes," a tribe, a village, or some other social unit with distinct boundaries and small enough to be encompassed in its entirety by direct observation.

When I thought about just what I was going to do, I kept in mind the job Richard Slobodin had done for the Child Rearing Study in the summer of 1960.[2] As part of the effort to get at community as well as family influences on child rearing, the director had assigned Slobodin to "make like an anthropologist" in a one-block enclave in northwest Washington. It seemed to me that I could use his work as a model and, in the course of a year, produce several such studies, each covering a strategic part of the world of the low-income male. I thought of doing a neighborhood study, then moving on, say, to a construction laborers' union, then a bootleg joint, and perhaps rounding these out with a series of genealogies and life histories. I was going to give myself about a month or so of poking around town, getting the feel of things, before committing myself to any firm plan of action.

In the Field

In taking up the director's suggestion that this would be "a good place to get your feet wet," I went in so deep that I was completely submerged and my plan to do three or four separate studies, each with its own neat, clean boundaries, dropped forever out of sight. My initial excursions into the street—to poke around, get the feel of things, and to lay out the lines of my field work—seldom carried me more than a block or two from the corner where I started. From the very first weeks or even days, I found myself in the middle of things; the principal lines of my field work were laid out, almost without my being aware of it. For the next year or so, and intermittently thereafter, my base of operations was the corner Carry-out across the street from my starting point.

The first time out, I had gone less than one short block when I noticed a commotion up the street. A man—Detective Wesley, I learned later—was dragging a kicking, screaming woman to a police call box. A small crowd had gathered on each of the four corners to watch. I approached two men and asked what the woman had done. Both were uncertain. The younger of the two said that he had heard two stories and proceeded to tell me both of them, concluding with the observation that he had known Detective Wesley for six or seven years and that he was "nobody to fool with."

I said that sometimes being a cop seems to do something to a man. This led to a discussion of policemen and each of us contributed personal experiences or anecdotes on the subject. After ten or fifteen minutes of this, the older man said good-bye and walked off. The younger man stayed on. Across the street from where we were standing was the Downtown Café. I suggested that we go in and have some coffee and he agreed. As we walked across the street he asked if I was a policeman. I told him no and explained that I was working on a study of family life in the city. There was no more discussion about who I was or why I was there. We sat at the bar for several hours talking over coffee.

I had not accomplished what I set out to do, but this was only the first day. And, anyway, when I wrote up this experience that evening, I felt that it presented a fairly good picture of this young man and that most of the material was to the point. Tomorrow, I decided, I would go back to my original plan—nothing had been lost.

But tomorrow never came. At nine the next morning, I headed down the same street. Four men were standing in a group in front of the Carry-out.

Three were winos, in their forties—all marked with old scars on face and neck, dressed shabbily, but sober. The fourth was a man of thirty-two or thirty-three, who looked as if he had just stepped out of a slick magazine advertisement. . . . One of the winos had a month-old puppy stuck in the front of his overcoat. Only the dog's head was exposed.

The group approached me and one of the older men said, "Isn't he a nice puppy?" I said yes, and began patting the dog. "He just bought him," one man said. "I wanted the female, too, to breed them," said the man holding the dog, "but that woman, she sold the female to her friend."

The puppy was whining. "Maybe it's hungry," said the older man, "let's get him some hamburger." "No man, he'll get worms from that stuff," said one of the others. I suggested milk and we all went into the Carry-out. I asked the waitress for a half pint of milk. The man asked for a saucer. "You can't feed him here," the waitress said, "the Health Department would close us up." She gave us a paper plate and the milk (paid for by me). We took the dog into a hallway next door. Everyone was pleased at how eagerly the puppy drank.

A man who had been in the Carry-out joined us in the hallway. "That's a shepherd, isn't he? Just what I want for my little boy." I said, "I wish I could get one for my little girl, but she's allergic to all animals, dust, and lots of things." "It's better that way," said one of the winos. "She'll outgrow it. But man, if you don't have that until you're full grown—man, look out." "Yes, that's right," the newcomer agreed. "I know a woman who got allergies after she was grown and she got bronica asthma with it."

The dog finished the milk. The owner put him back in his overcoat and I shook hands all around with the winos. We split up three ways. The winos went up the street, the well-dressed man down the street, and the newcomer—who turned out to be Tally Jackson—and I went into the Carry-out.

For more than four hours Tally and I lounged around the Carry-out, talking, drinking coffee, watching people come in and go out, watching other hangers-on as they bantered with the waitresses, horsed around among themselves, or danced to the jukebox. Everyone knew Tally, and some frequently sought out his attention. Tally sometimes participated in the banter but we were generally left undisturbed when we were talking. When I left at two o'clock, Tally and I were addressing each other by first names ("Elliot" was strange to him and we settled for "Ellix"), and I was able to address the two waitresses by their first names without feeling uncomfortable. I had also learned to identify several other men by their first names or nicknames, had gotten hints on personal relationships, and had a biographical sketch (part of it untrue I learned later) of Tally.

Back on the street, I ended up at the Downtown Café, this time by way of the morning's now very drunk owner of the puppy, who was standing near the entrance. The puppy was our bond and we talked about him with an enthusiasm that perhaps neither of us felt. Later, the well-dressed man who had also been part of the puppy episode came in and joined me at the bar.

Then, still drinking beer at the bar stool, I met two other men in quick succession. The first man had to leave shortly for his night-shift busboy job at the restaurant. The other was a surly man in his middle thirties who initiated the contact by taking the stool next to me and asking what kind of work I did, adding that he had seen me around the day before watching Detective Wesley drag that woman across the street.

I told him briefly what my job was.

"Well, if you hang around here you'll see it all. Anything can happen and it does happen here. It can get rough and you can get your head knocked in. You'll be okay though, if you know one or two of the right people."

"That's good to know," I told him, guessing (and hoping) that he was one of the "right people." He left me with the impression that he was being friendly and, in a left-handed sort of way, was offering me his protection.

By the end of the second day I had met nine men, learned the names of several more, and spent many hours in close public association with several men, at least two of whom were well known. And perhaps most important of all, in my own mind I had partly sloughed off that feeling of being a stranger and achieved that minimum sense of "belonging" which alone permits an ease of manner and mind so essential in building personal relationships.

Over the next three or four weeks, I made several excursions into other neighborhoods and followed up at the Downtown Café and the Carry-out shop on an irregular basis, getting to know some of the people better and many others for the first time. Frequently I ate breakfast and lunch at the Carry-out and began putting occasional dimes in the jukebox and in the pinball machine. Ted Moore, who worked at a liquor store nearby and whom I had first met in the Carry-out while he was waiting for the store to open, regularly alternated with me in buying coffee and doughnuts in the morning. At the Downtown Café the man who told me that I'd be okay if I knew "one or two of the right people" publicly identified me as his friend. ("Sure I know him," he told another man in my presence. "We had a long talk the other day. He's my friend and he's okay, man, he's okay. At first I thought he was a cop, but he's no cop. He's okay.")

All in all, I felt I was making steady progress. There was still plenty of suspicion and mistrust, however. At least two men who hung around the Carry-out—one of them the local numbers man—had seen me dozens of times in close quarters, but they kept their distance and I kept mine. Once, accidentally, I caught the numbers man's eye as I walked in. We held the stare for three or four seconds and I nodded slightly but he wouldn't let go. I went on about my business, determined that I wasn't going to be stared down next time and that he'd get no more nods from me unless he nodded first. As it turned out, I didn't have long to wait.

One mid-February day, I walked into the Carry-out.

. . . Tally was having a cup of coffee. "Look here," he said. "Where is this place?" Tally took out a sheet of paper from an envelope and handed it to me. It was a summons to appear as a witness for the defense in the case of the United States versus Lonny Reginald Small. A faint stamp indicated that Tally was to report to the United States District Court for the District of Columbia at 3rd and Pennsylvania Avenue, Northwest, at ten o'clock this morning. I read off the address. It was then 9:40. I suggested that Tally take a cab, but when Tally said he didn't have the money I offered to drive him down. He quickly accepted. On the way, Tally explained that Lonny was a friend of his. Lonny was being tried for murdering his wife last summer. "Lonny is a nice guy," he said. "He's one hundred percent."

Thus began a three-week odyssey into the world of Lonny Small, a young man of twenty-six who, according to the jury's subsequent verdict of "not guilty," had choked his wife to death accidentally. Upon his acquittal, Lonny was rearrested in the courthouse for a violation of probation (on a previous grand larceny conviction) in another jurisdiction. He waived extradition, was given a hearing, was released on an appearance bond, and after another hearing he was again placed on probation.

Almost imperceptibly, my association with Tally, and through him with Lonny, was projecting me into the role of a principal actor in Lonny's life. By being with Tally through the trial, I found that first Tally, then Lonny, were looking to me for leadership and, as in the question of waiving extradition, for decision making. Court officials, apparently taking their cues from Lonny, began looking to me as his spokesman.

The follow-up of Lonny, which took most of my time for at

least the next two weeks, carried me into dozens of places and into contact with scores of people. Throughout this period I stayed in close touch with the project director, getting clearance for and weighing the possible consequences of my growing involvement with the authorities. I went to three different jails during this time, sat through one murder trial and two hearings in judges' chambers, testifying at one of them. I went to bondsmen's offices, to the United States Employment Service, to the Blessed Martin de Porres Hostel (for homeless men), and into several private homes. I met policemen, judges, lawyers, bondsmen, probation officers, and one of Lonny's former employers. I talked with his friends and at least one enemy, his mother-in-law, whose daughter he had killed. I met in council several times with various members of his extended family (who accepted me, through Tally, as Lonny's friend, no questions asked) in their houses, and drove around with them to the houses of other members of the family trying to raise money for Lonny's bond.

Meanwhile, back at the Carry-out, where Tally and I were meeting regularly at night and where I tried to stop in during the day whenever possible, people I had never seen, or others I had seen but never spoken to, began coming up to me and asking, "Is Lonny out yet?" or "Did you raise his bail yet?" or simply, "How's it going?" Bumdoodle, the numbers man, one of those who had not known Lonny, was especially solicitous of Lonny's welfare. He, too, began calling me by my first name and, although I kept no record of it, I think it was at this time that he dropped all subterfuge in taking numbers in my presence and soon began taking bets from me.

By the middle of March, Tally and I were close friends ("up tight"), and I was to let him know if I wanted or needed "anything, anytime." By April, the number of men whom I had come to know fairly well and their acceptance of me had reached the point at which I was free to go to the rooms or apartments where they lived or hung out, at almost any time, needing neither an excuse nor an explanation for doing so. Like other friends, I was there to pass the time, to hang around, to find out "what's happening."

I switched my day around to coincide with the day worker's leisure hours: from four in the afternoon until late at night, according to what was going on. Alone, or with one, two, or half a dozen others, I went to poolrooms, to bars, or to somebody's room or apartment. Much of the time we just hung around the Carry-out, playing the pinball machine or standing on the corner watching the world go by. Regularly at five, I met my five "drinking buddies" when they came off from work, and we went into a hallway for an hour or so of good drinking and easy talk.

Friday afternoon to Sunday night was especially exciting and productive. I'd go to Nancy's "place" (apartment) where, at almost any hour, one could get liquor, listen to music, or engage in conversation. Or perhaps seven or eight of us would buy some beer and whiskey and go up to Tonk's apartment near the Carry-out where he lived with his wife. Occasionally, I'd pair up with one or two men and go to a party, a movie, or a crap game, which might be in almost any part of town. Sunday afternoon was an especially good time to pick up news or happenings of the preceding forty-eight hours. People were generally rested up from the night before, relaxed, and ready to fill one another in on events which involved the police, breakups of husband-wife relations and bed-and-board arrangements, drink-stimulated brawls, sex adventures, and parties they had witnessed, heard about, or participated in over Friday and Saturday.

By April most people seemed to be taking it for granted that I belonged in the area. At least two men did not trust me or like me, but by then I was too strongly entrenched for them to challenge successfully my right to be there, even had they chosen to do so. New people moved into the area, and I found myself being regarded as an old-timer, sometimes being asked to corroborate events which predated my arrival.

Throughout this period, my field observations were focused on individuals: what they said, what they did, and the contexts in which they said them or did them. I sought them out and was sought out by them.

My field notes contain a record of what I saw when I looked at Tally, Richard, Sea Cat, and the others. I have only a small notion—and one that I myself consider suspect—of what they saw when they looked at me.

Some things, however, are very clear. They saw, first of all, a white man. In my opinion, this brute fact of color, as they understood it in their experience and as I understood it in mine, irrevocably and absolutely relegated me to the status of outsider. I am not certain, but I have a hunch that they were more continuously aware of the color difference than I was. When four of us sat around a kitchen table, for example, I saw three Negroes; each of them saw two Negroes and a white man.

Sometimes, when the word "nigger" was being used easily and conversationally or when, standing on the corner with several men, one would have a few words with a white passerby and call him a "white motherfucker," I used to play with the idea that maybe I wasn't as much of an outsider as I thought. Other events, and later readings of the field materials, have disabused me of this particular touch of vanity.

Whenever the fact of my being white was openly introduced, it pointed up the distance between me and the other person, even when the intent of introducing it was, I believe, to narrow that distance.

. . . All of us left Tally's room together. Tally grabbed my arm and pulled me aside near the storefront church and said, "I want to talk to you." With no further introduction he looked me straight in the eye and started talking.

"I'm a liar. I been lying to you all along now and I want to set it straight, even if it means we can't be friends no more. I only lied to you about one thing. Everything else I told you is gospel truth but I did lie about one thing and that makes me a liar. I know that some white people think that if you catch a man in a lie one time you can't never trust him after that. And even if you feel that way about it I still got to tell you. You remember when you first come around here, I told you. . . . Well, that was a lie. . . . I didn't think nothing of it at first, but then you and me started going around together and when we started getting real tight, my conscience started whomping me. I kept looking for a place to tell you but it never seemed right. Then tonight . . . I knew this was the right time. I knew you were going to find out and I didn't want you to find out from somebody else. . . ."

Once I was with Richard in his hometown. It was his first visit in five years. We arrived in the middle of the night and had to leave before daybreak because Richard was wanted by the local police. We were in his grandmother's house. Besides Richard, there were his grandmother, his aunt, and two unrelated men, both long-time friends of Richard.

The group was discussing the possibility of Richard's coming home to stay and weighing the probable consequences. In the middle of the discussion, Richard interrupted and nodded to me. "Now Ellix here is white, as you can see, but he's one of my best friends. Him and me are real tight. You can say anything you want, right to his face. He's real nice." "Well," said his Aunt Pearl, "I always did say there are some nice white people."

Whether or not there is more to these citations than "Some of my best friends are . . ." or "Yes, but you're different," the wall between us remained, or better, the chain-link fence, since despite the barriers we were able to look at each other, walk alongside each other, talk, and occasionally touch fingers. When two people stand up close to the fence on either side, without touching it, they can look through the interstices and forget that they are looking through the fence.

The disadvantage of being white was offset in part by the fact that as an outsider, I was not a competitor. Thus, in the matter of skin color, I saw myself nowhere in the spectrum of black- to light-skinned (or "bright"); I was completely out of it, with no vested interest. It could be that this made it possible for some people to speak freely to me about skin color.

"You know, I'm the darkest one in my family. All my aunts, uncles, everybody is light-skinned and they were all down on me, except my grandmother. . . . She'd do anything for me, maybe because she saw everyone else against me. . . . All the time I was coming up, I kept hoping somebody would have a baby darker than me."

Looking at me, however, the people I came to know in the area probably saw more than a "white male adult." They saw or knew many other things as well, any one of which relegated me to outside status. Those with whom I was in regular contact knew, for example, that I was with them because it was my job to be with them, and they knew, according to their individual comprehension and my ability to communicate, just what my job was. They knew that I lived outside the area. They knew that I was a college graduate, or at least they associated an advanced education with the work I was doing. Moreover, it was apparent, certainly to me, that I was not fluent in their language. Thus, I was an outsider not only because of race, but also because of occupation, education, residence, and speech. The fact that I was

Jewish came up only twice. Once, a man who worked but did not live in the area threw some Yiddish expressions at me because "I thought you looked Jewish." The other time was when I met a soldier in a local bootleg joint. We had been talking for some ten minutes or so when he asked me whether I was "Eyetalian." I told him I was Jewish. "That's just as good," he said. "I'm glad you're not white."

The facts that I was married and a father, and that I was bigger than average size—6 feet, 1 inch, 185 pounds—probably didn't matter much, except as they entered incidentally into my personal relationship with one or another individual. Since the people I spent most of my time with ranged in age from twenty to the middle forties, I would guess that my age (thirty-seven) was not significant in itself.

On several different counts I was an outsider,[3] but I also was a participant in the full sense of the word. The people I was observing knew that I was observing them, yet they allowed me to participate in their activities and take part in their lives to a degree that continues to surprise me. Some "exploited" me, not as an outsider but rather as one who, as a rule, had more resources than they did. When one of them came up with the resources—money or a car, for example—he too was "exploited" in the same way. I usually tried to limit money or other favors to what I thought each would have gotten from another friend had he the same resources as I. I tried to meet requests as best I could without becoming conspicuous. I was not always on the giving end and learned somewhat too slowly to accept food or let myself be treated to drinks even though I knew this would work a hardship on the giver.

When in the field, I participated as fully and as whole-mindedly as I could, limited only by my own sense of personal and professional propriety and by what I assumed to be the boundaries of acceptable behavior as seen by those I was with.

Occasionally, when I wanted to record a physical description of, say, a neighborhood, an apartment, or a social event, I tried to be an observer only. In practice, I found it impossible to keep all traces of participation out of a straight observer role.

One Saturday night, with my observer role clearly in mind, I went to a dance at the Capitol Arena, where more than a thousand people were jammed together. I was the only white male, this was my first time at such an event, the music was so foreign to me that I picked out the wrong beat, and I was unable to identify several of the band instruments. I was, willynilly, an observer. But here are a few lines excerpted from the field observation:

> It was very hot, it was very noisy, it was very smelly, and it was all very exciting. It was impossible to remain simply an observer in a place like this, even for someone as phlegmatic as I. It was only a few minutes after Jackie Wilson started singing that I discovered that the noise wasn't nearly loud enough, the heat wasn't nearly hot enough, and the odor from more than a thousand closely packed people was not really strong enough at all. Like everyone else, I wanted more of everything.

Almost from the beginning, I adopted the dress and something of the speech of the people with whom I was in most frequent contact, as best I could without looking silly or feeling uncomfortable. I came close in dress (in warm weather, T- or sport shirt and khakis or other slacks) with almost no effort at all. My vocabulary and diction changed, but not radically. Cursing and using ungrammatical constructions at times—though they came easily—did not make any of my adaptations confusable with the speech of the street. Thus, while remaining conspicuous in speech and perhaps in dress, I had dulled some of the characteristics of my background. I probably made myself more accessible to others, and certainly more acceptable to myself. This last point was forcefully brought home to me one evening when, on my way to a professional meeting, I stopped off at the Carry-out in a suit and tie. My loss of ease made me clearly aware that the change in dress, speech, and general carriage was as important for its effect on me as it was for its effect on others.

In retrospect, it seems as if the degree to which one becomes a participant is as much a matter of perceiving oneself as a participant as it is of being accepted as a participant by others.

Notes

Preface

1. The mystery-mastery theme in social science has been discussed by David Bakan, *On Method* (San Francisco: Jossey-Bass, Inc., 1967), pp. 37–48.
2. Notably, this criticism has often come from Eastern Europeans of a Marxist persuasion: the Marxist tradition's emphasis on reification (i.e., overobjectification, fetishization of concepts and ideas) allows it to treat ideas, including sociological thinking, as historical phenomena in the same category as ideologies. For some examples of this view, see Peter L. Berger, ed., *Marxism and Sociology* (New York: Appleton-Century-Crofts, 1969).
3. The theme of surrender in sociological research has been developed by Kurt Wolff. See his "Surrender and Community Study: The Study of Loma," in Maurice Stein *et al.*, eds., *Reflections on Community Studies* (New York: John Wiley and Sons, Inc., 1964), pp. 233–63.
4. Herbert Blumer, "Foreword" to Severyn T. Bruyn, *The Human Perspective in Sociology: The Methodology of Participant Observation* (Englewood Cliffs, New Jersey: Prentice-Hall, 1966), p. vi.
5. Florian Znaniecki, *The Method of Sociology* (New York: Holt, Rinehart and Winston, Inc., 1934), p. 37.
6. Wolff, *op. cit.*, pp. 245–51.
7. Bruyn, *op. cit.*, p. 21.

Introduction: On Context and Relevance

1. A. McC. Lee, "Institutional Structures and Individual Autonomy," *Human Organization*, Vol. 26 (1967): 1–5; "Power-Seekers," pp. 667–78 in A. W. Gouldner, ed., *Studies in Leadership* (New York: Harper & Bros., 1950).
2. "Magna Instauratio," pp. 239–363 in R. F. Jones, ed., *Essays . . . and Other Pieces* (New York: Odyssey Press, 1937), p. 283.
3. "The Methodological Position of Symbolic Interactionism," pp. 1–60 in Blumer, *Symbolic Interactionism: Perspective and Method* (Englewood Cliffs, New Jersey: Prentice-Hall, 1969), pp. 39, 49.
4. C. M. Arensberg and A. H. Niehoff, *Introducing Social Change: A Manual for Americans Overseas* (Chicago: Aldine Publishing Co., 1964), pp. 185–89.

5. 2nd ed. (Chicago: University of Chicago Press, 1955), pp. 356–57.

6. *Op. cit.*, p. 40.

7. Lee, "The Challenge of the 'Clinic,' " chap. 22 in his *Multivalent Man* (New York: George Braziller, 1966).

8. See especially his *The Immigrant Press and Its Control* (New York: Harper & Bros., 1922) and "The Natural History of the Newspaper," chap. 4 in Park and E. W. Burgess, *The City* (Chicago: University of Chicago Press, 1925).

9. See especially Lee, *The Daily Newspaper in America: The Evolution of a Social Instrument* (New York: The Macmillan Co., 1937; Octagon Books, 1970) and "Freedom of the Press: The Services of a Catch Phrase," pp. 355–75 in G. P. Murdock, ed., *Studies in the Science of Society* (New Haven: Yale University Press, 1937).

10. F. R. Kluckhohn, "The Participant-Observer Technique in Small Communities," *American Journal of Sociology*, Vol. 46 (1940–41), pp. 331–343; B. D. Paul, "Interview Techniques and Field Relationships," pp. 430–51, and Oscar Lewis, "Controls and Experiments in Field Work," pp. 452–75 in A. L. Kroeber, ed., *Anthropology Today: An Encyclopedic Inventory* (Chicago: University of Chicago Press, 1953).

11. M. R. Stein, "Robert Park and Urbanization in Chicago," chap. 1 in his *The Eclipse of Community* (Princeton: Princeton University Press, 1960). For recent texts on the subject, see S. T. Bruyn, *The Human Perspective in Sociology: The Methodology of Participant Observation* (Englewood Cliffs, New Jersey: Prentice-Hall, 1966), and G. J. McCall, *Issues in Participant Observation: A Text and Reader* (Reading, Massachusetts: Addison-Wesley Publishing Co., 1969).

12. Marvin Harris, *The Rise of Anthropological Theory: A History of Theories of Culture* (New York: T. Y. Crowell Co., 1968), p. 617. Cf. G. P. Murdock, "The Cross-Cultural Survey," *American Sociological Review*, Vol. 5 (1940), pp. 361–70; Oscar Lewis, "Comparisons in Cultural Anthropology," pp. 259–92 in W. L. Thomas, Jr., ed., *Current Anthropology: A Supplement to Anthropology Today* (Chicago: University of Chicago Press, 1956); F. W. Moore, ed., *Readings in Cross-Cultural Methodology* (New Haven: HRAF Press, 1961); and C. S. Ford, ed., *Cross-Cultural Approaches: Readings in Comparative Research* (New Haven: HRAF Press, 1967), especially pp. 3–21.

13. *The Method of Sociology* (New York: Holt, Rinehart and Winston, Inc., 1934), pp. 37, 45.

14. Lee, "Problems: Social and Sociological," chap. 30 in Lee, ed., *Principles of Sociology* (3rd ed.; New York: Barnes & Noble, 1969), especially pp. 309–12.

15. Lee, "Sociologists in an Integrating Society: Significance and Satisfaction in Sociological Work," *Social Problems*, Vol. 2 (1954–55), pp. 57–66.

16. Lee, "Tissues of Orthodoxy and of Legitimacy," chap. 14 in his *Multivalent Man* (New York: George Braziller, 1966).

17. Lee, *How to Understand Propaganda* (New York: Rinehart & Co., 1952), pp. 165–70.

18. Daniel Walker and others, *Rights in Conflict . . . During the Week of the Democratic National Convention of 1968* (New York: Bantam Books, 1968), especially pp. 99–129, 287–331.

19. National Advisory Commission on Civil Disorders, *Report* (New York: Bantam Books, 1968), especially chap. 11; Urban America, Inc., and The Urban Coalition, *One Year Later* (New York: F. A. Praeger, 1969), especially chaps. 5–8.

20. Alcoholics Anonymous has long crusaded, and with some success, against police abuse of alcoholics.

21. The American Civil Liberties Union and various special defense

agencies have files full of specific cases of police brutality to members of underprivileged minorities, alcoholics, and alleged criminals.

22. H. E. Starr, *William Graham Sumner* (New York: Henry Holt and Co., 1925), chap. 15, pp. 297–301.

23. New York: D. Appleton & Co., 1874; reissued, Ann Arbor: University of Michigan Press, 1961.

1. How Black Enterprisers Do Their Thing

1. See Daniel Bell, *The End of Ideology* (New York: Collier Books, 1960, 1961, 1962), pp. 127–50.

2. *Ibid.*, pp. 149–50.

3. James Q. Wilson, *Negro Politics* (New York: The Free Press, 1960), pp. 312–14.

4. James Q. Wilson, "Introduction," in Harold F. Coosnell, *Negro Politicians* (Chicago: University of Chicago Press, 1935, 1967), pp. ix–x.

5. See Robert Ezra Park and Ernest W. Burgess, *Introduction to the Science of Sociology* (Chicago: University of Chicago Press, 1921); Robert Ezra Park, "Human Ecology," *American Journal of Sociology*, Vol. 42 (July, 1936), pp. 1–15; Robert Ezra Park, "The City as a Social Laboratory," in *Chicago: An Experiment in Social Research*, eds. T.V. Smith and Leonard D. White (Chicago: University of Chicago Press, 1929), pp. 1–19; and Robert E. Park, "Symbiosis and Socialization," *American Journal of Sociology*, Vol. 45 (July, 1939), pp. 1–25.

6. Norton E. Long, "The Local Community as an Ecology of Games," *American Journal of Sociology*, Vol. 64 (1958), pp. 251–61. Also see Gerald D. Suttles, *The Social Order of the Slum: Ethnicity and Territoriality in the Inner City* (Chicago: University of Chicago Press, 1968).

7. My entry into the environment was accomplished through securing the permission of the beauty parlor proprietor to perform odd jobs such as mopping the floor, running errands for customers, and answering the telephone. My presence was sufficiently unobtrusive to enable the clientele to interact without suspecting me of snooping. From a research standpoint, the beauty parlor proved to be a springboard into the assessment of the networks of group affiliations and activities predominating in a nine-block area of the Bedford-Stuyvesant section of Brooklyn.

8. Claude Harris, "Weavirama," *The Hair Weavers Magazine* (February, 1963), pp. 8–12. At present, the use of wigs and African hair styles has displaced the Weev.

9. I observed a total of ninety-five people with the aid of the appointment book. Since many of them were periodic visitors, I was able to observe them more than once. The twenty-seven professionals included twelve Americans, four Africans, and eleven West Indians; the fifty-three nonprofessionals, thirty-two Americans, twenty West Indians, and no Africans.

10. The emphasis on style among these people cannot be overstated. In the ghetto, one's identity is established in large part by his relative expertise in handling language so as to maneuver himself into a position of situational superiority. As Kenneth Burke points out, style is ingratiation, "an attempt to gain favor by the hypnotic or suggestive process of 'saying the right thing.'" See Kenneth Burke, *Permanence and Change* (2nd. rev. ed.; Indianapolis, Indiana: Bobbs-Merrill, 1954, 1965), p. 50. For a discussion of clothes as it relates to this matter, see Hugh Dalziel Duncan, *Communication and Social Order* (New York: Bedminster Press, 1962), pp. 190–94. For a perceptive analysis of the subject of style and language in the ghetto, see Thomas Kochman, "'Rapping' in the Black Ghetto," *Trans-action*, Vol. 6 (February, 1969), pp. 26–34.

11. William Foote Whyte, *Street Corner Society* (Chicago: University of Chicago Press, 1943, 1955).

12. Norbert Wiley, "The Ethnic Mobility Trap and Stratification Theory," *Social Problems*, Vol. 15 (Fall, 1967), pp. 147–59. The dynamics of this process are closely related to the phenomenon that the sociologist Edwin Lemert calls "self defeating deviance," for what occurs is the repetition of behavior, possibly behavior intended at the outset to mitigate certain consequences, but which finally reinforces that which it was intended to extinguish. See Edwin M. Lemert, *Human Deviance, Social Problems, and Social Control* (Englewood Cliffs, New Jersey: Prentice-Hall, 1967), pp. 55–57.

13. George J. McCall, "Symbiosis: The Case of Hoodoo and the Numbers Racket," *The Other Side*, ed. Howard Becker (New York: The Free Press of Glencoe, 1964), p. 61.

14. E. Franklin Frazier, *The Negro in the United States* (New York: The Macmillan Co., 1957), pp. 356–58.

15. We can almost take the analogy literally. For an interesting discussion of the nexuses between Negro religion and music, and the similarity of the preacher and bluesman role, see Charles Keil, *Urban Blues* (Chicago: University of Chicago Press, 1966).

16. See Ari Kiev, *Magic, Faith, and Healing* (New York: The Free Press of Glencoe, 1964); and Lee Sechrist and James H. Bryan, "Astrologers as Useful Marriage Counselors," *Trans-action*, Vol. 6 (November, 1968), pp. 34–36.

17. See St. Clair Drake and Horace Cayton, *Black Metropolis: A Study of Negro Life in a Northern Metropolis*, (rev. ed. New York and Evanston: Harper and Row, 1962), E. Franklin Frazier, *Black Bourgeoisie* (Glencoe, Illinois: The Free Press, 1957), and Harold M. Baron, "Black Powerlessness in Chiago," *Trans-action*, Vol. 6 (November, 1968), pp. 27–33. See also Edward C. Banfield and James Q. Wilson, *City Politics* (Cambridge, Massachusetts: Harvard University Press, 1965), pp. 293–312; Martin Rein, "Social Stability and Black Capitalism," *Trans-action*, Vol. 6 (June, 1969), pp. 4, 6.

18. For an understanding of how and why these are legitimating myths, see Elliot A. Krause, "Functions of a Bureaucratic Ideology: 'Citizen Participation.' " *Social Problems*, Vol. 16 (Fall, 1968), pp. 129–43.

2. *The Needle Scene*

1. Edwin M. Schur, *Crimes Without Victims: Deviant Behavior and Public Policy* (Englewood Cliffs, New Jersey: Prentice-Hall, 1965), p. 122.

2. Marshall B. Clinard, *Sociology of Deviant Behavior* (3rd ed.; New York: Holt, Rinehart and Winston, Inc., 1968), p. 319.

3. Harold Finestone, "Narcotics and Criminality," *Law and Contemporary Problems*, Vol. 22, No. 1 (1957), pp. 76–77, quoted in Clinard, *op. cit.*, p. 331.

4. Harold Finestone, "Cats, Kicks, and Color," Howard S. Becker, ed., *The Other Side* (New York: The Free Press, 1964), p. 282.

5. Marsh B. Ray, "The Cycle of Abstinence and Relapse Among Heroin Addicts," in Becker, *op. cit.*, p. 164.

6. *Ibid.*, p. 165.

7. Finestone, *op. cit.*, p. 297.

Notes 279

3. Birth of a Mini-Movement

1. Ted R. Vaughan, "The Landlord-Tenant Relation in a Low-Income Area," *Social Problems*, Vol. 16 (Fall, 1968), p. 210.
2. *Ibid.*, p. 210.
3. *Ibid.*, pp. 208–18.
4. Gerhard Lenski, *Power and Privilege* (New York: McGraw-Hill Book Co., 1966), pp. 87–88.
5. Herbert Blumer, "Collective Behavior," *Principles of Sociology,* ed. Alfred McClung Lee (2nd rev. ed., New York: Barnes and Noble, 1965), pp. 165–222.
6. Karl Mannheim, *Ideology and Utopia,* trans. by Louis Wirth and Edward Shils (New York: Harcourt, Brace and Co., 1936).
7. See Howard Becker, ed., *Social Problems: A Modern Approach* (John Wiley and Sons, Inc., 1966), pp. 11–14; Willard Waller, "Social Problems and the Mores," *American Sociological Review*, I (December, 1936), pp. 922–33; Richard C. Fuller and Richard R. Meyers, "The Natural History of a Social Problem," *American Sociological Review*, Vol. 6 (Time, 1941), pp. 320–29; and Howard S. Becker, *Outsiders: Studies in the Sociology of Deviance* (New York: The Free Press of Glencoe, 1963).
8. Blumer, *op. cit.*, p. 204.
9. See Lewis Coser, *The Function of the Social Conflict* (Glencoe, Illinois: The Free Press, 1956), p. 34.
10. Georg Simmel, *Conflict and the Web of Group Affiliations,* trans. by Kurt H. Wolff and Reinhard Bendix (Glencoe, Illinois: The Free Press, 1955), pp. 87, 88.
11. See Alfred McClung Lee, *Multivalent Man* (New York: George Braziller, 1966).
12. Blumer, *op cit.*, p. 211.
13. *Ibid.*, p. 203.
14. E. Franklin Frazier, *Black Bourgeoisie* (Glencoe, Illinois: The Free Press, 1957), p. 167.
15. See Lenski, *op. cit.*, p. 87, where he describes a similar example involving the interaction between a Negro doctor and a white laborer.
16. Allison Davis and Robert J. Havighurst, "Social Class and Color Differences in Child-Rearing," *American Sociological Review*, p. 708.
17. Lewis Coser, *The Function of Social Conflict* (Glencoe, Illinois: The Free Press, 1956), p. 157.

4. The Gilded Asylum

1. Erving Goffman, *Asylums* (Garden City, New York: Doubleday-Anchor Books, 1961), p. xiii.
2. *Ibid.*, p. 386.
3. This building, with one attendant only on night duty, is open when there is a patient, or patients, who will benefit by a less restricted and protective atmosphere than the main buildings provide; most often they are people who have found jobs and are about to be discharged.
4. *Op. cit.*, p. 244.
5. These figures are derived from *Action for Mental Health: The Final Report of the Joint Commission on Mental Health* (New York: Basic Books, Inc., 1961), chap. 1, which lists the state mental hospital personnel to

patient ratio as 0.32. The 2 to 1 ratio at PPH compares with the personnel-patient ratio of the private community general hospital listed as 2.1 or approximately 2 to 1.

6. See Ailon Shiloh, "Sanctuary or Prison: Response to Life in a Mental Hospital," *Trans-action*, Vol. 6 (December, 1968), pp. 28–35. The Joint Commission reported that the average daily amount spent for patients in state mental hospitals is $4.44, as compared to $31.16 in private community general hospitals and $12.00 for veterans' psychiatric or tuberculosis hospitals.

7. *Op. cit.*, p. 312 n.176.

8. *Ibid.*, p. 211.

9. *Ibid.*, p. 105.

10. *Ibid.*, p. 26.

11. Brewster Smith, "The Revolution in Mental Health Care: A 'Bold New Approach?' " *Trans-action*, Vol. 5 (April, 1968), pp. 19–23.

12. In one such case, a patient had written a letter to the President in Washington, D.C., and threatened his life. The hospital authorities received a call from the F.B.I. in response. The letter-writing career of this patient was quickly curtailed.

13. Goffman, *op. cit.*, pp. 101–4.

14. *Ibid.*, p. 41.

15. *Ibid.*, p. 3.

16. *Ibid.*, p. 29.

17. We commonly referred to PPH by an abbreviation of "Sanitarium" (i.e., "San"), this word, in the past, having been a part of its official name.

18. *Op. cit.*, p. 286.

19. I recall discussing at length with my doctor my desire to move to another table. I had, for ten months, put up with a meal-mate who was always either sarcastic or noncommunicative. She so disturbed my digestion that I began to dislike attending meals. Yet I had to plead to be allowed to transfer to a table of more congenial people, being told that I was trying to "escape" a situation that I should learn to handle.

20. I became friendly with a certain attendant at PPH, who, against all hospital rules, told me something about the training period he had to go through before assuming his duties on a unit. More time, he said, was spent on detailing the difficulties ensued in romantic attachments than on any other part of his training.

21. The terms "escape" and "elope" are used interchangeably and mean that the patient has left hospital property clandestinely or without the staff's knowledge of his action. The analogy is logical since elopement in all societies is escape, escape from social structural strictures on the individual's freedom to choose a partner outside of the institutional arrangements. When I said that going beyond the stereotyped family pattern in PPH was tantamount to incest, this represented a logical extension of the analogy itself.

22. *Op. cit.*, p. 11.

23. Conversely here, the staff experiences difficulties. Unit life often provides the patient with a less demanding and more satisfying group milieu than his own family does, thereby encouraging him to want to escape the necessity to adjust to and deal with the home situation.

24. *Op. cit.*, p. 362.

25. For an example of such a view, see Jerome D. Frank, "The Dynamics of the Psychotherapeutic Relationship," *Psychiatry*, Vol. 22 (February, 1959), pp. 17–34.

26. See H. J. Eysenck, *Fact and Fiction in Psychology* (Middlesex, England: Penguin Books, 1965), especially pp. 154–55. Of course, it can be objected that such research relies on diagnostic labels such as "cure," "spontaneous remission," and so on, but so do the agencies and personnel

Notes

that make the decisions and evaluations regarding commitment, treatment mode, release, and outpatient care.

27. See, for example, Barbara Wootton, *Social Science and Social Pathology* (New York: The Macmillan Co., 1957), especially chap. 7; and Michael Hakeem, "A Critique of the Psychiatric Approach," in Joseph Roueck, ed., *Juvenile Delinquency* (New York: Philosophical Library, Inc., 1958), pp. 79–112.

28. See Thomas S. Szasz, *The Myth of Mental Illness* (New York: Paul B. Hoeber, Inc., 1961); and Thomas J. Scheff, *Being Mentally Ill: A Sociological Theory* (Chicago: Aldine Publishing Co., 1966).

29. The following is a painfully small sample of this literature: Marvin K. Opler, *Culture and Social Psychiatry* (New York: Atherton Press, 1967); Jane M. Murphy and Alexander H. Leighton, eds., *Approaches to Cross-Cultural Psychiatry* (Ithaca, New York: Cornell University Press, 1965); E. Gartly Jaco, *The Social Epidemiology of Mental Disorders* (New York: Russell Sage Foundation, 1960); August B. Hollingshead and Frederick Redlich, *Social Class and Mental Illness* (New York: John Wiley and Sons, Inc., 1958); and Jerome K. Myers and Bertram H. Roberts, *Family and Class Dynamics in Mental Illness* (New York: John Wiley and Sons, Inc., 1969).

30. See Smith, *op. cit.;* and Eugene Heimler, *Mental Illness and Social Work* (Middlesex, England: Penguin Books, 1967).

31. *Op. cit.,* p. 355.

32. *Ibid.,* p. 11.

33. See Jaco, *op. cit.,* pp. 125–48; Murphy and Leighton, *op. cit.,* p. 10; Paul M. Roman and Harrison M. Trice, *Schizophrenia and the Poor* (Ithaca, New York: Cayuga Press, 1967), "Occupational Mobility and Schizophrenia: An Assessment of Social Causation and Social Selection Hypotheses," *American Sociological Review,* Vol. 32 (1967), pp. 104–13.

34. *Op. cit.,* p. 90.

35. *Ibid.,* p. 10.

36. I am using Shiloh's (*op. cit.*) term "institutionalized" patients, which refers to those who have resigned themselves to hospital life and have no desire to be discharged. "Noninstitutionalized" patients, on the other hand, desire and trust that they will leave.

6. Urban Samurai

1. Gregory P. Stone, "Appearance and the Self," *Human Behavior and Social Processes: An Interactionist Approach,* ed. Arnold Rose (Boston: Houghton Mifflin Co., 1962), p. 113. See also Hugh Dalziel Duncan, *Communication and Social Order* (New York: Bedminster Press, 1962), pp. 190–94.

2. Arnold van Gennep, *The Rites of Passage* (Chicago: Phoenix Books, University of Chicago Press, 1960), pp. 10–11, 65–115. On this subject, also see Bruno Bettelheim, *Symbolic Wounds* (Glencoe, Illinois: The Free Press, 1954); Hutton Webster, *Primitive Secret Societies* (New York: The Macmillan Co., rev. ed., 1931); Theodore Reik, *Ritual* (New York: Grove Press, 1946, 1962), pp. 91–166; John M. Whiting, Richard Kluckhohn, and Albert Anthony, "The Function of Male Initiation Ceremonies at Puberty," *Readings in Social Psychology,* ed. Maccoby *et. al.* (New York: Holt, Rinehart and Winston, Inc., 1958), pp. 359–70; Alfred McClung Lee, *Fraternities Without Brotherhood* (Boston: Beacon Press, 1955); and Duncan, *op. cit.,* pp. 257–61.

3. On the subject of status passage and careers, see Everett C. Hughes, "Cycles, Turning Points and Careers," in his *Men and Their Work* (Glencoe, Illinois: The Free Press, 1958), pp. 11–12.

4. E. J. Harrison, *The Fighting Spirit of Japan* (London: W. Foulsham and Company, Ltd., n. d.), pp. 59–60.

5. For an interesting philosophical discussion of the phenomenology of the social world, see Alfred Schutz, *Collected Papers: The Problem of Social Reality* (The Hague: Martinus Nijhoff, 1962), I, pp. 207–59.

6. One writer, in commenting on the cultural differences prevailing in the Japanese and American martial arts, notes that Westerners indulge in conversation and intellectual explanation during practice, whereas the Japanese frown upon this, insisting that too much talk and explanation in teaching and practice result in intellectual conceit. See Robert Frager, "The Psychology of the Samurai," *Psychology Today*, Vol. 2 (January, 1969), p. 50.

7. The wearing of such visible "masks," if not intended to sustain social distance, by its obvious hauteur at least results in maintaining distance. Nor is the situation drastically changed in Japan; it is only more subtle. While one might be tempted to make invidious distinctions vis-à-vis the purity of the arts in Japan versus their adulteration in the Western world, notice how the following quote, albeit laudatory, reveals the same elements of "face-making": "Discipline in all Japanese arts is so demanding that it reshapes the student completely—mentally and physically. A man who has attained mastery of an art reveals it in his every action." Frager, *op. cit.*, p. 49. For some revealing discussions on "face," see Erving Goffman, *The Presentation of Self in Everyday Life* (Garden City, New York: Doubleday Anchor Books, 1959), pp. 57–70; Ernest Becker, *The Birth and Death of Meaning* (New York: The Free Press of Glencoe, 1962), pp. 95–101; and Erving Goffman, *Interaction Ritual* (Garden City, New York: Doubleday Anchor Books, 1967), pp. 5–45.

8. In several talks with Mr. Urban, he was careful to enunciate this characterization of himself. This same point was brought out in a recent interview for a karate magazine. See Herman Petras, "Peter Urban: Founder of American Style Goju," *Official Karate*, Vol. 1 (June, 1969), pp. 30–35.

9. Willard Waller, *The Sociology of Teaching* (New York: John Wiley and Sons, 1932, 1965), pp. 116–17. James Coleman follows through on Waller's ideas in his analysis of the role of athletics in maintaining the identity of the school and the community in, "Athletics in High School," *The Annals of the American Academy of Political and Social Science*, 338 (November, 1961), pp. 33–43. Terry Southern's short stories "Red Dirt Marijuana" and "Razor Fight" carry on Twain's apotheosis of egalitarian peer group values. See his *Red Dirt Marijuana and Other Tastes* (New York: Signet Books, New American Library, 1968), pp. 9–38. Also see Duncan, *op. cit.*, pp. 326–45.

10. Alfred McClung Lee, *Multivalent Man* (New York: George Braziller, 1966), p. 236.

11. Peter Urban, *The Karate Dojo* (New York: privately published, 1964), pp. 8, 9.

12. Lee, *Multivalent Man*, pp. 230–37.

13. Herbert Bloch and Arthur Niederhoffer, *The Gang* (New York: Philosophical Library, 1958), p. 17.

14. Lee, *Multivalent Man*, p. 154.

15. Kenneth Burke, *Permanence and Change* (2nd rev. ed., Indianapolis, Indiana: Bobbs-Merrill Co., Inc., 1954, 1965), p. 276.

16. For an interesting discussion of this problem see Peter L. Berger and Thomas Luckmann, *The Social Construction of Reality* (Garden City, New York: Doubleday and Co., 1966), pp. 119–68.

17. Frederic M. Thrasher, *The Gang* (Chicago: Phoenix Books, University of Chicago Press, rev. ed., 1963), p. 55.

18. See W. A. Schofield, *Psychotherapy: the Purchase of Friendship* (Englewood Cliffs, New Jersey: Prentice-Hall, 1964).

19. Georg Simmel, *The Sociology of Georg Simmel*, ed. Kurt Wolff (Glencoe, Illinois: The Free Press, 1950), pp. 359–60.

20. The hippie phenomenon in some sense is indicative of this, as are the Esalen and encounter type therapies which have borrowed culture traits from the former.

21. The sociologist Orrin E. Klapp has come to some similar conclusions insofar as he recognizes that leisure pursuits often constitute identity-seeking activities outside the organizational and institutional channels (i.e., the regularized status passages) under the aegis of "fun." See his *Collective Search for Identity* (New York: Holt, Rinehart and Winston, Inc., 1969).

7. *Poker and Pop*

1. The data for this study were gathered from November, 1967, to May, 1968, by participant observation of card-playing groups in the midwest university center union. Midwest-university center is a two-year branch of a large university, and serves a city and metropolitan area of about 50,000 people in an eighty-mile radius. Most of the 600 students attending the center live at home, with the rest living in either a newly constructed dormitory or apartments.

2. Irving Crespi, "A Functional Analysis of Card Playing as a Leisure Time Activity" (Ph.D. dissertation, The New School for Social Research, 1955), p. 112.

3. *Ibid.*, p. 117.

4. *Ibid.*, p. 171; also Frederic M. Thrasher, *The Gang* (Chicago: University of Chicago Press, 1963), pp. 155–58, 170.

5. See Ned Polsky, *Hustlers, Beats and Others* (Chicago: Aldine Publishing Co., 1967), pp. 106–17.

6. Crespi, *op. cit.*, p. 32.

7. Lee, *op. cit.*, p. 33.

8. Erving Goffman, *Presentation of Self in Everyday Life* (New York: Doubleday Anchor Books, 1959), p. 104.

9. Lee, *op. cit.*, p. 132.

10. *Ibid.*, p. 133.

11. Goffman, *op. cit.*, pp. 58–66.

12. Edward C. Devereux, "Gambling and Social Structure: A Sociological Study of Lotteries and Horseracing in Contemporary America" (unpublished Ph.D. dissertation, Harvard University, 1950), pp. 200–2. Devereux defines three types of kibitzers: (1) the expert or aspiring expert who is silent and just watches and learns. "He constantly evaluates the group according to expert criteria"; (2) the non-card player whose presence is accidental; and (3) the excluded card-player—he would like to play, but because he is not playing, he lets you know how bad you play. He considers himself an expert and counteracts the integrating effects of the game. Thus he is viewed as as much a pest as the non-playing kibitzer can be at times. See also *Dictionary of American Slang*, eds. Harold Wentworth and Steward Berg Flexner (New York: Thomas Crowell Company, 1967), p. 302.

13. S. I. Hayakawa (ed.), *A Modern Guide to Synonyms* (New York: Funk and Wagnalls, 1968), p. 229. "*Arrivista*" refers to a person recently accepted into a group yet still largely unfamiliar with it.

14. Goffman, *op. cit.*, pp. 30–34.

15. See Wentworth and Flexner, *op. cit.*, pp. 122, 333. "Cooling the mark out" is defined as the appeasement of an easy victim, a sucker, etc. This expression and practice is defined by Erving Goffman in "On Cooling the Mark Out," *Psychiatry*, Vol. XV (1952), pp. 451–63.

16. Polsky, *op. cit.*, p. 62. See also Goffman, *Presentation of Self in Everyday Life*, pp. 58–66, on misrepresentation and false appearance.

17. See Wentworth and Flexner, *op. cit.*, p. 116.

18. Crespi, *op. cit.*, p. 146.

19. John McDonald, "Poker: An American Game," *Fortune* (March, 1948), p. 113.

20. Lee, *op. cit.*, p. 64.

21. F. P. Adams, "Women Can't Play Poker," *Good Housekeeping* (June, 1948), p. 113.

22. Thrasher, *op. cit.*, pp. 156–57.

23. Alfred McClung Lee, *Fraternities Without Brotherhood* (Boston: The Beacon Press, 1955), pp. 119–20.

24. For an interesting interpretation of adolescent delinquency, deviance, and other "autonomous" behavior, see Gerald Marwell, "Adolescent Powerlessness and Delinquent Behavior," *Social Problems*, Vol. 14 (Summer, 1966), 35–47.

25. Marwell, *ibid.*, p. 40.

26. Devereux, *op. cit.*, pp. 950–79.

27. Kurt Wolff, ed., *The Sociology of Georg Simmel* (New York: The Free Press of Glencoe, 1950), p. 48.

8. The Home Territory Bar

1. The concept of "territory" or "home territory" is used in the field of animal ecology to refer to the preferential treatment of an area by members of given species, sometimes including defense of that area upon invasion by others of the same species—see W. C. Alee *et al., Principles of Animal Ecology* (Philadelphia: W. B. Saunders Co., 1950), p. 412. In Barker and Wright's analysis of behavior settings they also note that for any setting there may be in addition an implicit or explicit exclusion of certain groups—*Midwest and Its Children* (Evanston, Illinois: Row, Peterson & Co., n.d.), pp. 99–147.

2. *San Francisco Chronicle*, May 10, 1962.

3. Maurice Gorham, *The Local* (London: Cassell & Co., 1939), p. x, writes that in England, collectivities that use pubs as home territories include waiters, artists, medical students, musicians, banknote engravers, ragpickers, used car salesmen, B.B.C., chorines, draymen, fruit salesmen, market porters, Negroes, and car thieves. A description of a home territory bar for fighters, fight managers, trainers, and ex-boxers can be found in "Neutral Corner Cocktail Lounge" (*The New Yorker*, December 18, 1954, pp. 71 *ff.*). Another description of a home territory bar for writers can be found in *Time*, May 3, 1963, pp. 65–66.

4. Cf. Margaret Chandler, "The Social Organization of Workers in a Rooming House Area" (unpublished Ph.D. dissertation, University of Chicago, 1948), p. 73.

5. Although the habitués of the bars around the football stadium and the opera house were in many respects similar, the outsiders who use their establishments were not, in a very apparent way. The regular patrons of the bars in both areas were characteristically dressed in a very informal manner, while those who came from the football stadium were typi-

cally in the same casual garb, and those who came from the opera house were in suits and ties. The difference in treatment that they were accorded may well have stemmed from the fact that the casual dress of the former group indicated that they were likely to fit in, while the formal dress of the latter indicated that they were less likely to fit in. For a discussion of dress and behavior, see Erving Goffman, *Behavior in Public Places* (New York: The Free Press, 1963), pp. 203–4.

6. Quite obviously, not all collectivities are equally acceptable in all establishments, and those who attempt to co-opt a public drinking place as their own may be discouraged by those who have a vested financial interest in the establishment. Thus, for example, when one of the small theatre groups in the city changed their theatre to a new location, they also sought a new bar that could function as a home territory for the members of the company after their shows. The one they more or less decided on was a respectable convenience bar right next to the theatre, but they had no sooner begun to use it as their own than they received a formal message from the manager stating that if, in the future, they desired to patronize the bar, the men must wear ties and suits and the women must be equally respectable in their dress. The message was taken as evidence of the management's lack of welcome for them, and after that they rarely used the establishment for anything other than a convenience bar.

7. Cf. Sherri Cavan, "Interaction in Home Territories," *Berkeley Journal of Sociology*, Vol. 8 (1963), pp. 17–32.

8. Herbert Gans, *The Urban Villagers* (New York: The Free Press, 1962), p. 341.

9. Chandler, *op. cit.*, pp. 97, 98.

10. Other examples can be found in Cavan, *op. cit.*

11. Donald W. Cory and J. P. LeRoy, *The Homosexual and His Society* (New York: The Citadel Press, 1963), pp. 105–6, provide a number of similar examples, although they imply that the masking of such bars is a much more general phenomenon than it appears to be in San Francisco.

12. Gordon Westwood *Society and the Homosexual* (New York: E. P. Dutton & Co., 1953), p. 126, writes that once a pub in England becomes known as a "homosexual hangout," those who are not homosexual avoid the establishment.

The suggestion has been made, at least with respect to homosexual home territory bars, that explicit information should be made public about the fact. Thus, one attorney said, "They should hang a sign out in front to keep the unaware out, so that unsuspecting innocents wouldn't walk into something. Homosexuals do have a right to congregate, but it should be apparent that the place caters to them" (The Question Man, "Should We Discourage Gay Bars?" *San Francisco Chronicle*, August 6, 1960). One tavern in Gottlieb's study actually did hang out a sign that said, "For Members Only" ("The Neighborhood Tavern and the Cocktail Lounge," *American Journal of Sociology*, Vol. 62, 1947, p. 562.)

13. The Question Man, "Should Gay Bars be Marked?" *San Francisco Chronicle*, June 23, 1964.

14. Anonymous, *Streetwalker* (New York: Viking Press, 1960), pp. 62–63.

15. See, for example, Harvey W. Zorbaugh, *The Gold Coast and the Slum* (Chicago: University of Chicago Press, 1930), p. 115, and Alan Lomax, *Mister Jelly Roll* (New York: Grove Press, 1956), p. 49. There is, of course, a notable exception—namely, the coffee houses of the bohemians.

16. There are lawful limits upon bar activities, of course, which are specified in the Alcoholic Beverage Control Act, but the extent to which these will be met within the home territory bar is variable. As noted above with respect to dancing, the ABC statutes specify that such activity

shall be engaged in only in establishments that have a special dancing license.

17. Helen Branson, *Gay Bar* (San Francisco: Pan Graphic Press, 1957), pp. 42–43.

18. Slow service is not always oriented toward excluding the outsider, for sometimes neutral patrons may be ignored to give priority to the habitués, as in the following incident:

P.C. had gone to the bar from the table to order. The bartender was at the other end of the bar, mixing drinks and chatting with one of the patrons. A man sitting next to where P.C. was standing called down to the bartender, "You have a customer here." The bartender replied, "Just a minute, there are some before you" (this was a hard line to distinguish). The other patron then said to P.C., "He had to take care of those he knows so they won't get mad."

19. When, for some reason, the police feel that a particular bar warrants particular attention, they sometimes also use ID checks as a method of control. These checks are similarly not necessarily for ascertaining that no one under legal drinking age is present but rather for assuring the management, and perhaps the patrons too, that the police have their eyes on the bar. Bartenders frequently mention such checks as one form of police harassment, along with men on the beat dropping in too frequently and stationing patrol cars or paddy wagons outside the bar.

9. Summertime Servants

1. The data for the analysis of social relations in the small resort hotels were gathered during the summers of 1959–1964 by participant observation as a busboy and waiter in three small resort hotels in the area. This analysis will be to an extent retrospective: accordingly, I have tried to minimize such factors as detachment, or distortions in recall which might have affected my analysis by making ample use of correspondence written to my wife (then fiancée) during the summers of 1963–1964. In addition, I have received invaluable comments and criticisms on my observations by friends who worked with me and who have worked in other hotels.

2. Erving Goffman, *The Presentation of Self in Everyday Life* (New York: Doubleday and Co., 1959), p. 238.

3. William Foote Whyte, "The Social Structure of the Restaurant," *American Journal of Sociology*, Vol. 54, No. 4 (January, 1949), p. 302.

4. Goffman, *op. cit.*, pp. 106–40.

5. William Foote Whyte, *Human Relations in the Restaurant Industry* (New York: McGraw-Hill Book Co., 1948), pp. 92–93.

6. *Ibid.*, p. 110.

7. Goffman, *op. cit.*, p. 188.

8. *Ibid.*, pp. 190–207.

9. *Ibid.*, p. 191.

10. See Goffman, *ibid.*, pp. 193–94, on redefinition of the situation involving unequal female-male statuses via emphasis of male superordination.

11. The following orientation has been borrowed from Goffman, *ibid.*, pp. 208–12.

12. *Ibid.*, pp. 212–228.

10. *The Hustler*

1. The Pascal quotation is from Penseés, V. Al Capone's remark is quoted in Paul Sann, *The Lawless Decade* (New York: Crown Publishers, 1957), p. 214.

2. The compendium of misinformation and cockeyed interpretation is Jack Olsen's "The Pool Hustlers," *Sports Illustrated*, Vol. 14 (March 20, 1961), pp. 71–77. Jack Richardson's "The Noblest Hustlers," *Esquire*, IX (September, 1963), pp. 94, 96, 98, contains a few worthwhile observations; but it is sketchy, ill-balanced, and suffers from editorial garbling—all of which make it both confusing and misleading for the uninitiated. One article conveys quite well the life style of a particular hustler: Dale Shaw, "Anatomy of a Pool Hustler," *Saga: The Magazine for Men*, Vol. 23 (November, 1961), pp. 52–55, 91–93. Useful historical data are in Edward John Vogeler's "The Passing of the Pool Shark," *American Mercury*, Vol. 48 (November, 1939), pp. 346–51. For hustling as viewed within the context of the history of pool in America, see Robert Coughlan's "Pool: Its Players and Its Sharks," *Life*, No. 31 (October 8, 1951), pp. 159 *ff.*; though Coughlan's account of the game's history contains errors and his specific consideration of hustling is brief (p. 166), the latter is accurate.

3. The only non-bettor whose payment is somewhat related to the size of the action is the rack boy (if one is used), the person who racks up the balls for the players after each frame. The bigger the action, the larger the tip he can expect; and if one player comes out very much ahead he tips the rack boy lavishly. The rack boy's position is thus analogous to that of the golf caddie, except that a rack boy is used in only about half of hustler-vs.-hustler contests and in but a tiny fraction of other contests. Sometimes he is an employee (sweeper, etc.) of the poolroom, but more often is a spectator performing as rack boy on an *ad hoc* basis.

4. When two high-betting hustlers agree to play each other there is often a real race among poorer spectators to offer rack-boy services because, as previously indicated, if one is engaged for such a session he can expect a good tip. I witnessed one six-hour session between hustlers in which the winning hustler came out $800 ahead and tipped the rack boy $50.

5. Its pool-hustler origin is noted by Vogeler (*op. cit.*, p. 347), a reliable observer. It is recorded in none of the slang source books (Mencken, Mathews, Berrey and Van den Bark, *et al.*,) except Harold Wentworth and Stuart Berg Flexner's *Dictionary of American Slang* (New York: T. Y. Crowell, 1960), p. 527. Wentworth and Flexner do not attempt to account for the phrase's origin. They claim that it dates to about 1835, but this seems impossibly early. The only source they cite is its use as the title of a 1941 W. C. Fields movie.

Actually, Fields used the phrase earlier in his "Poppy" (1936), where it is his exit line and the last line of the movie. Fields' partiality to the phrase is quite in keeping with Vogeler's account of its origin, as Fields spent much of his boyhood in his father's poolroom, was an excellent player, and built his funniest vaudeville act around his pool-playing skill (at the act's climax he sank fifteen balls with one shot). Cf. Douglas Gilbert, *American Vaudeville* (New York: Whittlesey House, 1940), pp. 273–74.

6. This sort of situation is unusual. One part of the poolroom code, adhered to by virtually all regular players, holds that a player is supposed to watch out for himself in the matches he gets into, find out for himself whom he can and cannot beat. Ordinarily one does not warn a player about who is superior or who the hustlers are, unless one is a close friend

of that player. (And even if one is a friend, the code demands that such warning be given only before any match is in prospect; that is, once a player has started to "make a game" with another, third parties are supposed to stay out.)

7. Under certain special circumstances dumping can also occur when there are no bets with spectators or such bets are approximately equal on both sides. See below.

8. Of course conning is only a matter of degree, in that all of us are concerned in many ways with manipulating others' impressions of us; and so one can, if one wishes, take the view that every man is at bottom a con man. This form of "disenchantment of the world" is central to Herman Melville's *The Confidence Man* (perhaps the bitterest novel in all of American literature) and to the sociological writings of Erving Goffman. Its principal corollary is the view expressed by hustlers, by professional criminals, and by Thorstein Veblen that all businessmen are thieves.

9. The kinds of structural problems faced today by the pool or billiard hustler are by no means all endemic. Some are the result of recent social change (see Polsky, *op. cit.*).

On the other hand, such change does not create structural problems for all types of hustling. Today the golf hustler, for example, finds that with precious little "acting" he can (a) get heavy action from non-hustlers, (b) lose the good majority of the eighteen holes and still clean up, and at the same time, (c) not be suspected as a hustler. The structure of the game of golf itself, the peculiar structurally predetermined variations in the betting relationship as one makes the round of the course ("presses," etc.), and the present setting of the game within the larger society—all these combine to create a situation that is tailor-made for hustling. But that is another story.

10. The latter two-thirds of this study deals mainly with hustlers' careers and the relationship of hustling to larger social structures and social change.

11. Life in the Colonies

1. Milton M. Gordon, "The Concept of the Subculture and Its Application," *Social Forces*, Vol. XXVI (October, 1947), p. 40. See also John T. Zadrozny, *Dictionary of Social Science* (Washington, D.C.: The Public Affairs Press, 1959), p. 334, where subculture is defined as "the culture that is peculiar to a particular group of people who form a part of a larger society, and who also share in much of the culture of the larger society." Also see Alfred McClung Lee, *Multivalent Man* (New York: George Braziller, 1966), pp. 38–76, for a more complete and systematic view using the concept of group culture.

2. With the guidance and suggestions of Alfred McClung Lee, Brooklyn College of the City University of New York, and Deborah Offenbacher, Ph.D., New School for Social Research, New York. Milton Kramer, Department of Social Services, New York, advised the author on an earlier draft.

3. Albert K. Cohen, *Delinquent Boys: The Culture of the Gang* (New York: The Free Press, 1955), p. 148. Following Cohen's prototypical usage, the concept was operationalized in the analysis of a drug subculture in Lexington, Kentucky, by John A. O'Donnell, "The Rise and Decline of a Subculture," *Social Problems*, XV (Summer, 1967), pp. 73–84.

4. Frederic M. Thrasher, *The Gang*, abridged by James F. Short, Jr. (Chicago: University of Chicago Press, 1963), pp. 23–24, 44, 117, 133.

5. Howard S. Becker, *Outsiders: Studies in the Sociology of Deviance* (New York: The Free Press of Glencoe, 1963); Edwin M. Lemert, *Social Pathology* (New York: McGraw-Hill Book Co., 1951); Kai T. Erikson, "Notes on the Sociology of Deviance," in *The Other Side: Perspectives on Deviance*, Howard S. Becker, ed. (New York: The Free Press of Glencoe, 1964), pp. 9–21; Harold S. Finestone, "Cats, Kicks and Color," in *ibid.*, pp. 281–97; and Lewis A. Coser, "Some Functions of Deviant Behavior and Normative Flexibility," *American Journal of Sociology*, XLVIII (September, 1962), 172–81.

6. Richard Korn, "The Private Citizen, the Social Expert, and the Social Problem: An Excursion Through an Unacknowledged Utopia," in Bernard Rosenberg, Israel Gerver, and F. William Howton, *Mass Society in Crisis: Social Problems and Social Pathology* (New York: The Macmillan Co., 1964), pp. 576–93.

7. C. Wright Mills, "The Professional Ideology of Social Pathologists," in Rosenberg, Gerver, and Howton, *op. cit.*, p. 105.

8. Korn, *op. cit.*, pp. 578–79.

9. *Ibid.*, p. 578.

10. *Ibid.*, p. 581.

11. *Ibid.*, p. 587. See also Kenneth Keniston, "How Community Mental Health Stamped Out the Riots (1968–78)," *Trans-action*, V (July–August, 1968), pp. 21–29.

12. Lewis A. Coser, "The Sociology of Poverty," *Social Problems*, XIII (Fall, 1965), pp. 140–48; Bernard Beck, "Welfare as a Moral Category," *Social Problems*, XIV (Winter, 1967), pp. 258–77; and Robert A. Scott, "The Selection of Clients by Social Welfare Agencies: The Case of the Blind," *Social Problems*, XIII (Fall, 1965), pp. 118–40.

13. Coser, *op. cit.*

14. Edgar May, *The Wasted Americans* (New York: Harper and Row, 1964), pp. 171, 176.

15. Korn, *op. cit.*, p. 592.

16. Glenn Jacobs, "The Worker-Client Relationship: Some Notes on the Interpersonal Dynamics of the Welfare Department," *The Scene*, I (December, 1965), pp. 18–20.

17. Korn, *op. cit.*, p. 593.

18. Lee Rainwater, "The Revolt of the Dirty-Workers" ("Comment"), *Trans-action*, V (November, 1967), p. 2; and Everett C. Hughes, "Good People and Dirty Work," in *The Other Side: Perspectives on Deviance*, Howard S. Becker, ed., pp. 23–36.

19. O. Mannoni, *Prospero and Caliban: The Psychology of Colonization*, Pamela Powesland, trans. (London: Methuen & Co., 1956).

20. Frantz Fanon, *The Wretched of the Earth* (New York: Grove Press, 1963).

21. Mannoni, *op. cit.*, p. 43.

22. *Ibid.*, p. 63, and chap. III.

23. Barry Schwartz, "The Social Psychology of the Gift," *American Journal of Sociology*, LXXIII (July, 1967), pp. 1–11.

24. *Ibid.*, p. 5.

25. "An Anxious Mother Writes," in the *Wayfarer*, XVII (August, 1965), p. 2.

26. Scott, *op. cit.*, pp. 255–56.

27. Beck, *op. cit.*, p. 275.

28. *Ibid.*, p. 275.

29. Bernard Rosenberg, "The Slum—'Internal Colonialism,'" in Rosenberg, Gerver, and Howton, *op. cit.*, p. 441.

12. *A Field Experience in Retrospect*

1. This chapter, in slightly different form, was originally written for the Child Rearing Study of the Health and Welfare Council of the National Capital Area.

2. Richard Slobodin, " 'Upton Square': A Field Report and Commentary."

3. From the outset, I had decided that I would never shoot crap, pool, or play cards for money, or bet money in any way (numbers excepted, since playing numbers is safely impersonal), and would meticulously avoid the slightest suspicion of a personal involvement with any woman. These self-imposed restrictions to some extent did underline my marginality. My explanation that I couldn't afford to chance a fight or bad feelings because of my job was usually accepted, and I was generally excused from participating in these activities rather than excluded from them.

Index

Addiction, *see* Drugs, Drug addiction

Advisers, religious, in ghetto culture, 43–45

Aikido, 140

Alcoholics, 15, 276n20, n21

Alcoholics Anonymous, 276n20

American Civil Liberties Union, 276n21

Amsterdam News, 25

Aqueduct race track, 36

Athletics, identity role of, 155, 282n9

Bacon, Francis, 7

Bar
  in ghetto culture, 34
  and numbers racket, 36
  see also Convenience bar; Home territory bar; Marketplace bar

Beauty parlor (ghetto enterprise), 23–31, 277nn7–9
  customers classified by status, 25–28, 277n9
  fencing stolen goods in, 28–31

Beck, Bernard, 249

Becker, Howard S., 248

Bedford-Stuyvesant, *see* Brooklyn, N.Y.

Behavior
  "autonomous," 284n24

rational vs. irrational, 131–132
  social and deviant, 72

Benway, Hascal, 79

Benzedrine, 129

Bernstein, Mr. (apartment house manager), 67, 71, 73, 74, 78, 83, 85, 86, 87, 88, 89, 90

Betting, *see* Gambling; Hustling, Hustlers; Numbers racket

Billiards, *see* Hustling, Hustlers: poolroom hustler

Black capitalism, 22
  city politics and, 20–23
  civic vs. political leaders and, 21
  and ghetto culture, 45–47
  Nixon philosophy of, 20
  see also Capitalism; Entrepreneurship

Blacks
  American vs. West Indian, 24–25
  nonprofessionals, in beauty-parlor study, 25–27
  professionals, in beauty-parlor study, 25, 27, 277n9
  segregation within black population, 25, 27–28
  social classes, 64–65
  street time, 133–135

Blessed Martin de Porres Hostel, 268

Bloch, Herbert, 158
Blumer, Herbert, 7, 8, 71, 72
Bootlegging, gangsterism and, 14–15
Bridge-playing (collegiate gambling) 162–178 passim
status in, 163, 164
Bronx, N.Y.
Lancaster-Bennet Apartments, Soundview, East Bronx, 65–91 passim
Lancaster Residents Association, 71–91 passim
North Bronx, 70
Brooklyn, N.Y., 85
Bedford-Stuyvesant, 28, 58, 277n7
drug-addiction studies in, 50–55
Gowanus, 59
Burke, Kenneth, 158, 277n10

Calvinism, 5
Capitalism
ethnic minorities and, 20
exploitation and, 19
see also Black capitalism
Capone, Al, 227
Caseworker, see Welfare services
Chandler, Margaret, 182
Chicago, Ill., 229
Chicago, University of, 9
"Chicago School" of sociology, 22
Church, storefront, 39–43
Cleveland, Ohio, 229
Cohen, Albert K., 248
College, gambling at, see Students, university
Colonialism
internal, 259
psychological aspects of, 256
Communism, Soviet, 5
Concentration camps, 259

Conflict, "dysfunctional," 91
Convenience bar, 183, 284n5, 285n6; see also Bar; Home territory bar; Marketplace bar
Coser, Lewis A., 91, 249
CPT, defined, 134
Crime
among drug addicts, 50–55
organized crime and ghetto politics, 22–23
victimless crime and prohibitory law, 37–38
Culture, see Group culture; Subculture; Street culture
Cynicism, 5

Danton, Richie, 75, 87
Davis, Allison, and Robert J. Havighurst
"Social Class and Color Differences in Child-Rearing," 89
Davis, Kingsley, 52
Daytop Village, Staten Island, N.Y., 55–61
Death and rebirth theme, in karate, 145
Democratic National Convention (1968), 15
Dependence factor, in drug addiction, 49, 50
Dexedrine, 129
Dickens, Charles, 155
Dixon, Greg, 75, 79, 80, 81, 82, 83, 85
Dojo, see Karate, Karate dojo
Dreambooks, and numbers racket, 38
Drugs; Drug addiction, 48–63, 129
addiction defined, 49

Index

Drugs
  case histories
    of addicts, 50–55
    of former addicts, 55–61
  community role in, 61–63
  dependence factor, 49, 50
  "joy popper," 54
  police and, 62–63
  social world of, 54–55
  street addicts, 50–55
  subculture of, 288n3
  as system of human inter-
    action, 63
  therapy for, 55–61
  tolerance process, 49–50
  see also Alcoholics; Benzedrine;
    Dexedrine; Heroin; Mari-
    juana
"Duking," 126
Durkheim, Emile, 42

Empiricism, viii–ix
Employment, for lower-class
    blacks, 24–25
Entrepreneurship (ghetto enter-
    prises)
  and aggression, 157–158
  and bars and speakeasies, 34–
    35
  beauty parlor study, 23–31,
    277nn7–9
  and ghetto culture, 45–47
  hustler as, 132
  numbers racket, 26, 35–38
  and pawnshops, 32
  peer groups and, 161
  poolroom, 33
  shoeshine parlors, 31
  see also Black capitalism;
    Ghetto; Hustling, Hus-
    tlers; Thief, professional
Erikson, Erik H., viii
Ethnic mobility trap, 26, 278n12

Fanon, Frantz, 256
Father role vs. peer group leader,
    155
Faustus, Dr., 13
Fields, W. C., 287n5
Fieldworker
  method of involvement, 263–
    273
  "outsider" status of, 269–272,
    290n3
  preparing for assignment, 262–
    263
  see also Welfare services: case-
    worker
Finestone, Harold
  "Cats, Kicks and Color," 53
Frazier, Franklin, 40
Freud, Sigmund; Freudianism,
    155

Gambling, 14
  college-student study, 161–178,
    283n1, n12, n13, 284n15,
    n16, n24
  see also Hustling, Hustlers;
    Numbers racket; Poker;
    Pool
Gang, subculture of, 159, 161
Ghetto
  language and style in, 277n10
  numbers man in, 22
  organization in, 22
  professional thief in, 22
  and welfare dependency, 259
  white profiteering in, 22
  see also Entrepreneurship;
    Street culture
Gig; Gigging, 126, 130, 131, 133–
    134
Goffman, Erving, 97, 98, 99, 102,
    103, 106, 114, 118, 119,
    167, 220, 241, 288n8
  Asylums, 95

Goldschmidt, Walter
  Exploring the Ways of Mankind, 120
Gowanus, *see* Brooklyn, N.Y.
Gray, Clara, 23
Group culture
  bureaucratic, 250
  concept of, 250
  groups within groups, 159
  and means of identity, 256–257
  worker-client relationship, 256–259

Hair-Weev, 23, 25, 27, 277n8
Havighurst, Robert J., *see* Davis, Allison
Henry, Jules
  "White People's Time, Colored People's Time," 134
Heroin, 49, 50, 51; *see also* Drugs, Drug addiction
Hingle, Mr., 86
Home territory bar
  collectivities, 181–182, 184, 285n6
  and convenience bars, 183, 284n5, 285n6
  and English pub, 180, 284n3
  habitués, 180–182, 183, 284n5
    behavior of, 184–188, 198–200
    territorial defense by, 188–195
  management
    attitude toward patrons, 195–198, 286n18, n19
    territorial defense by, 195–198
  and marketplace bar, 183, 186
  neutral persons, 182, 183, 286n18
  outsiders, 182, 188, 189, 190, 191, 192, 195, 196, 197, 198, 286n18
  profane and obscene language in, 185–186
  as second home, 180, 284n3
  sexual activity, 186–188, 188–189, 192–193, 285n11, n12
  uses of, 184–185, 195, 285n16
  see also Bar
Hospital, *see* Mental hospital, report on
Hotel, *see Shlockhaus* study
Hughes, C. E., 255
Hughes, Everett, 227
Human relations, clinical study, 8–10
Hustling; Hustlers, 126, 128–130, 132, 227
  golf hustler, 288n9
  poolroom hustler, 226–245
    backer for, 242–244
    betting, 230–232
    conning skill, 235, 244–245, 288n8, n9
    deception by, 233–235, 239–242, 287n5, 288n7, n8
    dumping, 239–242, 288n7
    hustled vs. nonhustled games, 232–233
    lemoning, 239, 240
    number of, 230
    rack boy, 287n3, n4
    research on, 228, 287n2
    structural problems faced by, 244–245, 288n9
    techniques of, 235–237
    traits required for success, 237–239, 287n6
Hustler, The (film), 228

Identity
  athletics and, 155, 282n9

Identity (cont.)
  group culture and, 256–257
Insurance companies, and drug-
    addiction areas, 62
Interaction, social, 8–9

Jackson, Tally, 265, 267, 268, 269
James, William, ix
Johnson, Lyndon B., 138
Jones, Donnie, 79, 80, 82, 85, 87,
    89
"Joy popper," 54
Judo, 140

Karate; Karate *dojo*, 140
  achievement of status, 144–
    145, 282*n*3
  aggressiveness, 156–158
  belt symbolism, 142–143, 149–
    151, 158
  caricature in, 152–154, 282*n*7
  discipline in, 146, 282*n*7
  dojo (class building), 141–142
  dojo bum, 149
  hierarchy within, 142–144,
    148–154, 158
  "karate poker face," 152, 154
  kata, 143
  katsu, 144
  kihon, 147
  kumite, 143, 156
  membership in, 142
  psychological significance, in
    American life, 148
  quasi-therapeutic role of, 160
  role of master of, 154–155
  training program, 146–148
  violence vs. control, 157
Korean War, 52
Korn, Richard, 248, 249, 253, 254

Lancaster-Bennet Apartments, *see*
    Bronx, N.Y.
Language, ghetto, 126, 277*n*10

Las Vegas, Nev., 164
Lee, Alfred McClung, 250
Lemert, Edwin M., 278*n*12
Lenski, Gerhard, 71
Lenz, Murray, 69
Lewis, Hylan, 262
Lexington, Ky., 52
Liebow, Elliot
  Talley's Corner, 260
Loans; Loan sharks, 29–30
Los Angeles, Calif., 126, 229
  Watts riots, 88, 138
Lynd, Robert S., 15

Madagascar, 256
Malcolm X, 138
Manhattan College, N.Y.C., 58
Mannheim, Karl, 72
Mannoni, O., 256
Marijuana, 129
Marketplace bar, 183, 186; *see
    also* Bar; Convenience bar;
    Home territory bar
Martial arts
  American vs. Japanese, 282*n*6
  see also Karate, Karate *dojo*
Marxism, reification and, 275*n*2
Maurer, David
  The Big Con, 244
May, Edgar, 252
McCall, George J., 38
Mead, G. H., ix
Melville, Herman
  The Confidence Man, 288*n*8
Mental hospital, report on
  acceptance of responsibility by
    patients, 106–108, 111
  case history of inmate of, 92–
    121
  creative activity in, 104–106
  family life atmosphere, 112–
    114, 280*n*23
  group-therapy sessions, 112–
    113, 280*n*25, *n*26

Mental hospital (cont.)
  Halfway House, 96, 279n3
  institutionalized vs. noninstitu-
    tionalized patients,
    281n36
  letter writing, 101, 280n12
  meals, 98–99, 107, 280n19
  patient privileges, 101–106
  prescribed dress, 100–101
  private vs. public, 95–97,
    279n5, 280n6, 99, 101,
    102, 115, 119
  psychotherapy, 96, 98, 114–116
  romantic attachment in, 108–
    111, 280n20, n21
  services provided, 98–100
  staff image, 101, 102
  "total institutions," 95
  visitors to, 102
  work as therapy, 116–121
Mental illness
  stigma of, 118
  work-sanity correlation, 116–
    121
  see also Mental hospital, report
    on
Mephistopheles, 13
Mills, C. Wright, 15, 248
Minnow, Ted, 71, 74, 75, 76, 77,
    79, 80, 81, 82, 83, 85, 88
Mitchell-Lama Law, 66
Moore, Ted, 266
Murphy, Michael J., 37
Murray, Ed, 85, 87
Muslims, 138
Mystery-mastery dualism, viii,
    275n1
Myth, see Success myth

NAACP, see National Association
    for the Advancement of
    Colored People

National Association for the Ad-
    vancement of Colored Peo-
    ple, 21
National Institute of Mental
    Health Child-Rearing
    Study Project, 261, 263
Nazis, 259
Negroes, see Blacks
"Never give a sucker an even
    break," origin of slogan,
    233, 287n5
New York, N.Y., 53, 58, 204, 205,
    220, 229, 230, 255
  Dept. of Welfare (Social Serv-
    ices), 247, 257
  see also Bronx; Brooklyn;
    Staten Island
New York State Division of Hous-
    ing, 83, 84, 85, 87
New York State Narcotic Addic-
    tion Control Commission,
    62
Newark, N.J., 56
Niederhoffer, Arthur, 158
Nixon, Richard M., 20
North Carolina, 230
Numbers racket
  beauty-parlor customers and,
    26
  in ghetto culture, 35–38
  numbers man, 22, 35–37

Observation
  clinical study of social inter-
    action, 8
  firsthand, 9
  see also Participant observation
Okinawa, bars of, 180
Order, authority and, 158
Outsiders, and home territory bar,
    182, 188, 189, 190, 191,
    192, 195, 196, 197, 198,
    286n18

Park, Robert E., 9, 21
Participant observation, 7–12
    crucial aspect of, 8–9
    defined, ix
    for in-depth information, 48
    methodology of, 260
    understanding one's role in, 273
    see also Fieldworker; Welfare services: caseworker
Pascal, Blaise, 227
Pawnshop, and ghetto culture, 32
Perry, Commissioner, 87
Philadelphia, Penna., 230
Playboy magazine, 142
Poe, Edgar Allan
    "The Purloined Letter," vii
Poker
    collegiate gambling, 161–178, 283n1
    status in, 163–164, 169
Police, 264
    and drug traffic, 62–63
    ghetto racketeers and, 22
    Narcotics Squad, 62
    and numbers racket, 37–38
    police brutality, 15, 276n20, n21
    and pool, 232
    professional thief and, 30–31, 34–35
Politics, and economic opportunity, 20–23
Polsky, Ned
    Hustlers, Beats and Others, 226
Pool; Poolroom, 229
    as focal point of ghetto activities, 33
    see also Hustling, Hustlers
Poppy (film), 287n5
Poverty
    category of, 249

subculture of, 246–247, 258–259
Press, participant observation and, 9
Prohibition era, 14, 21, 226
Prostitution, 14, 52, 59, 60, 227
Psychotherapy, see Mental hospital, report on
Pub, see Bar; Home territory bar

Rainwater, Lee, 255
"Rap," 127
Readers, religious, in ghetto culture, 43–45
Rebirth, see Death and rebirth theme
Reification, viii, 275n2
Relevance
    criteria of, for social science, 11
    need for, 10–16
Religion
    in ghetto culture, 39–45
    and music, 41, 278n15
    and numbers racket, 38
    readers and advisers, 43–45
    religious stores, 43
    storefront church, 39–43
    West Indian vs. American Black, 39
Remington, Bobbie, 79, 85, 87
Reno, Nev., 164
Research, integrity in, 12–16
Resort hotel, see Shlockhaus study
Reynolds, Arnold, 82
Rosenberg, Bernard, 259
Rubinstein, Sam, 75, 76
Runner, see Numbers racket: numbers man

St. Elizabeths Hospital, Washington, D.C., 97

San Francisco, Calif., 181, 191,
    193, 194, 229, 285*n11*
Schwartz, Barry, 256
Scott, Robert A., 259
Secret society, 159–160
Seeley, John R., 155
Segregation, within black popula-
    tion, 25, 27–28
"Set, the," 126, 127–128
Sexual mores, among black non-
    professional group, 26
Shlockhaus study
    dining room, 208–212
    food, 207
    guests, 205–206
    kitchen, 209, 211
    maitre d' role, 210–211
    performance pattern of em-
        ployees, 218–224, 286*n10*
    disruption of, 221–223
    as social establishment, 204,
        207–208, 220–221, 225
    staff, 206–207
    tipping system, 215–217, 218
    waiter-busboy roles, 210, 212–
        214
    waiter-guest relationship, 214–
        215, 216–218
Shoeshine parlor, as front for il-
    legal business, 31
Simmel, Georg, 159, 178, 249
Slumming, 194, 285*n15*
Small, Lonny Reginald, 267, 268
Small-group study, source of
    material for, 91
Smith, Brewster, 101
*Snow White and the Seven
    Dwarfs*, 261
Social activism
    among middle-class blacks, 64–
        91
    genesis of a movement, 67–72
    stages of a movement

formalization, 72, 78–82
institutionalization, 72, 82–
    86
popular excitement, 72–78
social unrest, 72
status insecurity and, 70–71
tenants' association, 65–91
Social science, context and rele-
    vance in, 6–16
Social world; Society
    gambling and, at university
        level, 177–178
    givenness, viii
    ideals vs. practical procedure,
        3–6
    phenomenology of, 282*n5*
    social interaction, 8–9
    see also *Shlockhaus* study
Soul, 136–137
Space, and human territoriality,
    179–200, 284*n1*
Spanish-American War, 15
Speakeasy, in ghetto culture, 34–
    35
Spencer, Herbert
    The Study of Sociology, 15
Staten Island, N.Y., 58
    Daytop Village, 55–61
Status
    bridge-playing and, 163–164
    and group-specific knowledge,
        169–170
    in one's group, 168–173,
        283*n12, n13*, 284*n15*
    "outsiders," 173
    and place of residence, 89
    poker-playing and, 163–164,
        169
    scapegoats, 172
    support of radical movements
        and, 70–71
    as symbolized in karate, 142–
        145

Status (cont.)
  tipping system and, 215–217
  see also Ethnic mobility trap;
    Karate, Karate *dojo;*
    Poker; Students, university
Stolen goods, fencing of, 28–35
Stone, Gregory, 143
Stores, religious, 43
Street culture, in ghetto, 125–139
  activities of, 126
  "future" orientation of, 136–
    139
  pimping, 129
  police trouble, 129–130
  rational vs. irrational behavior,
    131–132
  the "set," 126–130
    defined, 126
    financial situation, 128
    hustling, 126, 128–130, 132
  soul, 136–137
  street language, 126
  style in, 135–136
  time concept, 125, 130–135
  "woman game," 129
Students, university
  gambling-clique study, 161–
    178, 283n1, n12, n13,
    284n15, n16, n24
    argot in, 165–167
    cliques, 162, 168–169,
      283n1
    folklore in, 167–168
    group solidarity, 167–168
    motivation, 177–178
    status, 162, 163–164, 168–
      173
Style, in street culture, 135–136,
  277n10
Subculture, concept of, 246–249,
  250, 259, 288n1
Success myth, and social cultures, 47, 278n18

Sumner, William Graham, 15
Surrender theme, viii–ix, 275n3

Tenants' grievance committee, as
  microcosm of social activism, 65–91
Territoriality
  human, 179, 284n1
  see also Home territory bar
Therapy
  for drug addiction, 55–61
  work as, 116–121
  see also Mental hospital, report
    on
Thief, professional
  and beauty-parlor study, 26,
    28–29
  fencing stolen goods, 22, 28–35
Third World, 46, 249, 256, 259
Thomas, W. I., 16
Thomism, 5
Thrasher, Frederick M., 178, 248
  The Gang, 159
Time
  "alive time," 131
  CPT, 134
  "dead time," 131
  personal vs. clock time, 125,
    133–135
  street time, 130–135
Tokyo, Japan, 52
Tolerance process, in drug addic-
  tion, 49–50
Twain, Mark, 155

Uniform, significance of, 143–
  144
University, see College
Urban, Peter (karate master),
  142, 146, 148, 152, 154–
  155, 156, 157, 282n8

Veblen, Thorstein, 16, 288n8

Vietnam War, 138
Vocation, philosophy of, 5–6

Waller, Willard, 155
Washington, D.C., 261, 263
Watts riots, see Los Angeles, Calif.
Weber, Alfred, 19
Weev, see Hair-Weev
Welfare services
    agency-client relationship, 250
    caseworker
        and bureaucratic system, 251–255
        role of, 250
        strikes by, 255–256

worker-client relationship, 256–259
    confidentiality in, 252
    professionalizing of, 249, 255
    public assistance grants, 257
Wesley, Detective, 263, 264
Whyte, William Foote, 8, 217
    Street Corner Society, 7, 169
Winisk, Hudson Bay village, 262
World Health Organization, 49

Yale University, 15

Zeiger, Steve, 79, 80
Znaniecki, Florian, ix, 10

THE PARTICIPANT OBSERVER

Edited by GLENN JACOBS

"How can we best perceive social behavior in context?" asks Alfred McClung Lee in his introductory essay—"On Context and Relevance"—in the present book. By way of answer he quotes Harold Blumer: "We must go to a direct examination of actual human group life.... No theorizing, however ingenious, and no observance of scientific protocol, however meticulous, are substitutes for developing a familiarity with what is actually going on in the sphere of life under study."

Take, for instance, "black capitalism." Much has been said and written on the subject since the then presidential candidate, Richard M. Nixon, spoke of it in 1968. But when Desmond Cartey takes us on a fascinating journey through the ghetto in his survey of "How Black Enterprisers Do Their Thing," we see clearly that "black capitalism is at the very least naïve" and that "any attempt to ameliorate existing ghetto conditions must go beyond the formalistic thinking which has passed for problem-solving in public life."

"The clinical study of human relations is the crucial aspect of participant observation," writes Professor Lee. Or, as Charles Horton Cooley put it in *Social Process*: "The surest way to know men is to have simple and necessary relations with them."

The contributors to this volume, most of them of the younger generation of sociologists, have all participated in the encounters of